Bernard Herrmann's *Vertigo*

A Film Score Handbook

David Cooper

Film Score Guides
Kate Daubney, Series Adviser

GREENWOOD PRESS
Westport, Connecticut • London

Library of Congress Cataloging-in-Publication Data

Cooper, David, 1956–
    Bernard Herrmann's Vertigo : a film score handbook / by David Cooper.
      p. cm.—(Film score guides, ISSN 1527-7291 ; no. 2)
    Includes bibliographical references (p.) and index.
    ISBN 0-313-31490-X (alk. paper)
    1. Herrmann, Bernard, 1911–1975. Vertigo. I. Title: Vertigo. II. Title. III. Series.
ML410.H562C66   2001
781.5′42—dc21   00–049501

British Library Cataloguing in Publication Data is available.

Library of Congress Catalog Card Number: 00–049501
ISBN: 0-313-31490-X
ISSN: 1527-7291

First published in 2001

Greenwood Press, 88 Post Road West, Westport, CT 06881
An imprint of Greenwood Publishing Group, Inc.
www.greenwood.com

Printed in the United States of America

The paper used in this book complies with the
Permanent Paper Standard issued by the National
Information Standards Organization (Z39.48–1984).

P

Copyright Acknowledgments

The author and publisher gratefully acknowledge permission for use of the following material:

Excerpts from the score to *Vertigo* are reprinted by permission of Famous Music Corporation. Copyright © 1958 by Famous Music Corporation. Copyright renewed by Famous Music Corporation.

To Stephanie, Edward and Robert

CONTENTS

ILLUSTRATIONS

FIGURES

TABLES

EXAMPLES

ABBREVIATIONS AND ACKNOWLEDGEMENTS

Pitches are notated according to the ASA rather than the Helmholtz system. The following table converts between the two systems:

ASA	Helmholtz
C_1	CC
C_2	C
C_3	c
C_4	c'(Middle C)
C_5	c"
C_6	c'''
C_7	c''''

I am very indebted to a number of people and organisations who have assisted in the preparation of this book. The Faculty of Arts of the University of Leeds awarded me a period of study leave to complete the book and my Head of Department, Graham Barber, gave me his unstinting support. Bee Ong expertly typeset the manuscript, coping with the many problems that arose with good humour. Kia Ng and Ewan Stefani gave me technical assistance and undertook much of my teaching and administrative load. John Waxman of *Themes and Variations* was wonderfully supportive, acting as an intermediary with the Paramount Music Library and dealing patiently with my numerous enquiries. Sid Herman of the Famous Music Corporation generously allowed me to borrow a copy of the composer's autograph score of *Vertigo* for an extended period of study. Simon Launchbury of the BBC Music Library gave me access to the printed version of the score to the Prelude. Ridge Walker supplied hitherto unpublished information about the recording of *Vertigo*.

Special thanks must go to Kate Daubney for suggesting the project in the first place, reading my drafts and supplying very many helpful comments and corrections. Without her support and enthusiasm, the book would never have been conceived or completed.

INTRODUCTION

Alfred Hitchcock's *Vertigo* was released by Paramount in 1958 and in the subsequent years it has come to be regarded as a classic of the cinema. In this acknowledgement of the director as the primary author of a film which is, as much as anything, about directorial control — for both Gavin Elster and Scottie adopt this role with Judy, fabricating and refashioning her as Madeleine—let us not forget the technical virtuosity of the rest of the cast and crew. The fine performances of Kim Novak and James Stewart, the beautiful and evocative camerawork of director of photography Robert Burks, the meticulous editing of George Tomasini, the elegant art direction of Hal Pareira and Henry Bumstead, Edith Head's refined costume design, John Ferren's animation and Saul Bass's title design, along with Alex Coppel's final version of the script and Bernard Herrmann's score, all contribute to the realisation of Hitchcock's intentions. *Vertigo*, like many other successful films, seems to present an almost seamless integration of its components and its narrative is the synergistic outcome of their interaction.

In this book I examine in detail the musical component of *Vertigo*, showing how it connects to the rest of the narrative and how it can affect one's reading of the film. In the normal circumstances in which one views and hears films, as distinct from the special mode adopted when studying them, the musical element of the text is appreciated aurally, and often subconsciously, rather than mediated by a notated score. Because of the difficulty of obtaining scores, scholars often have had to rely on their aural ability to transcribe material and draw connections between cues— an approach that is also found in ethnomusicology and popular musicology. Whereas in these two latter branches of music, the "text"—in the sense of the set of performance instructions, rather than their realisation as sound—is often either not notated at all or entails relatively open and nonprescriptive forms of notation, for much film music there exist extremely detailed "closed" scores that can be very revealing to analytic scrutiny. Many film music composers working between the 1930s and

1960s, were highly literate musicians for whom the grid of manuscript paper was not simply a matter of convenience, but the interface between imagination and sound.[1] The translation of musical ideas into signs on paper is a complex process and usually involves continuous, if apparently unconscious, negotiation between mental representations and their reification. Although composers can be reluctant to talk publicly about this aspect of their craft, their scores can often reveal useful documentary evidence about the act of composition as well as simplifying musical analysis.

Herrmann was a classically trained musician who brought the conventions of "concert" music with him to the cinema. He did not distinguish between works such as his opera *Wuthering Heights* or his Symphony and the music he wrote for the cinema—both were equally respectable in his eyes and both involved the application of the same skills and techniques. With this in mind, I have approached his score to *Vertigo* in the same detail that I would consider an autonomous piece of Western art-music and have applied many of the same descriptive and analytic methods. In so doing, I hope to demonstrate that Herrmann's score is musically dense and sophisticated, and that it relies on similar devices to support and underline the development of the narrative in the film to those that have been consistently used by composers in the art-music sphere; it draws on an expressive vocabulary which has been established and refined over many centuries. Inevitably, much of the discussion involves the use of musical terminology to describe and analyse the score and it is hoped that this will not prove too great a barrier to the nontechnical reader.

The first chapter presents an overview of Herrmann's career up to 1958 when he composed the score for *Vertigo*. There have been a number of excellent studies of the history of film music, and it no longer seems mandatory to rehearse the maturation of the classical Hollywood film score through the 1930s and 1940s. Neither is it necessary to offer a comprehensive survey of Herrmann's life—Steven C. Smith's biography *A Heart at Fire's Centre: The Life and Music of Bernard Herrmann* is strongly recommended to readers who wish to delve further in this area. Graham Bruce's *Bernard Herrmann: Film Music and Narrative* offers a perceptive overview of Herrmann's career and compositional style, and also contains analyses of *Vertigo* and *Psycho*. It would have been tempting to elaborate a psychological profile of the composer, for from all accounts here was a man who on one hand could be coarse, irascible, vindictive, arrogant, splenetic, insensitive and opinionated and on the other could be sensitive, gregarious, refined, sentimental and supportive. I have resisted this temptation, feeling that amateur psychoanalysis is not particularly helpful in the explication of the composer's musical objectives. Instead, my intention is to isolate some of the important stages of his personal development and suggest the musical and intellectual milieu from which his score to *Vertigo* sprang.

I have already remarked that Herrmann was a composer of concert works as well as radio, television and film scores, and that in his estimation they were of equal importance. Thus, although the discussion of his musical technique in chapter 2 focuses on his film music, much of what I say is equally applicable to his "serious" music. As Herrmann remarked to Leslie Zador and Gregory Rose in an interview:

There's no difference between being a composer for one thing and the other. You just have a career as a composer. Whether you write occasionally for television, for films or for symphony, I don't see that there's any difference. It's all part of the life of being a composer.[2]

Like many of the famous Hollywood composers such as Korngold, Rózsa and Waxman, Herrmann had a hybrid professional life. However, his success outside the confines of radio, film and television was actually rather limited and he was never deemed to be in the "first rank" as a conductor or art-music composer either in America or Europe. This is not to suggest his achievement in these fields is insignificant, for *Wuthering Heights*, *Moby Dick* and the Symphony, in particular, are sadly neglected works which deserve more regular airings. Rather, he was out of step with fashion, and though within the context of film music, given the conservative ethos of Hollywood, he could seem at times to be a radical, he was never in sympathy with the lionised musical *avant garde*. He despised systematisation, and unfashionably relied on his musical instinct, opening himself to whichever influences seemed most appropriate. Difficult as he could be as an individual, what does seem to shine through all his work is an integrity which sets him apart from many of his peers in the profession for whom music was a mere commodity to be manufactured in an assemblyline process.

Issues surrounding the production and reception of *Vertigo* have been very widely discussed. Dan Auiler's recent *Vertigo: The Making of a Hitchcock Classic* presents the student of film with a wealth of information about the whole production process of the film from inception to release and is to be strongly recommended. The opening section of chapter 3 offers a concise comparative overview of the sources of *Vertigo* and delineates the main stages of production; it also provides a table which, to my best knowledge, summarises the sources of the recordings of the nondiegetic cues in *Vertigo* for the first time. I thank Robert Townson of Varese Sarabande for confirming the accuracy of this table. The second part of the chapter briefly reviews some of the critical readings of the film. I have deliberately stood back from offering a personal reading here for several reasons: first, because the film is a complex text, no single reading can hope to explain it; and second, because the discussion in the final two chapters is intended to suggest ways in which the musical score influences the interpretation of the narrative. I hope that readers, guided perhaps by Spoto, Wood, Brill, Sterrit and the very many others who have analysed and discussed the narrative, will come to their own determination of its meaning and relevance.

The fourth chapter examines the contribution of its various elements other than dialogue—music, both diegetic and nondiegetic and sound effects—to the shaping of the soundtrack, and provides the final components of the "toolkit" of information and techniques preparatory to the detailed discussion of the score in chapters 5 and 6. The opening section approaches the thorny issue of signification in music by considering the semiotics and semantics of film music. Whether it is considered as a series of acoustic events or their notational encoding, music is not semantically neutral and is able, at least in a partial and constrained sense, to carry some degree of meaning. If this were not the case, formulaic "genre music" such as that which musically encodes the "spaghetti Western," would not be able to elicit its near-Pavlovian response—consider how the rapid whistling of a motif such as $D_5-G_5-D_5-G_5-D_5$ can instantly invoke the image of Clint Eastwood! A theory of the construction of musical meaning in film music is tentatively proposed, according to the categories of context-derived associations, cultural referents, intracultural semantics, isomorphisms and intertextuality. It is freely admitted that this is by no means complete as a theory of signification, nor is it intended to be universal in scope—it is deliberately written from the perspective of Western music and with a Western audience in mind—and it may not be applicable to other cultural contexts in the same way. However, it is hoped that it may offer a handle on the ways in which "abstract," music can functionally be connected to the rest of the narrative.

An extremely important ingredient of Hitchcock's soundtracks is the shaping of the effects track—what in modern parlance would be described as *sound design*. The factory system still prevailing in Hollywood studios during this period, and the division of labour between sound recordists, composers, music and sound editors, and other staff, which reached its competitive conclusion in the final dub, tended to limit the extent to which directors were able to contrive the mutual interpenetration rather than mere overlapping of the fundamental constituents of the soundtrack, namely dialogue, effects and music. Few directors had the vision, the time or the technical expertise to explore the potential of sound *in toto* to enhance the cinematic experience, vision almost invariably being regarded as the primary sense. I suggest that Hitchcock attended extremely carefully to the possibilities of film sound in *Vertigo*, and that the effects track, whose editing he fastidiously supervised, subtly cooperates with Herrmann's nondiegetic score, rather than competing with it. Sound design and the interaction between effects and music is considered in a section which draws on Michel Chion's models of the auditory space of film sound.

In the final part of this chapter, which looks at the shaping of the soundtrack through music, a discussion of the use of diegetic music in the film is followed by an examination of Herrmann's nondiegetic score. All of the cues, whether diegetic or nondiegetic, are presented in tabular form in terms of cue number, title, motif employed, duration, metre, tempo, tonality and orchestration. The intention of this table is to provide an overview or outline map of the score before it is considered in detail in the following chapters and it offers a considerable amount of information to the inquiring reader; for example, it demonstrates Herrmann's tendency to employ slow tempi (most commonly lento), his metrical flexibility, the heterogeneity of his orchestration, and his use of descriptive titles for each cue. It also, in skeletal form, acts as a summary and index of the subsequent analysis. I have suggested a possible method for the study of the score, but would also strongly recommend that the reader considers the approaches described by Michel Chion in "Introduction to Audiovisual Analysis," chapter 10 of his *Audio-Vision: Sound on Screen*.[3]

The last two chapters represent the outcome of the in-depth study of the score and I make no apology for the detailed musicological consideration given to it there. As I have already remarked, Herrmann's score is sophisticated and dense, and while material is reused within it, it is always recontextualised when it reappears. The orchestration is invariably fascinating, and despite the fact that some fine detail is lost in the original soundtrack (less so in James Katz and Robert Harris's cleaned up version of the film reissued in 1996), subsequent recordings have demonstrated just how sensitive Herrmann's ear was. Of course, few readers will have the good fortune to be able to access the facsimile of Herrmann's autograph score, so I have explicitly *described* much of the material that might normally have been taken for granted in an equivalent study of an opera or concert work. It was decided to take a chronological approach, working from the beginning to the end of the film cue by cue (though it should be noted that the discussion of the prelude appears at the end of chapter 2 in the examination of Herrmann's strategy with regard to musical form in longer cues). This is partly for the convenience of the reader, to enable the discussion of individual cues to be found easily, and partly because the score's linear evolution mirrors the elaboration of the narrative—there is a musical design which unfolds in an ordered way. In order to contextualise the cues, the narrative events which they accompany are briefly described before the musical analysis. Although there are almost eighty minutes of music in a film running just over two hours in length, there will inevitably be discontinuities in the discussion because of the absence of music at various points . This is not intended to devalue these parts of the film, and in fact Herrmann's decision *not* to use music in a scene can often be just as significant as his decision to use it elsewhere.

The danger of the close study of a film score, as with the prioritisation of any of the other discrete elements of a film, is that we give it precedence, make it audible above the rest of the narrative to the extent that the images, the dialogue, and the sound effects seem to take on the status of accompaniments to the music. The effect of a score on the average member of the cinema audience is largely subliminal; my hope is to draw attention to, and thereby develop an awareness of, the *means* by which it is able to operate subliminally rather than to suggest that we should focus our whole attention on the score when viewing. The outcome of this, to my mind, would be to unravel the cinematic experience rather than to enrich it. Herrmann, citing Jean Cocteau, remarked that "a film score should create the sensation that one does not know whether the music is propelling the film, or the film is propelling the music."[4] I can only hope that, at the end of the process of analysis of the score, the essential mystery of *Vertigo* still remains.

NOTES

1. I am not trying to suggest by this that many composers working after the 1960s were not also classically trained and highly musically literate.
2. Leslie Zador and Gregory Rose, "A Conversation with Bernard Herrmann" in ed. Clifford McClarty, *Film Music 1* (Los Angeles, CA: The Film Music Society, 1998), pp. 211–13.

3. Michel Chion, edited and translated by Claudia Gorbman, *Audio-Vision: Sound on Screen* (New York: Columbia University Press, 1994), pp. 185–213.

4. Bernard Herrmann, "Bernard Herrmann, Composer" in ed. Evan William Cameron, *Sound and the Cinema: The Coming of Sound to American Film* (New York: Redgrave Publishing Company, 1980), p. 135.

CHAPTER 1

HERRMANN'S CAREER UP TO
THE COMPOSITION OF *VERTIGO*

> The music in the opening sequence as the camera glides up the iron-
> work of the Kane palace builds the atmosphere as macabre and terrify-
> ing. It continues to build with the images up to the climax of the se-
> quence, when the crystal rolls from the dying man's hand and crashes
> splintering on the floor with the last word "rosebud" declared from
> Kane's dying lips.[1]

What is interesting about this quotation from Roger Manvell's influential study,
Film, first published in 1944, is not so much his pertinent discussion of the relationship between score and picture in *Citizen Kane*, but his complete failure to identify
the composer. If the score is "inaudible," to adopt Claudia Gorbman's conceit in
Unheard Melodies: Narrative Film Music, then by this token its composer appears
to be anonymous.[2] A subsidiary and subservient function was never suited to
Bernard Herrmann, however, and throughout his career he managed to place his
personal imprint on the films for which he composed scores to a remarkable degree.

Bernard Herrmann was a first-generation American. His father, Abraham Dardick,
was born in Russia in March 1872 to a fairly prosperous Jewish family.[3] According
to Abraham's death certificate, he had been resident in the United States for 45
years when he died in 1933, which implies that he first arrived on U.S. territory (in
Hawaii) in 1888 at the age of 16, having absconded from a whaler that he had joined
in Odessa. For the next four years he worked as an overseer on a sugar plantation
in Hawaii and then in 1892 he joined the crew of another whaler called *The Alexan-*
der, which was shipwrecked for six weeks on St Paul's Island in the Baring Sea. He
settled permanently in the United States in the same year. Dardick changed his
name first to Herman and then to Herrmann during this early period of his life,
possibly because of the increased social cachet attached to a German surname.
After training as an optometrist by correspondence course, he settled down in New

York in 1903 and set up a successful practice.[4] Bernard Herrmann's mother, Ida Gorenstein, was also of Russian Jewish origin, but her background was much less well heeled than Dardick's. The couple married in 1909, and their first child, whose given name was actually Max though he was almost immediately called Bernard, was born two years later on 29 June, 1911.[5]

The Herrmann household was by no means an orthodox Jewish one. According to Bernard's brother Louis, his father was an agnostic who did not attempt to bring his children up in the Jewish tradition and culture, but strongly espoused the pursuit of music and literature instead. [6] All the children played musical instruments, Herrmann learning the violin until his early teens before moving to the piano. While his ability as a performer does not suggest any precocious talent in that area, he does seem to have had a remarkable propensity for composition and Louis remarks that he wrote an opera as early as his eleventh year.[7] It may be that the familial atmosphere, with its avoidance of religious dogma and pursuit of the fine arts, encouraged Herrmann's auto-didacticism; he certainly spent much of his time studying by himself in public libraries, developing a famously encyclopaedic knowledge of music.

Among the works that he discovered in these early days of exploration was Berlioz's *Treatise on Modern Instrumentation and Orchestration*, which apparently confirmed his interest in composition.[8] Although Berlioz's musical illustrations — which are largely drawn from his own compositions and those of Beethoven, Gluck and Meyerbeer — must have seemed rather dated from the perspective of a youth in the 1920s, his emphasis on timbre or tone colour had a profound influence on Herrmann, and it is this aspect of his film music, above all others, which is so innovative. In 1927 or 1928, Herrmann also came across some of the works of the maverick composer Charles Ives in the New York Library,[9] a man whom he was to describe in 1932 in a deeply passionate article, as "one of the most inspired of living composers."[10] For Herrmann, Ives's technical developments displayed a greater logic than those of either Schoenberg or Stravinsky, for their compositions were "built upon a set of mystical incantations, formulated under gaslight in the suburbs of Vienna, or upon a group of artificial, neo-classic rules."[11] Ives's modernism, however, sprang from the realities of everyday life and was "the result of his observation of town and country." From this point on, Herrmann championed his music, communicating with him by post, dedicating his cantata *Moby Dick* (1938) to him, performing many of his works and recording his Second Symphony. In the 1970 interview with Zador and Rose, Herrmann claims that he was responsible for a series of 30 concerts of Ives music with the CBS orchestra—"Five concerts a week for six weeks."[12]

While he was still a student at DeWitt Clinton High School, Herrmann attended classes at New York University (NYU), whose music department was still in its infancy, having been founded in 1923 by Albert Stoessel and Philip James. This was just one example of his chutzpah, for he seems to have insinuated himself into the company of many of New York's most illustrious musicians at this time, including Aaron Copland. When Stoessel moved to the Julliard Graduate School to take up the post of director of the opera and orchestra departments in 1930, he suggested to

Herrmann that he might apply to the Julliard School of Music. After an appropriately rigorous entrance examination, Herrmann was given a scholarship, but his studies at the Julliard did not prove to be a spectacular success and in less than two years he dropped out, apparently because he found the institution too conservative. He then returned, informally, to NYU during the academic year 1932–1933 to attend a course in composition and orchestration given by Percy Grainger, the chairman of the faculty of music. Grainger's eclectic approach seems to have struck a chord with the young Herrmann, revealing to him the range and diversity of the musical materials available to the contemporary composer.

Of, perhaps equal importance to his formal instruction at either the Julliard or NYU was his involvement with what became known as the Young Composers' Group, which was set up in emulation of "Les Six," established a decade earlier in Paris.[13] The group invited Copland to be its informal leader and figurehead, much as "Les Six" had Satie, and it met regularly through 1932 to discuss and perform compositions by its members.[14] It aligned itself to the radical tradition developing in America at that time, exemplified by such figures as Varèse, Ruggles, Cowell and, of course, Ives, whose First Orchestral Set "Three Places in New England" was premiered by Slonimsky and the Boston Chamber Orchestra in New York in January 1931. According to Henry Brant, one of the group's members, Herrmann was "the most voluble in expressing his views."[15] Brant illustrated Copland's benign and encouraging attitude by recounting a story involving Herrmann:

I can recall one episode in which Bernard Herrmann, who had the worst handwriting of anyone there, brought in a new piece that was just a scrawl. But he explained it, not hesitating to point out its significant qualities. He spoke in a flippant way about spilling coffee on it and so forth, and Aaron said, "Now look, Benny, you've taken the trouble to do it. It's not right for you to be flippant about what you do, because it clearly means a lot to you to do it. And you mustn't give others the impression that it shouldn't mean much to them."[16]

Like its Parisian prototype, the Young Composers' Group was a fairly short-lived affair, suffering from internal tensions and disagreements. It dissolved soon after its first formal public concert in January 1933.

On the group's demise, Herrmann set about finding another outlet for his talents as both composer and conductor, and in 1933 he formed The New Chamber Orchestra from a group of unemployed musicians. The ensemble's premiere, which was intended to be held on 10 May, 1933 but had to be delayed because of the death of Herrmann's father, included a mixture of English and American works, the former (pieces by Elgar and Purcell) being performed under the auspices of the Permanent Commission for International Exchange Concerts. The American element included compositions by his teachers Grainger and Philip James, his friends from the Young Composers Group, Moross and Heilner, his heroes, Ives and Cowell, two composers working in the field of popular music, Robert Russell Bennett and Vladimir Dukelsky (or Vernon Duke as he became known), and his own "Prelude to Anathema." The concert received considerable critical approval and Herrmann's talent as a conductor was widely praised.

The twenty-two-year-old Herrmann seemed to be developing his credentials as a modernist composer, and he might well have continued in this track had it not been for a break into the world of radio broadcasting. In 1934, he was recruited by the conductor and composer Johnny Green to act as an assistant on the CBS series "Music in the Modern Manner." This soon led to the opportunity to provide music for some of the company's radio programmes, the first being in May 1934 when he composed a score to accompany Keats's "La Belle Dame Sans Merci." Lucille Fletcher, who worked in the CBS Music Clearance Department and became Herrmann's first wife in 1939, noted how Herrmann, even in these early scores, made use of novel instrumental techniques, such as muting the harp by running paper between the strings and using a twelve-inch ruler to play piano cluster chords (a technique influenced by Ives's *Concorde* Sonata, no doubt).[17] He had, she remarked, "raised musical sound effects to the status of a fine art."

In the years from 1934 to 1939, Herrmann worked on numerous radio shows, and in 1935 was appointed a staff conductor for CBS, which provided him with the opportunity both to further develop his technique in that field and to publicly air the repertoire which lay closest to his heart. What Herrmann discovered in radio drama was the importance of economy of gesture, of well-chosen timbre, and of the interaction between the various sonic elements which make up radio, for the same ingredients which form the film soundtrack are present—dialogue, effects and music—but without visuals to elucidate the ambiguous moments. If music or effects drowned out the dialogue, then the play became totally incomprehensible and thus all the elements had to work together harmoniously rather than compete with each other. This was an invaluable lesson for any incipient film composer, and its influence is perceptible from Herrmann's first forays into the cinema. Herrmann continued to compose concert music during this time, including the *Currier and Ives* suite (1935) based on pictures by Currier and Ives, the famous firm of popular printmakers (with a rather Charles Ivesian rendition of "Jingle Bells" in the "Torchlight Finale"), and the cantata *Moby Dick* (1938), one of his most successful pieces, and a work which harks back to his father's nautical career.

From the creative perspective, the relationship he developed with Orson Welles was particularly significant. In 1937, the twenty-two-year-old Welles narrated the radio show "Fall of the City" and directed *Macbeth* for "The Columbia Workshop," and in the subsequent year he took responsibility for a series called "First Person Singular." Welles's infamous Halloween broadcast of 30 October, 1938, *The War of the Worlds* in "The Mercury Theater on the Air" series, cemented the reputation of the twenty-three-year-old director as one of radio's hottest properties. When he was made an offer of $225,000 by RKO in 1939 to write, direct and act in two films, he brought Herrmann with him as his composer. Although Herrmann was a complete novice in the field of film music composition at this stage, Welles demanded that he should receive the same fee for his first film, *Citizen Kane* as Max Steiner, the doyen of composers at that time, would have done—the very substantial sum of $10,000.[18]

The War of the Worlds achieved its remarkable effect through its blurring of the normal frame of the radio play in its first part (up until the intermission) by having a radio show within a radio show. Although listeners who had switched on their wirelesses at the start of the broadcast had to be aware that they were listening to a dramatic piece, Welles's narrative technique, which involved the use of the characteristic forms of nondramatic broadcasting such as the concert, the newscast and the interview, was so well contrived that credulous listeners coming to it later on could be persuaded that they really were hearing an extraordinary piece of breaking news. Music in this context had to be diegetic in order not to rupture the illusion of authenticity, and the sounds of dance music and light classical favourites are common in the score—in fact, Herrmann's contribution to this show in terms of original composition was very slight. For *Citizen Kane*, Welles adopted a not dissimilar premise, but here newsreel footage provided the means of blurring the frame, and the score was split between original nondiegetic music composed by Herrmann and material from the RKO library to accompany the newsreel sequences and provide the rest of the diegetic music. Other composers whose cues or arrangements appear in the soundtrack include Max Steiner, Alfred Newman, Anthony Collins, Roy Webb and Frank Toups.[19]

The experience of scoring *Citizen Kane* seems to have been a remarkably positive one for Herrmann. In *The New York Times* of Sunday 25 June, 1941, he wrote a fascinating piece discussing the process of writing and recording the music for the film. He noted that three particular conditions were supposed to characterise this process: the very short time frame composers were allocated for composition (as little as two weeks for a feature film) the farming out of orchestration and the unwillingness of directors and editors to allow composers to take an active role in the final mixdown. In fact, Herrmann suffered none of these problems or limitations and was given a full twelve weeks to write the score, which allowed him to orchestrate and conduct it, as well as planning it in some detail. He had the advantage of being able to work on the score as the film was photographed and edited, rather than in postproduction, a necessity given that a number of the scenes were cut to music. Most unusually for the period, he was even allowed to take an active role in the mixdown of the score onto the soundtrack. He remarks that:

Too often, in Hollywood, the composer has little to say about this technical procedure, and the result is that some of the best film music is often submerged to scarcely audible levels. Welles and I felt that music which was intended only as atmospheric background should be originally written for that purpose, and not toned down in the dubbing room. In other words, the dynamics of all music in the picture should be planned ahead of time so that the final dubbing is merely a transference process.

With this in mind two full weeks were spent in the dubbing room and music under our supervision was often re-recorded six or seven times before the proper dynamic level was achieved. The result is an exact projection of the original ideas in the score. Technically no composer could ask for more.[20]

Although in his later film scores he tended to avoid the wide-scale use of a leitmotivic technique—the classical mode in film music of identifying a character, event, or property with a musical theme—Herrmann employed two such leitmotivs in his score, feeling that they were "practically imperative, because of the story itself and the manner, in which it is unfolded": a four-chord brass figure which represents Kane's power; and a solo idea for vibraphone which signifies Rosebud, the sled Kane played with as a child before receiving his inheritance.[21] The specific influence of the radio work he had done for CBS was clearly explained by Herrmann in *The New York Times* piece:

In handling these motifs I used a great deal of what might be termed "radio scoring." The movies frequently overlook opportunities for musical cues which last only a few seconds — that is, from five to fifteen seconds at the most—the reason being that the eye usually covers the transition. On the other hand, in radio drama, every scene must be bridged by some sort of sound device, so that even five seconds of music becomes a vital instrument in telling the ear that the scene is shifting. I felt that in the film, where the photographic contrasts were often so sharp and sudden, a brief cue—even two or three chords might heighten the effect immeasurably.[22]

While *Citizen Kane* was by no means a box office success on its release, it earned Herrmann an Academy Award nomination. It was soon followed by a second score, for William Dieterle's film *All That Money Can Buy*, also known as *The Devil and Daniel Webster* (1941), and for this he received an Academy Award—the only one of his career. He was generous in his praise of Dieterle; in a symposium titled "The Coming of Sound to the American Film" held in New York in October 1973 he described him as "a man of great musical culture."[23] Herrmann's sensitivity to the potency of well-chosen sonorities and his interest in technical innovation is clear in this score. By overdubbing four optical audio tracks containing performances on the violin of "Pop goes the weasel," some arco and some pizzicato, laced with double and triple stopping and glissandi, he was able to create an astonishingly virtuoso sound for the barn dance. He also used an electronic effect which predates Miklós Rózsa's employment of the theremin in *Spellbound* (1946), for Mr. Scratch, the devil, is accompanied on each appearance by "the sound of singing telephone wires at 4 a.m."[24] In musical style, the score betrays the influence of both Copland and Ives. In particular, the exquisitely orchestrated cue "Sleigh-ride," which reappears as the second movement of the orchestral suite from the film, involves a melody in the vernacular "hoe-down" mode superimposed on a four-note descending chromatic figure in the bass register repeated as an ostinato. Several of the cues in *Vertigo* make use of a similar four-note figure, especially "The Necklace," which accompanies Scottie's discovery of Judy's true identity.

Herrmann's second film for Orson Welles for RKO, *The Magnificent Ambersons* (1942), similarly involves sleigh-ride cue, this time scored for the bizarre ensemble of three glockenspiels, two celestes, two harps, piano, triangles and jingles. The film, written, directed and produced by Welles, examines the fading fortunes of the patrician Amberson family, partly brought about by the efforts of the vain and spendthrift only son, George. While the Ambersons represent the values of the upper classes with inherited wealth in turn-of-the century America, the inventor Eugene Morgan, a former beau of George's mother who has returned to town as a widower with his beautiful daughter Lucy, stands for technological, meritocratic and capitalist modern America. Eugene has invented a new "horseless carriage," and the antinomy between this vehicle and the sleigh that George drives, accompanied by Lucy, is established in a key scene near the beginning of the film. Kathryn Kalinak provides a very pertinent analysis of the scene in *Settling the Score*, but there are several features which require further comment.[25] First, like much of the musical material both diegetic and nondiegetic used during the opening of the film, the cue derives from Waldteufel's Waltz No. 1 from the set *Toujours ou Jamais*, op. 156. Herrmann employs a similar variation technique in the opening scenes of the film to the one he used in *Citizen Kane*, the Waldteufel waltz reappearing in many guises in accordance with the on-screen action. At the beginning of the sleigh-ride cue it is pared down to its bare essentials, the first six pitches transposed to A Lydian mode $(A_5 - B_5 - E_6 - D\sharp_6 - B_5 - C\sharp_5)$ initiating a brilliant *moto perpetuo*. Second, the melodic fragment $(D_4 - E_4 - F_4 - A_4 - G_4 - C_5)$ which accompanies George and Lucy's kiss when they fall off the sleigh prefigures the first five pitches of Madeleine's theme from *Vertigo* as it appears in the "Graveyard" cue. In *The Magnificent Ambersons*, the motif achieves closure by resolving upwards to the C_5 whereas in *Vertigo* its ascent and resolution are thwarted by a return to its opening pitch, before a varied sequential repetition.

In Welles's version, *The Magnificent Ambersons* ran to almost two and a quarter hours.[26] At a first preview on 17 March, 1942, the public response was largely unfavourable, and some of the audience even left the cinema during the showing. Although it was rapidly cut by some seventeen minutes for a second showing, which had a more enthusiastic reaction, the RKO management was still not satisfied, and the film was shortened yet again and new scenes shot. By its final version, it was only eighty-eight minutes in length, a butchered torso of the original conception. In the re-editing process, Herrmann's score was truncated to less than half its length—to just twenty-seven minutes—and Roy Webb was brought in to compose several new cues that were completely out of character with the rest of music, being written more in the hyper-romantic mode of Max Steiner.[27] Enraged by the treatment of both the film and his music, Herrmann threatened to sue the company if his name appeared in the credits and RKO agreed to his demand, fearing litigation.

Herrmann's next score was for another project in which Welles featured prominently, but this time only as an actor. *Jane Eyre*, based on the Brontë novel with a screenplay commissioned from Aldous Huxley, was originally devised by David O. Selznick. In 1942, Selznick sold the complete package to Darryl Zanuck at Fox, including the set designs, the director Robert Stevenson and the actress Joan Fontaine, with the suggestion that Welles should play Rochester against Fontaine's Jane.[28] Welles had already worked with Herrmann on a radio version of *Jane Eyre* in a "Mercury Theater on the Air" broadcast of 18 September, 1938, and he recommended, via Selznick, that Herrmann should be hired as the film's composer, although Zanuck apparently wanted Stravinsky.[29] The film marked the beginning of a close working relationship both with Fox and with Alfred Newman, the head of the studio's Music Department; only one of his next thirteen film scores (released between 1945 and 1955) would be written for another company (*On Dangerous Ground* for RKO).

The score for *Jane Eyre* is rather different to those of the previous two films.

Now, appropriately, English music becomes an important influence, and in particular that of the Bradford-born composer Frederick Delius. Delius (1862–1934) counted among his closest friends Percy Grainger, to whom he had dedicated his orchestral work *Brigg Fair* (1907), and it was probably during his studies with Grainger at New York University that Herrmann first discovered Delius's music. The title theme for *Jane Eyre*, which is later used in association with Rochester and Jane's developing love for each other, can usefully be compared with music from Delius's opera *A Village Romeo and Juliet* (1900–1901). Herrmann's harmony in the set of cues derived from the title theme material, like Delius's in *A Village Romeo and Juliet*, widely employs chords involving sevenths, ninths and above, displays a penchant for parallelism and stepwise motion in voicing and progression, and is conspicuous for its modal flexibility. This is not to suggest that Herrmann's musical language is derivative of Delius's—as a composer, he assimilated those elements of other people's style that he found appropriate and as much as any other Hollywood composer he was able to maintain a personal identity.

Rochester and Jane's theme from *Jane Eyre* returns almost wholesale in Cathy's aria, "Oh I am burning," from the third act of Herrmann's opera *Wuthering Heights*, which was composed between 1943 and 1951. Here it is associated with Cathy's love for Heathcliff, rather than for her husband Edgar and sets the text:

Oh I am burning. A thousand hammers are beating in my head. I wish I were out of doors. I wish I were a girl again, half savage and hardy and free and laughing at injustices, not mad'ning under them. Why am I so changed? Why does my blood rush into a hell of tumult at just a few words?[30]

The reuse of material from his film scores in the concert music is indicative of the extent to which both were intertwined in Herrmann's creative consciousness. Undoubtedly, his art-music has not had anything like the public success of his cinema works and has been regarded as of inferior quality by some critics. For instance, without offering any supporting evidence, David Thomson's estimate is that "as a 'serious' composer, Herrmann was pretentious and derivative."[31] As far as Herrmann was concerned, however, there was no distinction between the two categories, and in the interview with Zador and Rose, recorded in September 1970, he answered Rose's question "But you say that your concert music comes first?" rather indignantly:

I didn't say that at all. I mean I'm a composer. You write what you're writing, that's all. It doesn't make any difference. Concert music isn't any more sacred than any other music. You just write music as you want to write it.[32]

In 1945, Herrmann was given the opportunity to compose a score for another, but very different, film set in England—John Brahm's *Hangover Square* starring Laird Cregar as the turn-of-the-century composer George Harvey Bone, a Jekyll and Hyde figure whose murderous "lapses" are sparked off by a strange, shrill screeching sound (played by three piccolos) that only he can hear.[33] Bone's diegetic, "Concerto Macabre," which ends the film, was composed by Herrmann before filming began so that the final twelve minutes of the picture, which involve a complete performance of the work, could be shot to the music.[34] Conflating the three movements of a conventional concerto into a single span in much the same way that Ravel's Concerto for the Piano Left Hand does, the work speaks through a musical style that invokes both Liszt and Rachmaninov, its opening descending diminished fifth conventionally intimating notions of evil. Claudia Gorbman has brilliantly analysed music's function in *Hangover Square* in *Unheard Melodies: Narrative Film Music*, and she notes there that in the final scene of the film it "seems to have taken the story into its own hands."[35] For Gorbman, the piano concerto "motivates the events themselves: the causality of 'musical illustration' is reversed when, for example, the three doors open, each revealing a Scotland Yard detective—as if these events are obeying the dictates of three accents in the music."[36] If Herrmann is nodding his head towards modernism and in particular the expressionism of Schoenberg in this score, it is perhaps less in the "Concerto Macabre" than in the extraordinary and fantastic sonorities he conjures up to represent the dissonances that trigger George's attacks, and in the robotically manic music (described as being "anempathic" by Gorbman) of the organ grinder near the start of the film.

After *Hangover Square*, *Anna and the King of Siam*, directed by John Cromwell and starring Rex Harrison and Irene Dunne (1946), gave Herrmann the opportunity to play with musical exoticism, though characteristically within the framework imposed by a Western instrumentation. According to Smith, Herrmann did considerable research on Siamese (now Thai) music, though in fact relatively little was published explicitly about this field in English by the mid 1940s. Herrmann may have seen Strickland's piece in *Etude*, "Music and Dancing in Siam,"[37] but he is more likely to have come across Colin McPhee's fairly widely disseminated writings on the related music of Bali, which influenced, among other composers, Béla Bartók.[38] Given that Thai music is characterised by the use of a scale pattern in which only the octave has the same interval as that found in Western music, the seven-note modes involving the division of the octave into seven rather twelve equal intervals, it would not have been feasible for Herrmann to accurately transcribe Siamese melodic patterns into a form that was playable by a Western orchestra. His score is thus a compromise that sounds suitably South-East Asian to the indiscriminate Westerner but cannot really be taken as a faithful and authentic reproduction of the music of the region. That being said, Herrmann was probably more assiduous than most other Hollywood composers would have been in his attempts to ground his style in the autochthonous practices of Thailand, and at least the music does go beyond the simple use of pentatonicism to signify anything from the "East." In the 1953 Fox film, *White Witch Doctor*, directed by Henry Hathaway, Herrmann similarly attempted to emulate "African" music, particularly through his use of percussion instruments (various types of membraphone, tuned percussion and so on). Yet again, the success of the score is dependent on Herrmann's ability to catch some of the more superficial musical features shared by the continent of Africa with its multiplicity of artistic practices in a way that was digestible by a mass Western audience.

Herrmann's score for *The Ghost and Mrs. Muir*, directed by Joseph L. Mankiewicz for Fox and released in 1947, presents a partial return to the world of *Jane Eyre*, though more controlled and consistent, and it remained a personal favourite of the composer's. In mood, orchestration, and even to some extent thematic identity, it seems to foreshadow his music for *Vertigo*. Set in England in the early decades of the twentieth century it stars Rex Harrison as the ghost of a seafaring captain and Gene Tierney as a young widow who moves into his former home. The consequence of the film's romantic conceit is that the two, who grow to love each other, will be united after Mrs. Muir's death at the end of the film, and much of the nondiegetic music has an appropriately yearning and elegiac quality. Like *Jane Eyre*, it shares material with Herrmann's opera *Wuthering Heights*: the musical description of sunset which "breaks forth in its final expiring splendour" from the first act of the opera (just after Heathcliff and Cathy's duet "On the moors"), first appears during the title sequence of *The Ghost and Mrs. Muir* accompanying images of the sea.[39] This intensely lyrical music, which is dominated by a falling 8–7–6–5 melodic pattern supported by rippling arpeggiations, follows an idea that is distinctly redolent of Britten's "Dawn" Sea Interlude from *Peter Grimes*.[40] The entire first section of the cue "Andante cantabile" towards the end of the film, reappears in the fourth act meditation from *Wuthering Heights*. Among the many beautiful moments of this highly wrought score, "The Apparition" presents a most extraordinary texture in which an enormous musical space separates high from low sounds, a kind of orchestration which features in those cues in *Vertigo* in which Madeleine is presented to us as an otherworldly figure.

In the period between the completion of *The Ghost and Mrs. Muir* and 1950, Herrmann did not finish any film scores. This was partly because of the breakdown of his marriage to Lucille Fletcher (the divorce was settled in July 1948), his near total nervous collapse and an ensuing loss of faith in commercial music. Although his mental health began to recover by summer 1948 and he remarried in August 1949, it was the following year before he wrote his next score—for RKO rather than Fox—for Nicholas Ray's *On Dangerous Ground*. Smith notes that Herrmann represents the elements of good and evil in the film by contrasting musical characteristics.[41] His association of the viola d'amore, a fourteen-string relative of the viola that has seven sympathetic strings, with the blind character Mary Warden came about because of the "veiled" quality that he perceived in the instrument, Herrmann feeling that the "colour of the music was like her character."[42] The cue "The Death Hunt," which involves a particularly dazzling scoring for two antiphonal horn quartets, is one of the few sections of the film to receive concert airings, and looks forward in style to the prelude to *North by Northwest*.

Herrmann returned to Fox in 1951 to compose the score for Robert Wise's science fiction film, *The Day the Earth Stood Still*. Although it predates Louis and Bebe Barron's soundtrack for *The Forbidden Planet* (widely regarded as the first fully electronic "score," though the Barrons avoided that term) by some five years, Herrmann's music has stood the test of time rather better than theirs. In his interview with Ted Gilling, Herrmann remarked that it was his film "with the most experimental, avant-garde techniques ... at that time, we had no electronic sound, but the score had many electronic features which haven't become antiquated at all: electric violin, electric bass, two high and low electric theremins, four pianos, four harps and a very strange section of about 30-odd brass."[43] Particularly imaginative use is made of recording technology in the sequence accompanying Klaatu's "demonstration" in which electricity is neutralised and the world comes to an effective standstill, Herrmann using reverse-track techniques and adding oscillator tone to the melange. Despite the electronic resources employed, however, some of the most impressive writing is found in the cue "Radar" in which ostinato figures scored for pianos and timpani recall Stravinsky's *Les Noces* and Bartók's Sonata for Two Pianos and Percussion.

Of the subsequent eight films for Fox (*Five Fingers,* 1952; *The Snows of Kilimanjaro,* 1952; *White Witch Doctor,* 1953; *Beneath the Twelve Mile Reef,* 1953; *King of the Khyber Rifles,* 1953; *Garden of Evil,* 1954; *The Egyptian,* 1954—a collaboration with Alfred Newman; and *Prince of Players,* 1954) the second, *The Snows of Kilimanjaro* (1952) directed by Henry King and starring Gregory Peck, is probably the most powerful and compelling. The significance of Herrmann's treatment of the title music is considered in chapter 2, and his use of a figure in the opening scene both to indicate and confuse the musical point of view is discussed in chapter 4. This latter idea, composed of two distinct and contrary elements, is characteristic of a type of music found in a number of Herrmann's scores, including *The Magnificent Ambersons,* in which neighbouring figures are used to represent the ancient technology of the sleigh and the modern technology of the motor car, and Scorsese's *Taxi Driver,* where an accelerating rhythmic idea played by the percussion lies beside a tender saxophone theme, underlining the disturbed nature of Travis Bickle's psyche. The cue accompanying the scene in *The Snows of Kilimanjaro* that follows Harry's meeting with Cynthia Green (Ava Gardner) in the Paris jazz club simultaneously looks back to *The Ghost and Mrs. Muir* and forward to *Vertigo* in its subdued lyricism. Although the score does involve some touches of exoticism, for instance in the scene set around the campfire after the first successful big game hunt in Africa, they are generally quite tastefully done, and like the two films just discussed go far beyond the usual Hollywood attempts at the reproduction of ethnic music.

In a journal entry written in January 1955, the composer and friend of Herrmann, Lyn Murray, wrote:

Hitchcock is shooting another picture, *The Trouble with Harry.* He told me he doesn't have a composer for it yet. I now make what is probably the biggest mistake of my life. I recommend Herrmann for it. Hitch does not know Herrmann. I introduce them.[44]

In an editorial note, Murray adds, "It was love at first sight." By the beginning of March 1955, Herrmann had completed the score and recorded it in the second week of that month. Murray recorded Herrmann's treatment of the Paramount musicians and their response to him:

I introduced him to the orchestra. He had a hassle immediately with Charlie Strickfaden, the first oboe. He is a saxophone double and is not really the best first oboe in the world, but we all love him, he is such a nice man. But Herrmann is a martinet. Charlie did not please him. After the session Steve Czillag, head of music cutting, said to me. "He may be your friend but he is a prick." Herrmann has always been very superior about our complaints concerning the acoustics of the stage at Paramount. He said "You guys who can't conduct always blame it on the acoustics." Then they did this picture and they recorded it very close. After the dubbing session he admitted he was physically ill.[45]

Not only did *The Trouble with Harry* give Herrmann the chance to work with one of the world's most prestigious directors, it also allowed him to write a score for a comic film (albeit the comedy is rather black because it concerns the disposal of the eponymous Harry's body). In signing up for a Hitchcock film, Herrmann was join-ing a stable production team including director of photography Robert Burks and editor George Tomasini, and he would work with this group on most of Hitchcock's films up to the disagreement and fallout over *Torn Curtain* in 1965. Herrmann's score for *The Trouble with Harry,* composed for strings and woodwinds, has a number of clean-cut Stravinskyan and French neo-classical turns of phrase, and the dry acoustic and close microphone placement previously alluded to serve to accentuate them (and perhaps highlight some deficiencies in the Paramount or-chestra). Equally, some elements of the score hark back to the music Herrmann wrote for *The Magnificent Ambersons* thirteen years before, in particular the cue played as the doctor trips over Harry's body without being aware of its presence is reminiscent of the passage that accompanies George and Lucy's horse and trap ride.

Although Herrmann's name was regularly associated with television westerns (including the theme for *Gunsmoke*), he only wrote scores for two such films, the last (perhaps better described as a pre-western) being *The Kentuckian* in 1955, directed by Burt Lancaster for United Artists. Smith notes that the film's title music is adapted from Herrmann's youthful concert work "A Shropshire Lad" and thus, curiously, alludes to rural America in a style derived from the composer's English enthusiasms.[46] Herrmann certainly employs a modal melody initially based on the pitches C_4–$E\flat_4$–F_4–G_4–$A\flat_4$ with phrase endings marked by the pattern G_4–$E\flat$–F_4, that has many of the characteristics of English folk song as used, for example, by Vaughan Williams in his 1923 Folk Song Suite for military band. To describe the ensuing passage as a "vigorous fugue" as Smith does, is somewhat misleading, however.[47] Overall, it is one of Herrmann's more conventional scores and conforms to the classical model of film music identified by Gorbman.[48]

The following year, 1956, was to prove one of the most productive of Herrmann's career, with four film scores, including two for Hitchcock—*The Man Who Knew Too Much* (Paramount) and *The Wrong Man* (Warner). The first of these, *The Man Who Knew Too Much,* was a remake of Hitchcock's 1934 thriller involving the kidnap of Hank, the young son of doctor Ben McKenna (James Stewart) and his wife Jo (Doris Day), a popular singer.[49] The original version had at its climax a performance of the Australian composer Arthur Benjamin's stirring *Storm Clouds* cantata, and Herrmann decided to reuse this (albeit with an extra eighty seconds of music specially commissioned from Benjamin and some slight tinkering with the orchestration) rather than composing a new cue for the film. The sequence leading to the climactic shooting of the ambassador (in which we see Herrmann conducting the London Symphony Orchestra) is both brilliant and absurd, Hitchcock using every trick to wind up the tension. However, when the barrel of the assassin's gun appears from behind the curtain, it as likely to generate amusement as much as horror. Hitchcock is, as always, entirely self-aware and is, at least to some extent, parodying the genre in which he is working. Unfortunately, the film seems at times to be simply a prop for Doris Day's singing talents, her rather tawdry song "Que Será, Será" which went on to win an Oscar, sowing the seeds which would eventually end in Hitchcock's and Herrmann's break-up in 1965. Herrmann's contribution to the soundtrack is relatively slight, but the music used in the sequences around and in Ambrose Chapel is, as Royal Brown notes, close in mood and style to that associated with Madeleine/Carlotta in *Vertigo*.[50] It involves a very similar figure doubled in major thirds, slithering around high above a repeated D_4, and the descending pattern (Bb_3–A_3–Ab_3–Eb_3) also returns wholesale in the nightmare sequence in *Vertigo*.

Herrmann's score for the semi-documentary *The Wrong Man* is even sparer and more terse. The film concerns dance band bass player Christopher (Manny) Balastero (played by Henry Fonda) who is wrongly arrested for larceny. For much of the soundtrack, sound design usurps the role that might normally have been taken by music and a sense of unease is established by the careful orchestration of sound effects, especially those with a substantial noise content, such as those produced by subway trains and motor vehicles. The title music, a diegetic cue supposedly played by the Stork Club band, is illustrative of Herrmann's problems composing authentic sounding popular dance music, for it sounds rather limp. Sterritt offers an interesting critical reading of its function, however:

The music has a significant structure: fully voiced passages alternating with thinly orchestrated interludes. If they came occasionally, these interludes might serve as appealingly whimsical respites from the full passages, but heard with unsparing predictability, they become compulsive lapses into a weak and wan monotony. The stagnant pattern of Manny's life, which we will soon observe for ourselves, is echoed here all too vividly.[51]

The rest of the score seems brilliantly contrived, largely making use of the sounds of the instruments from the dance band and prioritising the double bass. The veiled tone of the bowed bass in high register set against low register pizzicati as Mannie enters his house after leaving work near the opening of the film is extraordinarily beautiful yet disturbing, as are the combinations of muted trumpet and plucked bass. Much of this seems to be *radio* scoring at its best, the small ensembles of carefully chosen colour surreptitiously underlining the narrative with discrete gestures such as the ostinato figure (F–Eb–Db–C) which escorts Mannie as he leaves the police cell, and the tense appoggiaturas from B to C in muted trumpets. The panic attack he suffers in his cell, which makes use of a spiralling camera movement, is supported by an accelerating figure in the trumpet, and as a musical gesture this prefigures Herrmann's accompaniment to Scottie's attacks of acrophobia in *Vertigo*.

Of the two other films Herrmann scored in 1956, *The Man in the Gray Flannel Suit* directed by Nunnally Johnson for Fox, and *Williamsburg — The Story of a Patriot* directed by George Seaton for Paramount, the former, starring Gregory Peck as an ex-serviceman, is the most significant, being among the most successful box office hits of the year. The cues "The Rain," "Farewell," and "Finale," which are suffused with a nostalgic, yearning quality, anticipate the music that Herrmann would compose to characterise Madeleine in *Vertigo*. After the intense activities of 1956, Herrmann only composed one film score in 1957— *A Hatful of Rain* for Fred Zinnemann (Fox). Like Hitchcock's *The Wrong Man* of the previous year, it is written in a quasi-documentary style and tells the story of a dope addict played by Don Murray. Herrmann's music foregrounds string tone in much the same way that *Vertigo* does, and there are several points of thematic connection, such as the falling appoggiaturas in the bass clarinets that reappear in *Vertigo* as Scottie stands looking at Carlotta Valdes's gravestone. Although there were good performances from many of the actors, the film was not a box office success and failed to make the $1.8 million it cost to produce.

In 1957, the year that *Vertigo* was filmed and when he was first approached to compose the score by Hitchcock, Herrmann was forty-six and at the height of his creative powers. He had established himself as one of the pre-eminent musical figures in Hollywood, though one who remained in many ways an outsider, partly because of the seriousness of his intent and partly because of his difficult and irascible manner. As Norman Corwin remarked:

His romantic ideals were integrity and the purity of his art. He was extremely intolerant of dictation from producers and directors who didn't know a damned thing about his music, and he sacrificed commissions and friendships over that.[52]

As a composer, he remained passionately concerned about music and its role in the drama of film, and in *Vertigo* he took the opportunity to demonstrate his artistry in a score which remains one of the high points of all film music.

NOTES

1. Roger Manvell, *Film* (Aylesbury and London: Penguin, 1944, rev. 1950), p. 76. This is taken from a section examining "the importance of film music."

2. Claudia Gorbman, *Unheard Melodies: Narrative Film Music* (Bloomington: Indiana University Press, 1987).

3. According to Herrmann's great nephew Steven E. Rivkin, Herrmann's father was born Avram Dardik, but called himself August Dardek when he first arrived in the United States. The date of birth is taken from his death certificate which actually gives his Abraham's father's family name as Herrmann. His Hebrew gravestone names him Avraham ben Moshe Yosef. Http://www.uib.no/herrmann/articles/family/rivkin01.html.

4. The death certificate notes that he had been a resident in New York for thirty years.

5. Rivkin.

6. Steven C. Smith, *A Heart at Fire's Center: The Life and Music of Bernard Herrmann* (Berkeley and Los Angeles: University of California Press, 1991), pp. 11–12.

7. From a conversation between Louis Herrmann and Craig Reardon of 4 June, 1979 quoted by Smith, p. 12.

8. Christopher Palmer, *The Composer in Hollywood* (London, New York: Marion Boyars, 1990), p. 243.

9. Vivian Perlis, *Charles Ives Remembered: An Oral History* (New Haven and London: Yale University Press, 1974), p. 155.

10. "Charles Ives," *Trend: A Quarterly of the Seven Arts*, vol. 1 no. 3, 1932, pp. 99–101.

11. Ibid.

12. Zador and Rose, "A Conversation with Bernard Herrmann," p. 229.

13. Members of the group included Herrmann and his old school friend Jerome Moross, Elie Siegmeister, Irwin Heilner, Henry Brant, Israel Citkowitz, Lehman Engel, Vivian Fine and Arthur Berger. See Smith p. 30.

14. Aaron Copland and Vivian Perlis, *Copland: 1900 through 1942* (London and Boston: Faber and Faber, 1984), p. 192.

15. Ibid.

16. Ibid., p. 193.

17. Lucille Fletcher, "One Iceberg Please: The Strange Case of Radio's Music Cue Man," *Detroit Free Press*, 14 May 1939. Cited in Smith, *A Heart at Fire's Center*, p. 46. Christopher Palmer reproduces the entire article but gives its source as *Screen and Radio Weekly*, 1936.

18. Smith, *A Heart at Fire's Center*, p. 72.

19. From an RKO cue sheet.

20. Bernard Herrmann, "Score For A Film: Composer Tells of Problems Solved in Music for 'Citizen Kane'," *The New York Times*, 25/5/41.

21. Ibid.

22. Ibid.

23. Herrmann, "Bernard Herrmann, Composer," p. 120.

24. Ted Gilling, "The Colour of the Music: An Interview with Bernard Herrmann," *Sight and Sound*, Winter 1971/2, p. 36.

25. See "The "hysterical cult of the director" *The Magnificent Ambersons*: Music and Theme," Chapter 6 of Kathryn Kalinak, *Settling the Score: Music and The Classical Hollywood Film* (Madison: University of Wisconsin Press, 1992), pp. 135–158.

26. This and subsequent information about the cutting of *The Magnificent Ambersons* is from David Thomson's *Rosebud* (London: Abacus, 1997), pp. 214–217.

27. Smith, *A Heart at Fire's Center,* p. 94.

28. Thomson p. 239.

29. Smith, *A Heart at Fire's Center*, p. 105.

30. Bernard Herrmann, *Wuthering Heights*, libretto adapted from Emily Brontë by Lucille Fletcher (London: Novello, 1965), pp. 192–94.

31. Thomson, *Rosebud*, p. 98.

32. Zador and Rose, "A Conversation with Bernard Hermann," p. 215.

33. The film's title refers to the address 12, Hangover Square, the composer's London residence.

34. The edited film includes pictures of a real pianist's hands cross-cut with Cregar's often less than convincing attempts to synchronise his hand and body movements to the music.

35. Claudia Gorbman, *Unheard Melodies: Narrative Film Music* (Bloomington: Indiana

University Press, 1987), p. 161.

36. Ibid.

37. *Etude*, lvi (1938), p. 440.

38. See my discussion of Bartók's use of Balinese music in the finale of his Concerto for Orchestra in *Béla Bartók: Concerto for Orchestra,* Cambridge Music Handbook, (Cambridge: CUP, 1996).

39. Bernard Herrmann, *Wuthering Heights*, pp. 50–52 and 69–72.

40. Britten's opera received its US premiere at Tanglewood in August 1946, conducted by Leonard Bernstein.

41. Smith, *A Heart at Fire's Center*, p. 157.

42. Gilling, "The Colour of the Music," p. 37.

43. Ibid., pp. 36–37.

44. Lyn Murray, *Musician: A Hollywood Journal of Wives, Women, Writers, Lawyers, Directors, Producers and Music* (Secaucus: Lyle Stuart Inc., 1987), p. 152.

45. Ibid. p. 153.

46. Smith, *A Heart at Fire's Center,* gives the date of this work as both 1934 (p. 195) and 1932 (p. 370).

47. Smith, *A Heart at Fire's Center,* p. 195.

48. See Gorbman, *Unheard Melodies*, p. 73 for a discussion of the classical model of film scoring.

49. In the original version the film involves the kidnap of an English couple's daughter.

50. Royal S. Brown, *Overtones and Undertones: Reading Film Music* (Berkeley and Los Angeles: University of California Press, 1994), pp. 156–57.

51. David Sterritt, *The Films of Alfred Hitchcock,* (Cambridge: Cambridge University Press, 1993), p. 69.

52. Directed by Joshua Waletzky, *Music for the Movies: Bernard Herrmann* (Sony, 1995).

CHAPTER 2

OVERVIEW OF HERRMANN'S MUSICAL
STYLE IN *VERTIGO*

As a serious composer, Bernard Herrmann was concerned as much with the intrinsically musical characteristics of his film scores as with the connections between music and images. It is my intention in this chapter to consider his musical style, particularly as it is demonstrated in his score for *Vertigo*, largely independently from its narrative function in the film, as this aspect is discussed in detail in chapters 5 and 6. Herrmann was a cultivated musician with a wide range of interests and an encyclopaedic knowledge of his subject. He was regarded in the industry as a consummate professional, but one who would not be cowed by criticism, or in Lyn Murray's words, "conform to the opinions, dogmas, policies and restrictions" placed on him by others.[1] He revelled in the creative possibilities of music, refusing to restrict himself to a single mode of expression or technique, and thus the score to *Vertigo* moves from Wagnerian chromatic harmony, through Pucciniesque diatonic *bel canto* to Schoenbergian atonal *Klangfarbenmelodie*. Although he was undoubtedly influenced by many other composers including Copland, Stravinsky and Delius, this should not to be taken to suggest that he was simply a talented *pasticheur* only capable of composing through the styles of others, for his is one of the most individual voices of the cinema. Rather, he adopted the mode of expression that he felt most appropriate to the individual cue in much the same way that his hero and friend Charles Ives availed himself of all the available musical resources in his works. The following overview considers the contribution of the various conventional parameters (melody, rhythm and metre, harmony and counterpoint, orchestration and form) to his style in preparation for the discussion of links between music and the narrative in later chapters.

MELODY

The words melody and melodic have been widely misused in the nontechnical literature to indicate the employment both of tonality and of a *cantabile* (singing) style. In *The Hitchcock Romance: Love and Irony in Hitchcock's Films*, for example, Lesley Brill remarks that the title music to *Vertigo* is "neither melodic nor atonal," suggesting thereby that these terms are somehow contradictory in meaning.[2] In the most basic sense however, melody is simply the consecutive placement of pitches in time. Thus, the title music has many elements which can be described as melodic, from the repeating two-bar arpeggiated figure which underpins the entire cue, through the falling pattern D_4–C_4–$E\flat_3$–D_3, to the statement of the four-note "love motif" (D_5–C_5–B_4–E_4). What distinguishes melodic lines one from another, whether tonal or atonal, is their internal construction, and in an interview conducted by Ted Gilling and published in *Sight and Sound* in 1972, Herrmann recalled Georges Auric's advice about the danger of using popular song melodies built from four or eight bar phrases in the context of a film score.[3] Once such a melody, very often composed in an AABA form, has begun, it continues largely under its own momentum. To break it off mid-stream prevents the realisation of the expectations inherent in the structure, and this may be detrimental to the rest of the narrative. This is not to suggest that Herrmann invariably avoids regular forms, for instance, in *The Three Worlds of Gulliver* (1961), stock eighteenth century dance movements such as the Minuet and Hornpipe with strict eight-bar phrases are used. However, his preferred method of melodic construction is from short units, generally one, two or four bars in length, which are often repeated or treated imitatively or sequentially.

The cue "Madeline" from *Vertigo* (Example 2.1) offers an interesting illustration of one—and perhaps the most elaborate—class of Herrmann's lyrical melodies.[4] It is thirteen-and-a-half bars in length, and is built from three four-bar phrases, the last of which is extended. If the first phrase is considered by itself (the bracketed passage at the beginning of Example 2.1), it will be seen that the elementary melodic unit is a four-note figure or cell and that four of these cells are organised in a balanced arrangement that can be compared to a poetic ABCB' rhyme scheme. Where a gap greater than a major or minor second appears within a cell, it is immediately filled by the subsequent note. The second phrase begins with same initial five pitches as the first ($F\sharp_4$–G_4–B_4–A_4–G_4) but its continuation is adjusted so that it forms a descending scale pattern the effect of which is to coalesce the two cells. Herrmann sequentially repeats the first two bars of the second phrase a perfect fourth higher while retaining the opening two pitches ($F\sharp$–G), the leap of a major sixth seeming all the more dramatic because of the narrow intervals used up to that point. The third phrase upsets the regularity of the melody hitherto by the insertion of a transposed partial repetition (marked x on the example). This retards the eventual climax with its ecstatically rising major seventh and decorated couplet $C\sharp_6$–B_6 (marked y), and moves the phrase structure back onto the strong beat so that the final two bars, which restore the register of the opening, now lie in accented positions.

Example 2.1
"Madeline."

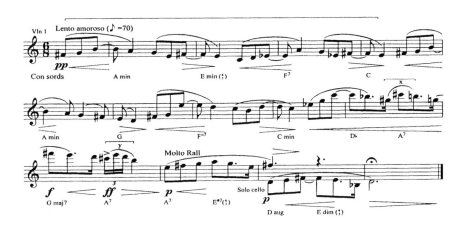

If the second phrase is regarded as a variant of the first, the overall structure of the cue is closer to *bar form* (the term used by the musicologist Alfred Lorenz to describe the AAB shapes he found in Wagner's works) than the homogenised standard song form (AABA). Herrmann is, of course, working under the specific constraints imposed by the film here, and his cue brilliantly supports the development of the narrative. The first phrase begins as the camera zooms into Madeleine (drawing our attention to her), the second on the medium shot of Scottie that prepares for his point of view of her framed by the doorway, and the third as she starts walking towards him from the door, the climax falling on her close-up in profile.

"Madeline's Car," the subsequent cue, accompanying Scottie's tailing of Madeleine through the streets of San Francisco, exhibits a less elaborate form of melodic construction. Here a five-note motif or cell, possibly derived from the last two bars of "Madeline" (Example 2.2) is the source of a series of very simple variants and extensions treated in an antiphonal manner. The phrase structure is regular, each of the first three ten-bar sections being composed of a two-bar introduction followed by four two-bar phrases based on the five-note cell. The pitch set that Herrmann employs in the first section (D–E–F–G♭–A♭–B♭–C♭) is not found in any diatonic scale, but neither is it chromatic, outlining five of the notes of a whole tone scale on D with two additional neighbour notes (F and C♭). Unlike "Madeline," there is a less clearly tonal focus and the harmonic underpinning provided by the ostinato accompaniment changes very slowly, with whole tone harmonies that have the same pitch content as augmented sixth chords rising by a semitone every ten bars during the first three sections.

Example 2.2
The Generating Five-Note Cell from "Madeline's Car."

In "Carlotta's Portrait," heard during the first scene set in the art gallery of the Palace of the Legion of Honour as Madeleine stands looking at the picture of Carlotta Valdes (Example 2.3), the chromatic melody played by the first flute has a compressed compass, all the pitches lying within the interval of a diminished fourth between $G\sharp_4$ and C_5. This melody can be seen to be a variant of the opening five notes of "Madeline" ($F\sharp$–G–B–A–G), transposed up a tone, modally adjusted and prefaced by A_4 (A–G$\sharp$–A–C–B–B$\flat$–A). No attempt is made at melodic development in the subsequent phrases and they simply repeat the figure at different levels and in different instrumentation, the guitar-like repetition of D_4 in the harp ensuring the tonal orientation of the cue, and the G$\sharp$ alluding to the sharpened fourth found in some flamenco modes. This type of suspenseful figure is a recurrent device in Herrmann's repertoire and a very similar one appears in *The Man Who Knew Too Much* (1956) in the scene in the Ambrose Chapel already alluded to in chapter 1 where Ben (James Stewart) regains consciousness after being attacked.

Example 2.3
"Carlotta's Portrait" Bars 5–12.

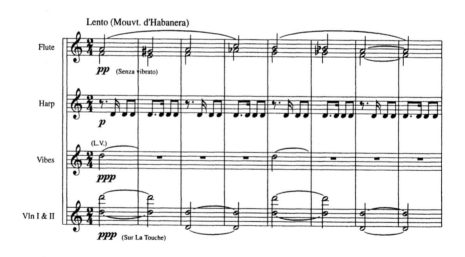

The use of repetition in "Carlotta's Portrait" is indicative of Herrmann's melodic writing at its most minimal. Two other simple methods of melodic extension and continuation commonly found in his scores are sequential repetition and cellular reordering. An example of the former technique can be seen in Example 2.4 in the development of the opening four-note cell from "Madeline" that brings the cue "The Beach" to its conclusion (accompanying the scene at Cypress Point where Madeleine and Scottie first kiss). It will be noted that the third sequential repeat of the figure (bar 7) is modified, the A_4 being altered to C_5 to maintain an unbroken melodic line between E_5 and B_4. The effect of this very subtle change is to make the descent to $E\flat_4$ in bar 9 of the example all the more dramatic. Herrmann eliminates the penultimate pitch ($A\flat$) from the final repeat in order to reinforce the sense of closure created by the cadence. This removes the irresolute appoggiatura $A\flat$ and pushes the G_4, the fifth of the C major chord that closes the cue, onto the first beat of the bar, the strongest accentual position.

Example 2.4
The Final Ten Bars of "The Beach."

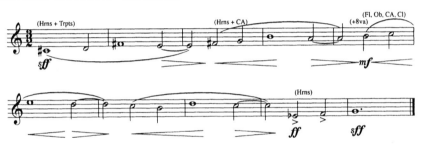

On this melody's reappearance in "Farewell" (at the Mission San Juan Bautista) it initiates a waltz-like passage in which the four-note cell is first reordered and then contracted to a three-note figure in a series of transformations that eventually leads to the crowning moment at the presentation of the "love motif" (D_5–C_5–B_4–E_4). Example 2.5 illustrates the succession of permutations of the figure, the double barlines demarcating bars which are not contiguous in the score.

Example 2.5
Stages in the Development of the Love Motif in "Farewell."

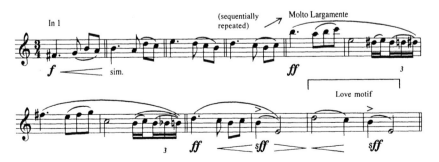

I have described the idea that appears in the last four bars as a "love motif" and this may suggest to the reader that it is treated in a leitmotivic fashion by Herrmann. In John Warrack's definition, a leitmotif is

A theme, or other coherent musical idea, clearly defined so as to retain its identity if modified on subsequent appearances, whose purpose is to represent or symbolize a person, object, place, idea, state of mind, supernatural force or any other ingredient in a dramatic work.[5]

In his 1941 *New York Times* piece, which was extensively quoted in chapter 1, Herrmann remarked that he was "not a great believer in the 'leitmotiv' as a device for motion picture music," though he had made use of them in *Citizen Kane*. Towards the end of his life, in the *Sight and Sound* interview with Ted Gilling, he commented that "I don't think that the leitmotif is the only way of writing a film score, because I think you can do it using the operatic principles of Verdi where each number is separate and not derived from the others."[6] Specific motifs do make very regular appearances in the score of *Vertigo*, however. For example, in the first half of the film (up to Madeleine's "death") close derivatives of the cue "Madeline" are heard in "The Flowershop," "Graveyard," "The Nosegay," "The Catalogue," "The Bay," "By The Fireside," "Exit," "The Outing" and "Farewell." Similarly, "Carlotta's Portrait" exerts its influence on a large number of other cues up to "The Necklace." These figures *do* seem to function as leitmotifs in the normally accepted sense defined by Warrack, namely as narrative devices, and demonstrate clearly that Herrmann did not turn his back completely on the compositional apparatus of the classical cinema.

Herrmann's remarks in the *Sight and Sound* interview were framed in the context of title music and the necessity or otherwise of thematic connection with the rest of the film. He noted that the main title music of *The Snows of Kilimanjaro* (which represents Harry Street's problems) is not used elsewhere in the film, and "other material has to evoke their solution."[7] In *Vertigo*, Herrmann builds almost the entire prelude out of what might seem to be a throwaway moment—the very brief cue accompanying the scene in the beauty parlour where Judy Barton is transformed back to Madeleine. The ostinato figure which dominates it embodies, in musical terms, three of the key motifs of the film — mirror images, spirals and obsession – by means of the constant repetition of a two-bar arpeggiated figure that has a number of axes of symmetry. Each of the four arpeggios of E♭ minor with major seventh (and, in the lower voice in the first bar, an added major 6th) is internally symmetrical and a looser symmetry, both horizontal and vertical, is found between pairs of bars. The melodic fragment in the brass, woodwinds and lower strings that follows is derived from the "mirror points" of the superimposed arpeggios, D and C in the first bar and E♭ and D in the second (circled in Example 2.6, see also Example 2.7). Arpeggiations of this kind are widely used by Herrmann and other examples can be found in the scores of *The Day the Earth Stood Still*, *The Man Who Knew Too Much* and *Beneath The Twelve Mile Reef.*

Example 2.6
The Ostinato Figure from "Prelude."

Moderato (misterioso)

RHYTHM, METRE AND HYPERMETRE

The rhythmic profile of Herrmann's music tends to be clean cut, sharp edged and relatively inflexible— that is, he prefers to use simple repeating units that are, in general, regular rather than irregular to support the underlying melodic characterisation. In much of the score to *Vertigo*, strings of even quavers, crotchets or minims dominate the surface of the music and the modernist tendency towards rhythmic complexity is avoided. A highly irregular rhythmic surface is liable to draw the viewer's attention towards the music, whereas recurrent patterns, and in particular ostinati (in which uniformity is the rule), establish a continuity that may be less likely to cause distraction. It is at least partly because of the stability of the motoric ostinato rhythms and the steady underlying pulse that the virtually aleatoric moments of "Roof-Top" and "The Tower" that disrupt it are so highly charged. However, Herrmann does employ figures with specific rhythmic features that will be familiar to his audience to help characterise a location, individual or mood (see the section on cultural referents in chapter 4). The baroque dance rhythms used in *The Three Worlds of Gulliver*, the waltz of *The Magnificent Ambersons* and the habanera of "Siesta" from *Garden of Evil* are but three examples of such "prepackaged" materials, and in *Vertigo*, waltz, habanera, and residual tango and cha-cha-cha rhythms are found.

An examination of Table 4.1 in chapter 4 demonstrates that the shorter cues tend to be more metrically regular, with unchanging time signatures throughout their course, whereas some of the longer ones, such as "The Letter," which draws on fragments from earlier cues, can be considerably more complex. Though Herrmann tends to restrict himself to the most common metres (simple duple, triple and quadruple and compound duple times), two cues, "Good Night" and "The Necklace," briefly involve quintuple time signatures. In both cases, there is a musical and narrative reason for the use of the quintuple metre, rather than simply for the technical convenience of the timing of the cue.

If Herrmann's score tends towards uniformity on both rhythmic and metrical levels, it does occasionally display a disparity between metrical and hypermetrical levels. Hypermetre denotes the hierarchical metrical organisation of the music on levels below the music's surface, describing the grouping of bars and phrases in an analogous way to beats within a bar. Figure 2.1 illustrates four hypothetical hypermetrical levels in a sixteen-bar phrase: in the uppermost cells of the table are the sixteen individual bars; in the subsequent row, the first hierarchical level of the hypermetre is shown, bars being grouped in pairs with the odd numbers marking strong hypermeasures and the even numbers weak hypermeasures. This pattern is repeated in the higher levels of the structure.

Figure 2.1
Hypothetical Hypermetrical Levels in a Sixteen Bar Phrase.

1	2	3	4	5	6	7	8	9	10	11	12	13	14	15	16
1		2		3		4		5		6		7		8	
1				2				3				4			
1								2							

The hypermetrical structure of the first sixteen bars of "Prelude" is schematised in Figure 2.2. While the two lowest levels (one and two bars, respectively) are regular, presenting the ostinato pattern shown in Example 2.6, the third row of the figure introduces a degree of hypermetrical complexity. It is seen that the bars are grouped (after the first two bars) in units of three, the shaded hypermeasure representing a strong hyperbeat at that level. To complicate matters further, the onset of pitches halfway through a bar subdivides the three-bar groups into two (see Example 2.7). In the subsequent level the three-bar units are themselves initially grouped in threes establishing a further triple hypermetre. Clearly there is a kind of metrical "dissonance" between the second and third rows of the figure, and this dissonance helps to propel the music powerfully through the "Prelude." This type of organisation is, in fact, rather unusual in the score to *Vertigo* and nowhere else is it used to create such ambivalence and ambiguity, though it does play a role in "Roof-Top" and its derivatives.

Figure 2.2
The Hypermetrical Structure of the First Sixteen Bars of "Prelude."

1	2	3	4	5	6	7	8	9	10	11	12	13	14	15	16
1		2		3		4		5		6		7		8	
1		2			3			4				5			6
1		2										3			

Example 2.7
The Figure in Long Notes from Bars 3–8 of "Prelude."

Obs, C.A., Hrns,Tbns

B. Cls, Bsns, C. Bn.,
Hrns, Tbns, Tuba,
Vla, Vcl, C.B.

TONALITY, HARMONY AND COUNTERPOINT

The Western art-music tradition, at least until the rise of Modernism, tended to favour consistency in the treatment of dissonance within a work, whether a song, a sonata, a symphony, an opera or whatever. Generally speaking, up to the beginning of the twentieth century, the interaction between dissonance and consonance was an important means by which musical form was established and projected through time, more dissonant events requiring resolution onto more consonant ones. Of course, the definition of dissonance was subject to constant revision and what was deemed unacceptable by a composer writing in one era might be freely used by later generations. Like his mentor Charles Ives, however, Herrmann managed to accommodate a range of approaches to dissonance treatment in his scores such that at one moment cues may be unequivocally diatonic, at another display an impressionistic penchant for parallelism and at yet another come close to atonality. This requires an unconscious re-evaluation of the status of consonance and dissonance according to the context, a characteristic that may seem to align Herrmann's approach with Postmodernism in the absence of a single tonal and harmonic metanarrative. Thus, a major ninth over a major or minor chord may be regarded as a dissonance requiring resolution in one situation (e.g., in "Madeline") or a relative consonance in another (such as those instances of the love motif, where an A min^9 chord harmonises the falling fifth B – E). Likewise, the A♭/B♭ dyad that permeates "The Mission," the cue that accompanies Scottie and Madeleine driving to the Dolores Mission in the first quarter of the film, is felt to be a stable, if disturbing, event within the context of the cue, for we do not expect the A♭ to fall to G.

The most unambiguously diatonic cue in *Vertigo* is "The Park," a Puccinian *bel canto* melody that accompanies Judy and Scottie as they walk together past the Golden Gate Park (the first eight bars are shown in Example 2.8). Although, like the rest of the score, it is written without key signature, it is obviously in the key of G♭ major; however its harmonic palette is restricted to chords of G♭, A♭ min^7, C♭^{7}, E♭^{7} and F^{ø7}, the latter leading-note seventh chord bringing the cue to its end. It will be noticed that Herrmann actively steers clear of the dominant chord with its powerful cadential function here. The avoidance of closure seen throughout *Vertigo* is a feature of much film music, for the perfect cadence effects a forceful point of resolution that can improperly or incongruously punctuate the narrative. Where

Herrmann does finish a cue with a root position tonic chord, there is generally a good narrative reason for it—for example, at the end of "The Beach," just after Scottie and Madeleine have kissed for the first time, and the end of "Scene d'amour" the parallel point in the second part of the film. Even in these places, however, Herrmann does not use a conventional (V–I or IV–I) cadential structure, but prefaces the tonic with a chord of the flattened submediant major (A♭ major in C major).

Example 2.8
The First Violin Part of Bars 1–8 of "The Park."

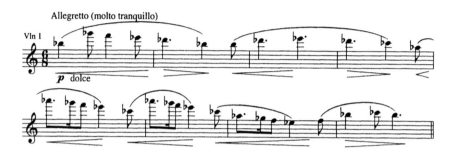

This cadential figure (♭VI–I), which can be seen as a kind of substitute plagal cadence, develops into an important device in the cues subsequent to "The Beach" forming one of the principal musical fingerprints of the score and appearing in a number of guises including the final cadence of the film.[8] In the very brief cue "3 A.M." which follows "The Beach" (Example 2.9), three different harmonisations of the love motif appear, involving progressions from A♭ to E min[6], to an implied A min[9] and to Cmaj7 respectively. The more conventional resolution of the A♭ chord would have been to E♭ major (requiring the B and E to be flattened) and the uplift created by the progression between A♭ major and the tonally "brighter" chords that Herrmann actually uses is palpable.

Example 2.9
Short Score of "3 A.M."

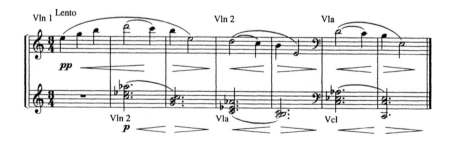

The voicing of the cue is arranged so that the chords in the second violins, violas and cellos do not progress smoothly, the parts moving between notes by large jumps, but in sections of *Vertigo* (for example, in the cue "Farewell") and other film scores, Herrmann adopts "nearest-neighbour" motion between voices. In the prelude to *Psycho*, for instance, an oscillation between chords containing the pitches $A\sharp_3–C\sharp_4–G_4–B_4$ and $B_3–D_4–F\sharp_4–A\sharp_4$ is established in which every instrumental part moves by semitone step. Similarly, in *Citizen Kane*, the so-called "power" figure involves nearest-neighbour movement between a first inversion chord of E minor $(G_2–B_2–E_3)$ and a root position chord of A♭ minor $(A\flat_2–C\flat_2–E\flat_3)$, the $B_2/C\flat_3$ forming a pivot tone. In the cue "Good Night," which is heard in the scene following Scottie and Judy's meal at Ernie's, a simple example of the technique can be observed in the alternation between chords of $F\sharp^{\circ 7}$ and $A\flat^7$ in the second violins, violas and cellos (Example 2.10). In this pairing of chords, the first, half diminished, chord is the weaker partner and sounds harmonically indecisive, while the second, a dominant seventh chord on A♭ is more potent and dynamic and the interplay between the two harmonic units mirrors and supports the interplay between Scottie and Judy (see chapter 6 for a fuller discussion).[9]

Example 2.10
"Good Night" Bars 10–19.

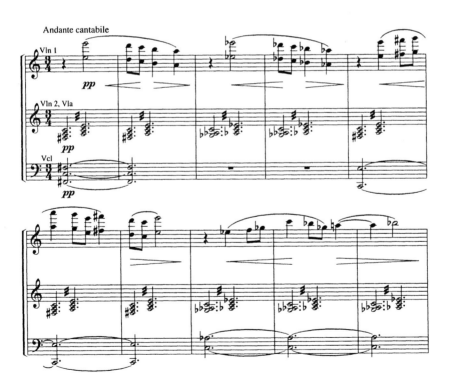

The opening bars of the cue "Farewell" involve harmony that, using Schoenberg's term, might be described as *roving*, in other words, no stable tonality is expressed by many of the chords.[10] This passage cannot be regarded as modulatory in effect, and it certainly does not prepare the way for the subsequent section in which the habanera rhythm on D is reiterated. Instead, it is underpinned by tonic (E minor) and dominant (B[7]) chords connected by more or less remotely related harmonies (a number of which are *vagrant*, with multiple meanings), and part writing involving motion by small intervals (tonic and dominant chords are marked in bold):

E min^{16} – Cmaj^7 – D^{ø7} –
B^7/F – A aug – C♯^{9} – C^7 (= German 6th in E) – C$^{7-♭5}$ (= French 6th in E) – D♭ aug♭^{7}/E♭ –
C♭^{7} (= B^7) –
E min^{16} – Cmaj^7 – D^{ø7} – **B^7/F**

"Madeline," the melody of which was discussed previously, offers a further example of Herrmann's exploitation of functional diatonic harmony. The first two four-bar phrases both proceed from species of A minor chords to harmonies on C (major in the first case and minor in the second) by way of conventional progressions. In the continuation of the third phrase, however, Herrmann moves the melodic line and its harmonisation a tone higher than might have been expected, so that the cue ends on D rather than C. The feeling of uplift this creates further supports the shot of Madeleine in profile. In this cue, Herrmann avoids closure by failing to harmonise the last note at all, leaving the unison D unaccompanied. As well as sustained unisons, other common strategies for the evasion of closure include:

1. Diminished seventh chords ("The Flowershop," "The Nosegay");

2. Tonic chords with minor seventh ("The Alleyway," "The Mission");

3. Half-diminished seventh chords ("By The Fireside," "Farewell");

4. Augmented triads ("Exit").

The final two species of chords listed above tend to promote a weaker tonal orientation. The half-diminished seventh chord (or "Tristan chord"), a mainstay of the late-Romantic harmonic repertoire — which, it is often stated, prepared the foundations for the break up of tonality — saturates the harmony from the cue "Sleep" onwards. The augmented triad, and other chords derived from the whole tone scale, was a favourite of the so-called impressionist composers because of its harmonic ambiguity and the sense of "suspension" that it can suggest. Herrmann uses augmented triads widely in the cue "The Alleyway," heard as Scottie waits for Madeleine in the alley behind Podesta's flower shop, where their effect is to amplify his feelings of confusion and concern.

A particular trait of Herrmann's writing in *Vertigo* is the use of parallelism, whether involving the doubling of a melody or the parallel motion of block chords, and in this respect it displays the influence of French impressionism. The melody of "Carlotta's Portrait" (see Example 2.3) is doubled a major third below throughout,[11] and the subsequent cue, "The Hotel," finishes with the repetition of a pair of apparently unrelated root position minor triads (A min and F min) played first by three trombones and then by a trio of trumpets. This chord sequence is extended further in "The Hallway" by the addition of a G minor chord that leads back to an A minor triad (A min – F min – G min – A min). Parallel and semi-parallel motion are also fundamental aspects of the mysterious cue "The Forest" (see Example 2.11). The basic harmonic unit of the opening seven bars is a major seventh chord in second inversion (e.g., Cb–Eb–Fb–Ab), though this is briefly transformed to a minor chord with sharpened elevenths for the two chords in the third bar, and an altered augmented sixth for the first chord in the fourth bar before reverting to strict parallel motion. Tonal directionality is obscured by the chromaticism of the upper voice and by the lack of differentiation between individual harmonies in terms of their construction, for it is the difference in the modality of chords as well as their hierarchical position that produces the sense of progression in tonal harmony. In "The Forest," perhaps more than in any other cues, Herrmann's language comes closest to atonality in the Schoenbergian sense.

Example 2.11
The Opening Seven Bars of "The Forest."

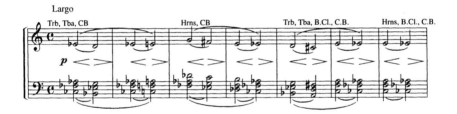

The chord built from a minor triad with a major seventh has been described as the "Hitchcock chord" by Royal S. Brown because of its frequent appearance in the scores Herrmann wrote for Hitchcock.[12] This harmonic unit was also particularly favoured by Bartók in his early music and has been labelled hyperminor by the Hungarian analyst Erno Lendvai. For Bartók, the chord, and its unfolding as a rising arpeggio, was a symbolic representation of his friend Stefi Geyer and of his love for her, whereas in Herrmann's scores it seems to represent a state of intense apprehension. We first find it in *Vertigo* as the initial event of the Prelude, the opening triplet figure spelling out the pitches Eb –Gb–Bb–D, and subsequently in bar 12 it is sustained for four bars by brass and woodwinds. This chord would seem to be the matrix of the "Vertigo chord," the superimposition of Eb minor and D major triads heard in "The Tower" at the climax of the first half of the film as Scottie is repeatedly racked by acrophobia (Example 2.12). The lower five notes spell out a chord of Eb min[17] (the upper F♯ being the enharmonic equivalent of Gb) while the upper note (A)

is a sharpened eleventh. It has been suggested that this should be considered as a bitonal chord, in other words as a harmony that has two simultaneous roots.[13] Bartók, among others, has demonstrated the inherent problem of the notion bitonality, for the ear will invariably tend to prioritise a single pitch, and in the case of the "Vertigo chord," it is hard to escape the influence of E♭ as the root of the chord.

Example 2.12
The "Vertigo Chord" as It Appears in Bar 32 of "The Tower."

Herrmann's avoidance of conventional cadential structures, and his employment of parallel progressions, roving harmonies and vagrant chords, results in considerable tonal ambiguity. An examination of Table 4.1 in chapter 4 reveals that the tonality of a number of the cues is at best difficult to establish and relatively few employ single, unequivocal and stable key centres. While, like Stravinsky's, the music regularly alludes to the practices of tonality, it often employs them in unorthodox ways. Similarly, Herrmann does not seem to have been interested in codifying his compositional technique; he was, rather, an empiricist who relied on his experience and instinct rather "mystical incantations" or "artificial neoclassic rules."

Very little of Herrmann's writing in *Vertigo* can be regarded as contrapuntal in the normal sense. Brill claims that there is a "tranquil fugue in the Mission Dolores," but this is incorrect, the cue simply involving a sequentially-repeating pattern which sounds rather like a student exercise in fifth species counterpoint in three voices.[14] Otherwise the cues are largely homophonic except for the very simple descants found in "Carlotta's Portrait," "The Gallery" and "The Dream," and the textural overlay in "Roof-Top," "The Tower" and "The Letter."

ORCHESTRATION AND INSTRUMENTATION

Herrmann was one of the most brilliant orchestrators working in Hollywood, and unlike the majority of his peers, did not pass this aspect of his work over to others. As explained in chapter 1, he learnt his trade working for radio shows and developed a keen sense of the dramatic possibilities of music. Some of the radio scoring was for very small ensembles—the CBS series *Crime Classics* (1952), for instance, involved just three musicians, with an occasional fourth when finances allowed. Herrmann's film instrumentation was often eccentric: the "Sleigh ride" from *The Magnificent Ambersons* is scored for three glockenspiels, two celestes, piano, two harps, small and large triangles and jingles; *The Day the Earth Stood Still* uses two theremins, electronic violin, bass and guitar, four harps, four pianos, percussion and brass; *Psycho* is scored for string orchestra; *Journey to the Center of the Earth* requires five organs; and *On Dangerous Ground* has a solo part for viola d'amore. In the score to *Vertigo* a conventional large symphony orchestra is called for, but rarely used as a tutti. Table 3.1 in chapter 3 demonstrates that only nine cues involve the full orchestra, the others being scored for carefully selected smaller ensembles.

The radio work also instilled in Herrmann an awareness of how music could interact with speech effectively. In the context of *Citizen Kane*, sound engineer, James Stewart, reminisced that "Bernie understood the type of orchestration that would go under dialogue. It made it possible for you to have more music underneath dialogue, and very effectively."[15] Although the score to *Vertigo* is strongly characterised by the use of string tone, as the violinist and personal friend of Herrmann, Louis Kaufman, remarked in 1992:

[He] had his own conceptions of sound. We tried to please him of course and be expressive as we possibly could — a lot of vibrato and so forth — and [he] immediately shut down on it. "Oh no, this is wrong. Cool it down. I don't want a hot sound. I want it very cold and very factual." There had arisen by this time what we call the Hollywood style, which was to play beautifully and with a lot of expression and vibrato, especially with a master like Al. Newman. But he didn't want that. He'd say "no, forget about your old conceptions."[16]

Interestingly, apart from a few of the passages written for the full orchestra, almost every cue in *Vertigo* involving strings requires them to be muted. Muted string tone has both of the features mentioned by Stewart and Kaufman: its thinner timbre means that it is less likely to interfere with dialogue and it is "colder," more distant and less intense than the natural sound.

Herrmann employs a variety of conventional colouristic techniques in his string writing, ranging from tremolo, both *sul pont* (bowing near the bridge—producing an eerie, glassy sound) and *sul tasto* (on the fingerboard—creating a much softer, gentler and flute-like sound); through pizzicato (the use of this effect in the last section of "Madeline's Car" is particularly impressive); to double and triple stopping. Rarely does he use solo strings, probably because of their particularly expressive tendencies, the brief cello phrase in the last two bars of "Madeline" and the final appoggiatura played by a single first violin at the end of "The Bay" being the sole exceptions. Where solo writing might have been expected because of his use of the extreme high register, for example in the cues "Graveyard" and "The Flowershop," Herrmann explicitly requires the full complement of violins.[17]

Example 2.13 presents the first nine bars of "Good Night," the second section of which was already discussed. Here the strings are muted and multiply divided, and for the first eight bars, the melody lies in the first violins against a sustained accompaniment. The voicing initially places the first violins high above the rest of the ensemble, and in the course of the opening section, melody and accompaniment work towards each other, gradually filling in the musical space between the two elements. At the beginning of the fifth bar, the first desks of violas and cellos join the first violins, the cellos adapting the melody in bar 6. As is the case throughout the score, expressive markings are highly specified, the crescendo-diminuendo figure being particularly characteristic.

Example 2.13
The First Nine Bars "Good Night."

   Although string tone is the foundation of Herrmann's orchestration of *Vertigo*, woodwind timbre, and particularly that of the flute, clarinet and bass clarinet in their lower, darker and richer registers, is a significant component of many of his textures. The use of three flutes to double the chromatic ostinato figure *ff* at the beginning of "Roof-Top" starting from C_4 is an audacious touch, and although the passage is awkward to play, it is remarkably effective. Similar use of the extreme low register is found in "The Streets" (as Scottie follows Madeleine through San Francisco for the second time). Here the resonant $E\flat_4$ is sustained by two flutes doubling the upper-most pitch of the repeated chords in clarinets and bass clarinets; and later, in "The Nightmare," Herrmann asks for awkward trills between $D\flat_4$ and $E\flat_4$ to be performed *sff*.[18] Two further interesting examples of the use of low-register flute tone are found in "Carlotta's Portrait" (Example 2.3), in which the flutes are required to play without vibrato, creating a thin, spectral sound, and in "Dawn" where three flutes and three clarinets provide the initial harmonic support to the violin melody. Occasional use is made of fluttertonguing in "The Nightmare"—a chromatically rising passage which recalls Stravinsky's use of the technique in "Danses des Adolescentes" from *Le Sacre du Printemps* — and "The Return." Herrmann uses the piccolo and alto flute sparingly, the former appearing particularly dramatically in the "Vertigo chord" (see later) and in "The Forest," where it eerily doubles the flutes at the octave *senza vibrato*, and the latter, briefly, in "The Dream."

The oboe is commonly treated as a lyrical instrument and it is possibly because of its highly expressive connotations that Herrmann uses it so seldom in *Vertigo*, though his rather unfortunate experiences with the Paramount orchestra's oboist in *The Trouble with Harry* may have rather warned him off it.[19] Like the flute, he utilises it in its low register in "Roof-Top," "The Tower" and "The Nightmare," and it makes brief solo appearances in "Madeline's Car" and "The Necklace," but otherwise its main employment is in orchestral tuttis. Herrmann seems to prefer the even richer tone of the cor anglais to that of the oboe, and in "The Forest" he scores an exceptionally intense passage (which reappears three times in the cue) for three cor anglais, two bassoons and a contrabassoon.

Clarinets and bass clarinets are essential voices in Herrmann's orchestra and they figure in many of the small ensemble cues either as melody instruments (in "The Window," "The Alleyway," "The Catalogue," "The Streets" and "The Dream") or supplying the accompaniment (in "Madeline's Car," "The Flowershop," "Carlotta's Portrait," "The Mission," "Graveyard," "Tombstone," "The Outing" and "The Past"). Again, he prefers the lower chalumeau and clarino registers, and rarely lets them climb into the highest octave, even in orchestral tuttis. Particularly characteristic combinations of clarinets and bass clarinets are found in the gently throbbing ostinato figure from "Madeline's Car" (Example 2.14) and the sinister cue "Tombstone," with its falling appoggiaturas in the second bass clarinet. Much of the clarinet writing is marked *quasi subtone*, a jazz technique that involves breathing, rather than blowing, into the instrument in the "hollow" chalumeau register. A notable example of this technique is found at the beginning of the cue "The Letter" (as Judy begins writing the letter to Scottie explaining to him who she really is) where close-voiced five-part chords played subtone descend chromatically.

Example 2.14
The Clarinet Ostinato Figure from "Madeline's Car."

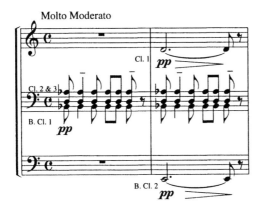

Herrmann seldom uses bassoons and contrabassoons in any role other than in tuttis in *Vertigo*, and they are almost never heard solo.[20] However, horns are very widely employed, sometimes as a foil to flute and clarinet tone, as in "Carlotta's Portrait" and often in a full-blooded melodic function, as at the end of "The Beach" (Example 2.4). The most scintillating effect is probably that found in "The Bay," at the moment when Madeleine throws herself into the water, three unison horns becoming involved in the antiphonal interplay of an arpeggiated wave-like figure with the strings (Example 2.15). Elsewhere, muted tone and hand-stopping (often with sforzatos and crescendos) predominates. The pedal tones played by four unison horns on C_2 immediately prior to the vertigo chords from, and at the end of, "Roof-Top" solidly support these climactic moments.

Example 2.15
The Horn Figure from "The Bay."

While the heavy brass appears regularly in the full orchestral cues, they make infrequent appearances in the score otherwise, and very rarely in solo roles. Striking use of a brass nonet (three each of horns, trumpets and trombones, all muted) is found in "The Hallway," heard as Scottie follows the manageress of the McKittrick Hotel up to Carlotta Valdes's room. Here, in an extremely simple but effective gesture, three-part chords are antiphonally passed between trios of trombones, trumpets and horns. Of the percussion, the vibraphones are the most frequently and effectively used, playing throughout "Prelude" and "Roof-Top" and supplying delicate bell-like touches in other cues. Harps supply colouristic touches such as the free glissandi of the vertigo chord and the guitar-like reiterations of "Carlotta's Portrait" as well as more conventional arpeggiations in "The Park" and "Farewell." The Hammond organ is sparingly, but brilliantly used, and the sonority found at the heart of "The Forest" where a B♭ minor "Hitchcock chord" is sustained against bass clarinets, vibraphones, cymbals and basses is particularly remarkable for its spine-chilling quality.

ORCHESTRATION OF TUTTIS

Despite his employment of a very large orchestra, Herrmann rarely exploits the full forces simultaneously, preferring to ration his resources and often making use of antiphonal interplay between smaller subgroups. Example 2.16 illustrates his treatment of foreground and background elements at the climax of "Scène d'amour" one of but a few passages scored for the complete orchestra. The melodic material presents a variant of the figure discussed in Example 2.5, adapted so that the

Example 2.16
The Climax of "Scène d'amour."

opening pitches of the its three bars rise rather than fall. The unison melody is played by strings (except double basses) and all but the lowest woodwind, with a slight simplification of its contour by the removal of the turn in the oboes, cor anglais, second and third clarinet and cello. Harmonic support is supplied by the rest of the woodwind, brass, harp and basses.

Trumpets and timpani are reserved until the culminating moment of the final cadence onto a chord of C major at the end of the cue, some seven bars later. The combination of bass clarinets, bassoons, contrabassoon, tuba and double basses playing the bass notes creates a powerfully deep and substantial sound, a solid foundation for the resonant chords in trombones and horns.

The avoidance of trumpets in a melodic role is, in fact, very typical of the scoring of the full orchestral cues in *Vertigo*, and only for very brief moments does Herrmann allow them that function. Instead they are used in a small number of specific contexts:

1. In the "Vertigo chord" ("Roof-Top," "The Tower," "The Nightmare" and "The Return") where high, sustained chords are played with hard mutes;

2. At the climax of "The Bay," where the descending sequence of chords is doubled;

3. In "The Forest," where they provide a colouristic effect through the employment of cup mutes against a quiet oscillating figure in flutes and piccolo;

4. At the very end of longer cues ("The Beach," "Dawn" and "Finale") where they supply harmonic support by playing block chords in low register.

FORM

The musical form of film cues is usually constrained by narrative requirements. However, Herrmann tends to avoid close synchronisation with on-screen events, and his cues are generally fully wrought even if they finish ambiguously with a diminished seventh chord or augmented triad. The structure of "Madeline" was previously discussed in the context of melodic writing and in chapters 5 and 6 attention is drawn to the musical construction of other individual cues. As an example of large-scale form in the film, "Prelude," the overture to *Vertigo*, will now be considered in some detail. Herrmann's attitude to the role of title music varied from film to film — in some it was entirely independent from the rest of the score and in others it was integrally related. In *Vertigo* it has clear thematic links with two ideas used later in the film, the "love motif" (Example 2.5) and the ostinato figure heard in the very short scene in the Elizabeth Arden beauty salon as Judy is transformed to Madeleine (Example 2.6). In the examination of the latter melody above it was noted that this idea has a number of axes of symmetry and could be taken as a musical embodiment of a mirror, one of the key props in the film (mirrors appear on very many occasions, and it is by means of a mirror that Scottie realises the truth in Judy's hotel room as she puts on the necklace). Equally, its insistent repetition, first in triplet crotchets and later in triplet quavers, intimates an obsessional neurosis.

The Prelude (cue **1A**) is written in two unequal length but closely related sections, the second beginning as the triplet quavers make their appearance. Although the arpeggios played by flutes, clarinets, harps and tremolando violins have the pitch content of E♭ min^{17} (with an added major 6th in the first bar of each pair) — Royal Brown's "Hitchcock chord" — the opening phrase (D–C–E♭–D) and the final note of the cue prioritise the note D. The instability of the hypermetre has already been considered, and its effect is to generate a feeling of uncertainty and anxiety. As James Stewart's name appears in the credits, the brass, oboes, cor anglais, bass clarinets and bassoons play *sff*, a sustained chord of E♭ min^{17}, a shock after the previous three-and-a-half bars of quiet and brittle arpeggios in the harps and celesta supported by a regular triangle stroke every minim (like the delicate chiming of a distant bell) that accompanies the partial view of a woman's face. The musical model that has been established is now repeated, this time leading to a chord of A♭ major in first inversion as Kim Novak's name appears. As will be remembered from the discussion of the harmony of "3 A.M.," the chord of A♭ major is an important element of the love theme, and the final cadences of both the pivotal cue "Scène d'amour" and "Finale" use A♭ as the penultimate chord, functioning as a substitute subdominant in a kind of plagal cadence. With the arrival of Alfred Hitchcock's card, the E♭ min^{17} chord is played an octave lower than before, continuing the downward trend of the block chords, tubas and lower strings adding further weight to the proceedings. A clinching chord which coalesces A♭ min and E♭ min^{17} over a low C natural accompanies the film's title *Vertigo*. (The same conjunction of A♭ and E♭ minor accompanies Scottie's fainting fit in Midge's flat when he tries to look down from the chair he has climbed.) Despite the simplicity of Herrmann's musical gestures the ear and brain are by now thoroughly confused by the accumulation of contradictory signals.

In the second stage of the first part of the prelude, trilling flutes and violins accompanied by rolls on the two vibraphones play a rising scale of E♭ minor in seconds (D–E♭, E♭–F, G♭–A♭, A♭–B♭, B♭–C♭ repeated an octave higher) against the emerging image of a spiral on screen. This leads to a statement of the love motif (Example 2.17), opening with the same falling figure (D–C) that was heard at the start of the prelude, the extension in the figure (B–E) seeming to be a logical development of it. Both the ostinato figure and the orchestration have been adapted to their new harmonic context, and the arpeggios in strings, flutes and clarinets (joined by harps on the A min^9 and Cmaj7 chords) are clearly derived from the underlying harmony. The first section ends on an augmented triad, a conventional marker for suspense.

Example 2.17
Love Motif from "Prelude."

The second part of the prelude is a varied recapitulation of elements from the first. It begins with the arpeggios heard at the beginning of the cue, inverted and played at double speed by harps and celesta (Example 2.18). In the course of the subsequent eighteen bars, the figure, variously reworked, is antiphonally bounced between, on one hand the harps and celesta and on the other the violins, flutes and clarinets. The D–C–E♭–D idea is split into its four component pitches, each lasting for two bars and separated by two bars of the ostinato played by harps and celesta. A duple hypermetre has by now been firmly established, and the love motif (Example 2.17) is now repeated in two-bar units rather than three. The final seven bars form a brief codetta that brings together the ostinato figure in both triplet crotchets and triplet quavers (in pizzicato strings, woodwind, harps and celesta) and settling, via a second inversion chord of A♭ with an inverted pedal on D in the brass, to the note D as tonic.

Example 2.18
Triplet-Quaver Figures from the Second Part of "Prelude."

Overall, the prelude can be seen as a binary form with two vestigial subjects, in which the hypermetrical irregularity of the first part, produced by the superimposition of duple and triple hypermetres, is resolved by the regularity of the second. Table 2.1 summarises the structure of "Prelude."

Table 2.1
Summary of the Form of "Prelude."

Part 1			Part 2		
Bars	Motif	Image	Bars	Motif	Image
1–2	Ostinato	"Paramount"	53–4	Ostinato (triplet quavers)	Spiral "Art direction ... "
3–8	D–C–Eb–D	"Vistavision"	55–70	D–C–Eb–D	
12.5–15.5	Eb min⁷	"James Stewart"			
18.5–20	Ab	"Kim Novak"			
22.5–24	Eb min⁷	"Alfred Hitchcock's"			
27.5–29	Ab min/Eb min⁷	"Vertigo"			
30.5–35	Rising Eb minor scale	Spiral shape from eye			
39–52	Love motif	Cast List	71–82	Love motif	"Costumes ... Herrmann... Mathieson"
			83–89	Codetta	Eye/Spiral

If individual cues can be seen to have their own individual forms, what of the whole score itself — can it be said to have an overall structure? Table 4.2 of chapter 4 demonstrates that the tonalities of C and D are central to work, and that the final resolution at the end of the film is onto a C major chord, settling it as the score's tonic. Two earlier major points of musical and narrative closure appear at the end of "The Beach" and "Scène d'amour," both in C major and employing the progression from Ab to C and the penultimate cue, "The Return" has a G pedal for almost its entire course, and seems to function as a dominant preparation for the C major of "Finale."

On a more localised scale, the appearances of the crowning moment of the love motif (see Example 2.16) are organised throughout the score so that its last manifestation forms a point of culmination.[21] Similarly, the score exhibits a considerable degree of thematic unity, "Madeline" being the matrix from which many of the subsequent motifs are developed. All things considered, however, the structure of a film score is intimately tied to the structure of the narrative, and while its musical form supports the narrative development, it is not normally independent of it. It should not be imagined or assumed that Herrmann's score for *Vertigo*, because it makes use of some of the elements that contribute to the establishment of large-scale form, functions like an autonomous orchestral work such as a symphonic poem. In the formulation of analyst Hans Keller, symphonic form is founded on the "large-scale integration of contrasts" and more especially *"the contrast between statements* (whether monothematic or polythematic) *and developments* (whether they concern themselves with statements or not)."[22] It is arguable that symphonic form in this definition was never of much compositional interest to Herrmann even in his concert works. Instead, we find in *Vertigo* a subtle process of variation and transformation of a small group of related ideas, as if they are constantly being relit and recoloured rather than rigorously thematically developed. To invert Keller's definition, one might assert that Herrmann's form in *Vertigo* is actually premised on the localised differentiation of similarities and the correspondences between statements and developments.

NOTES

1. Murray, *Musician: A Hollywood Journal*, p. 69.

2. Lesley Brill, *The Hitchcock Romance: Love and Irony in Hitchcock's Films* (Princeton, NJ: Princeton University Press, 1988), p. 205.

3. *Sight and Sound*, Winter 1971/2, pp. 36–39.

4. William Darby and Jack Dubois in *American Film Music: Major Composers, Techniques, Trends* (Jefferson, NC: McFarland, 1990), pp. 364–65, clearly not having access to the score, wrongly transcribe both this cue and the love motif. More problematically, they describe the cue "Madeline" as "Carlotta" and the love motif as "Scottie" claiming, among a number of other errors, that this latter idea is heard when Scottie first sees Madeleine. Interestingly, adopting Herrmann's error, Madeleine is called Madeline by these authors.

5. Ed. Stanley Sadie, *The New Grove Dictionary of Music and Musicians* (London: Macmillan, 1980).

6. *Sight and Sound*, Winter 1971/2, p. 37.

7. Ibid.

8. A♭ major is the relative major of F minor, the subdominant of C minor.

9. The indecision associated with the half-diminished seventh chord is probably related to its ambiguity. The chord F♯–A–C–E can be treated as a VII^7 in G, or like the "Tristan chord" resolve onto a French sixth in B♭ (G♭–B♭–C–E), or as in the *progression* Herrmann uses in "Sleep," onto a C♯ minor chord.

10. "The Bay" begins with the same sequence.

11. Such writing is found in many other film scores of Herrmann, including *The Man Who Knew Too Much*, and *The Day the Earth Stood Still*.

12. Brown, *Overtones and Undertones*, p. 158.

13. Graham Bruce, *Bernard Herrmann: Film Music and Narrative* (Michigan: UMI Research Press), p. 139.

14. Brill, *The Hitchcock Romance*, p. 212.

15. Waletzky, *Music for the Movies: Bernard Herrmann*.

16. Ibid.

17. It is a characteristic of the holograph that, for most cues involving strings in the first half of the film, Herrmann marks the number of players requested in the score at the beginning of the cue.

18. The difficulty of this trill lies in the fact that both notes are played with very similar fingering, the flautist being required to rapidly move the little finger of the right hand between the C♯ and E♭ keys.

19. Though he does use it in other scores. The sound of the instrument can be subject to painful distortion on poor quality sound reproduction or where optical tracks are damaged.

20. Though again he does use them prominently in other scores, for example *The Ghost and Mrs. Muir* and *The Trouble with Harry*.

21. In "Farewell" the first pitch of each bar is B_5–E_5–$F\sharp_5$–C_5, in "Scène d'amour" it is B_6–E_6–$F\sharp_6$–C_6 and then B_5–E_6–$F\sharp_6$–C_5 and finally in "Finale" it is B_5–E_6–$F\sharp_6$–C_7.

22. Hans Keller, "The State of the Symphony: Not only Maxwell Davies," *Tempo* 125 (June 1978), pp. 8–9. Keller's emphasis.

CHAPTER 3

CONTEXT OF THE PRODUCTION OF
VERTIGO AND READINGS OF THE FILM

SOURCES: *ORPHEUS AND EURYDICE* AND *D'ENTRE LES MORTS*

In 1954, the French authors Pierre Boileau and Thomas Narcejac co-authored the novella *D'Entre les Morts* (*From Among the Dead*). Their first collaboration, *Celle qui n'était*, translated into English as *The Woman Who Was No More*, was adapted to form the screenplay of Henri-Georges Clouzot's *Les Diaboliques*, released in 1954. *D'Entre les Morts* is very loosely based on the classical myth of Orpheus and Eurydice brought up to date and set in wartime Paris. The story of Orpheus, best known in the version by Ovid in his *Metamorphoses*, tells of the poet and musician Orpheus, whose young bride, Eurydice, dies from the bite of a snake lying hidden in the meadow flowers. Heartbroken, Orpheus travels to the underworld to try to find her, and so moves Hades with his grief and the beauty of his song, that he is permitted to bring Eurydice back to the world of the living. Hades sets a single condition for Eurydice's return — that Orpheus must not look at her until they have reached the light of the living world. Before they have completely left the under-world, however, Orpheus breaks his side of the bargain by turning round to see Eurydice and embrace her. As he does so she fades away, leaving him bereft again. This time there is no going back:

> Now to repass the Styx in vain he tries,
> Charon averse, his pressing suit denies.
> Sev'n days entire, along th'infernal shores,
> Disconsolate, the bard Eurydice deplores;
> Defil'd with filth his robe, with tears his cheeks,
> No sustenance but grief, and cares, he seeks:
> Of rigid Fate incessant he complains,
> And Hell's inexorable Gods arraigns.[1]

Orpheus rejects the rest of womankind and wanders the barren hillsides. Hearing his song from afar, trees uproot themselves and come to surround him and Orpheus is metamorphosed to their form.[2]

In Boileau and Narcejac's thriller, lawyer Roger Flavières is invited by ship-builder Paul Gévigne, a fellow student from his time at law school, to follow Gévigne's wife, Madeleine, about whom he is worried. Madeleine has been capriciously wan-dering round Paris and seems to lapse into dream-like states although her specialist can find nothing wrong with her. According to Gévigne, Madeleine's grandmother, Pauline Lagerlac, had committed suicide when she was twenty-five — Madeleine's current age — and Madeleine has been increasingly modelling her appearance on Pauline's self-portrait. Flavières, who has been forced to leave the police force because of a bout of vertigo that resulted in the death of a fellow officer, agrees to place Madeleine under surveillance and report back to Gévigne. The following evening he goes to the Marigny theatre and sees Madeleine for the first time. He is immediately attracted by her and is sickened that someone like Gévigne should have such a beautiful wife. The next day, he follows her into the Cimitière de Passy, and watches her as she stands over a gravestone, staring at it for nearly a quarter of an hour. When she has left and he is able to look at the grave, he notes, with little surprise, that the name on it is that of Pauline Lagerlac, who was born in 1840 and died in 1865.

Subsequently, Flavières tails Madeleine again and this time she goes to the Family Hotel, where, according to the manager, she regularly visits room 19 on the third floor. He does not go up to investigate, but waits outside, and in less than half an hour, she has emerged and set off again, this time to the Pont de Neuilly. Oppo-site the Ile de la Grande-Jatte, she sits at a table outside a bistro and writes on a piece of notepaper before going to the edge of the river and tearing it up. She then calmly throws herself into the water. Flavières rushes to the quay edge, jumps in, and rescues her. For the next week or so, they are inseparable, and they go for excursions to Versailles and the forest of Fontainebleau they take, trips to the cinema, and drives to the country. Flavières has now fallen head over heels in love with her and is ecstatically happy. During their time together, Madeleine tells him of her dreams or visions of a place to which she claims never to have been and Flavières realises that she has given a strikingly accurate description of the town of Saintes, but as it must have been a century before, in the time of Pauline Lagerlac. She also tells him of her sense of being out of time, which he puts down to simple feelings of *déjà vu*. As she leaves him after one of their liaisons, he makes her a present of a lighter and cigarette case insidewhich he has left a card with the words *A Eurydice ressuscitée*—to the risen Eurydice —a very direct reference to the Orpheus legend.[3] A few days later, Madeleine suggests that they should go for a long drive into the country. They arrive at the little village of Saint-Nicolas, north of Mantes, which has a square and a church with a tall tower that seems completely out of proportion to the building. Madeleine and Flavières enter the church, and Madeleine decides to explore the tower and belfry. Flavières follows her up the stairs but is overcome with nausea and vertigo. He manages to work his way up the stairs to the locked landing, not knowing how he will get down again. Calling out to her, he hears a cry and a thud and realises that she has fallen to her death. Sick to the heart, he cannot look at the body and leaves the scene without reporting the crime or telling Gévigne, whom rings him later to tell him that Madeleine is dead.

The second part of the novella is set some years later. Flavières has been practising in Dakar in North Africa, but has just returned to Paris. His health is poor and he has been suffering from an obsessional belief that Madeleine is not dead—after all, she has risen from the dead once already (as the reincarnation of Pauline Lagerlac) and he believes that she may well do so again. His psychiatrist's advice is clear and simple—he must put the thought of Madeleine out of his mind altogether and take a vacation. Visiting a cinema that evening, he watches a newsreel and notices, among the crowds of spectators cheering General de Gaulle on a visit to Marseilles, a woman who looks remarkably like Madeleine. The next morning, he sets off to Marseilles by train and discovers soon after his arrival that the woman is actually called Renée Sourange and is the girlfriend of a spiv called Almaryan. Flavières meets Renée and questions her about her past, but she denies having ever lived in Paris before the occupation. When Almaryan grows tired of her, Flavières steps in to offer his protection. He almost immediately begins to try to make her over as Madeleine, buying her the same grey suit, shoes and Chanel No. 3 perfume that Madeleine wore, so that she may rediscover herself, because, as he says, "I want to know the truth."[4] Flavières' treatment of Renée is at times brutal; he often makes her cry and he drinks too much. One night, as she lies sleeping, he looks in her handbag and finds Pauline Lagerlac's necklace, which more than ever convinces him that she must indeed be Madeleine.

From this point on, Flavières increasingly talks to her of their time together in Paris, fervently believing that he will eventually unlock her memory of the past. He decides that her hair should be fastened in a bun and inexpertly ties it up, temporarily restoring, in his eyes, the Madeleine he once knew. The next day he claims to feel ill and secretly follows her as she visits the Central Hotel. When Flavières asks the desk clerk for the name of the woman who just came in he is told that she is Pauline Lagerlac. In a scene parallel to one from the first part of the novella, he trails Renée to the Quai de la Joliette where she sits down at a table and writes a letter, presumably to him. He rushes over and tries to grab the note, knocking her bag over as he does so and losing the letter, which blows away in the wind. Under extreme pressure, she finally gives in to Flavières back in their hotel room and admits that she is Madeleine, telling him the full story of how she and Gévigne duped him. He cannot admit the truth, however, and strangles her, in his madness saying:

You're lying. . . . You've never stopped lying . . . but can't you see that I love you, that I've always loved you—right from the start—because of Pauline, because of the cemetery, because of your dreamy eyes. ... A love like a marvellous tapestry—on one side it told a wonderful legend, on the other ... I don't know ... I don't want to know. ... But when I first put my arm round you I knew you were to be the only woman in my life ... Madeleine. ... And our drives in the country together—don't you remember them? And the flowers, the Louvre, the lost country. ... Madeleine! I beg you—tell me the truth.[5]

The novella ends with the arrest of Flavières for Renée's murder, his last words in the novel, as he kisses her forehead, being "I shall wait for you."[6]

PREPRODUCTION

Don Auiler has provided evidence that Boileau and Narcejac's book was not actually written for Hitchcock, though the rights were purchased from them by Paramount for $25,275 in 1955.[7] The first writer commissioned to realise a screenplay was Maxwell Anderson in June 1956, and already by this stage the action had been transported from Paris and Marseilles to San Francisco. According to Auiler, Anderson's script (which was titled *Darkling, I Listen*) stayed very close to Boileau and Narcejac's novella and was inherently weak—"a standard B detective picture that would have seemed creaky during the late forties."[8] Hitchcock was dissatisfied, and after offering the job to Angus MacPhail, who demurred, turned in September 1956 to Alex Coppel.[9] Coppel's script introduced, among many other details that appeared in the final film, the opening scene on the rooftops of San Francisco (dramatising the brief discussion between Flavières and Gévigne in the first chapter of *Between the Dead*), the nightmare sequence following the scene in the coroner's inquiry and the famous 360-degree kiss in Judy's hotel bedroom.

However, neither Hitchcock, his agent Lew Wasserman, nor actor James Stewart was happy with Coppel's script and Hitchcock contacted Anderson again with a list of suggested changes and amendments in the belief that he might be able to supply a new version of the screenplay. Anderson declined and Samuel Taylor was approached in January 1957. Initially, Taylor seemed to think that the script was a lost cause but was keen to have the opportunity to work with Hitchcock and so agreed to be involved in the project. While, according to both Spoto and John Russell Taylor, Samuel Taylor did not read either the original book or the earlier screenplay, Auiler cites him as saying "I studied the screenplay on the train going out [to the Paramount Studio]. ... By the time I got there I had a pretty good idea what to do with it."[10] Despite a fairly severe illness suffered by Hitchcock, the director and writer liased through much of January and February, adding the figure of Midge to the narrative and tightening up the characterisation and dialogue considerably. A second, even more serious illness prevented Hitchcock from taking a role in script development during most of March and April 1957, Taylor's third draft being completed at the beginning of the latter month. Taylor's most contentious addition was in scene 227, where Judy reveals to the audience, by way of the letter she writes to Scottie and then destroys, that he was the victim of Gavin Elster's plot to murder his wife. This was sold to the director as a Hitchcockian touch—very much what the audience would expect in one of his films—though until almost the last moment in postproduction the arguments raged as to whether the scene should be included. The scene does, in fact, have the great advantage of making the second half of the film into a psychological thriller in which we are able to sympathise with both Judy and Scottie. Taylor's final screenplay, from which the film was shot, is titled *From Among the Dead* and is dated 12 September, 1957.

A brief résumé of the story as finally shot demonstrates the similarities with, and points of divergence from, *D'entre les Morts*. The film opens with a chase sequence across a series of San Francisco rooftops in which a uniformed officer and a plain-clothes detective pursue a criminal. The detective slips when jumping onto a slop-ing roof but manages to grab onto a guttering. In an attempt to save him, the officer holds out his hand, but the detective is overcome with vertigo and cannot move. The officer then slips and falls to his death. We soon discover, in a scene set in the apartment of his friend Midge, a commercial artist, that the detective is called Scottie Ferguson and that he has been forced to resign from the police department because of his acrophobia. He confides in Midge that he has been contacted by an old college friend, Gavin Elster, whom he has not seen for many years. In an office in Elster's shipbuilding yard, Scottie learns of his concern about Elster's wife, Madeleine, who has been acting strangely and whom Elster believes to be pos-sessed by someone dead, but does not at this stage say by whom. Scottie is deeply sceptical, reminding Elster that he is now retired, but reluctantly agrees to take on the job, and arranges to go to Ernie's restaurant that evening to identify her.

The next day, Scottie follows Madeleine as she drives through the streets of San Francisco, first to Podesta's flower shop, where she buys a nosegay, and then to the Mission Dolores where she stands for some time over the grave of a certain Carlotta Valdes. Madeleine next visits the art gallery at the Palace of the Legion of Honor, where she gazes at a painting that Scottie discovers to be the "Portrait of Carlotta," before her final port of call, the McKittrick Hotel. After seeing Madeleine open a first-floor window, Scottie enters the hotel and interrogates the manageress who informs him that the woman is called Miss Valdes—Carlotta Valdes—and that she regularly visits the hotel and sits by herself in her room. Scottie is confused by her claim that "Carlotta" has not recently come into the hotel, and when he sends her up to investigate, it is clear that Madeleine has already gone. After driving back to Madeleine's home at Brocklebank Apartments, he discovers that her car is parked outside.

On Midge's advice, Scottie visits local antiquarian bookshop owner and local historian, Pop Leibel, who supplies details of Carlotta's life and death in nineteenth-century San Francisco. Elster, in a further meeting with Scottie, explains that Carlotta, his wife's great-grandmother, is indeed the person whom he believes possesses her, but that Madeleine is totally unaware of her existence and according to him, when she goes to the Mission Dolores or the art gallery she is no longer his wife. Even more worrying to him is the fact that Carlotta went insane and took her own life, and he is insistent that Scottie should look after her carefully. Scottie subse-quently follows Madeleine again, this time from the art gallery to Golden Gate Bridge, where, after throwing petals from her nosegay into the water, she jumps in. Scottie quickly dives in and rescues her, and it is clear from his response to what seems to have been a suicide attempt that he is now totally infatuated with her.

Bringing her back to his apartment he puts her in his bed and dries her clothes. When she has fully regained consciousness, she is apparently completely unaware of her fall into the bay, but is very thankful and responsive to Scottie and, as he takes a phone call from Elster, she slips away. The next day, he follows her again and is surprised to find her driving to his own apartment. After accepting the letter of thanks that she has brought, he suggests that they should spend the day together and they set off in her car to Big Basin Redwoods State Park. Here, Madeleine points at the dated rings of a tree cross-section and, as if in a trance, mysteriously remarks that she was born and died many years before. They drive off again, this time to Cypress Point, where Madeleine tells him more of her dream-like memories of an earlier life, and her fears of insanity, before they embrace and kiss passionately. Later, Scottie visits Midge's flat and is thoroughly nettled by her caricature of the "Portrait of Carlotta Valdes" in which her face replaces that of Carlotta.

Madeleine wakes Scottie up early on a subsequent morning to tell him about a dream she has had, and he immediately recognises in her description the old Spanish San Juan Bautista Mission, south of San Francisco and arranges for a trip there later that day so that he can to prove to her that she is neither mad nor possessed. When they arrive at the mission, they go to the livery stable, where she sits in a surrey and recalls bygone days while Scottie attempts to convince her that she has been there before in her present incarnation. They declare their love to each other and embrace once again before Madeleine rushes off into the church and up the tower steps. Scottie tries to follow, but is overcome by vertigo, and before he can reach the top of the stairs he sees, through a small window in the tower, a body falling onto the roof below. In a state of shock, he makes his way back down the stairs and leaves the scene. A coroner's inquest ensues, and although Scottie is not held directly responsible for Madeleine's death, the coroner insinuates that he was at least partly culpable. The outcome of this is a total nervous breakdown, Scottie ending up in a sanatorium in a near catatonic state.

The second part of the film is set some time later. Although Scottie has now been released from the hospital he is unable to stop himself from obsessively thinking about Madeleine and searching for her in all her old haunts—Brocklebank Apartments, Ernie's and the art gallery. While standing outside Podesta's flower shop he notices a shop girl who, despite her different coloured hair and brighter clothes, looks remarkably similar to Madeleine. He follows her to her room in the rather seedy Empire Hotel and asks her who she is and where she is from. The girl is easily able to prove to Scottie that she is in fact called Judy Barton and has been living at this address for the last three years. Somewhat embarrassed, he asks her out to dinner later that evening, and she reluctantly agrees. When he has left, she takes a suitcase from the wardrobe and begins to pack it. In a flashback sequence, as she writes a confession to Scottie, we discover the truth, that she had been Elster's mistress and was an accomplice in his scheme to murder his wife—the real Madeleine—making use of the Scottie as a witness to her suicidal tendencies and knowing that he would not be able to save her because of his acrophobia. However, Judy decides that the possibility of love with Scottie is worth the risk and destroys the note, deciding that she will stay.

Although the two soon appear to be a happy couple, Scottie develops an obsessive desire to make her over as Madeleine. Judy reluctantly agrees to wearing the same style of clothes and shoes that Madeleine wore but resists Scottie's demands for her to dye her hair. Eventually, she acquiesces, though when she returns from the salon she is still not entirely to Scottie's satisfaction, for her hair has not been tied up in Madeleine's familiar bun. In the hope that Scottie will finally love her (as Madeleine even if not as Judy), she goes into the bathroom to adjust her hair. When Scottie sees her emerging into the room, suffused in the green neon glow from the Hotel Empire sign, he is completely entranced and the two embrace again in a scene which connects in Scottie's mind with the kiss in the livery stable at the Mission San Juan Bautista. For a while both Judy and Scottie are happy, but then she makes the fatal mistake of putting on Madeleine's necklace—a parting gift from Elster—which Scottie immediately recognises from the portrait of Carlotta. The truth suddenly strikes home, though he does not immediately tell her of his realisation that he has been the victim of her intrigue. Instead, he drives her back to the Mission San Juan Bautista to reconstruct the moments leading up to the real Madeleine's death and to "complete his cure." As Scottie forces her up the stairs to the bell tower, Judy admits her guilt, still hoping that Scottie can love and forgive her, but he tells her it is too late. During a final kiss—Scottie being equally attracted and repelled by her—Judy sees a dark shadowy figure from the corner of her eye. Imagining, perhaps, that this is her retribution she throws herself down from the tower. In the final shot, Scottie stands at the top of the tower in a cruciform pose, a shattered man, but cured of his vertigo at last it seems.

PRODUCTION

James Stewart had taken the principal role in Hitchcock's *Rear Window* (1954) and *The Man Who Knew Too Much* (1956). He was cast as the male lead early in preproduction and he took an active role in the development of the script, offering advice, criticism and support. Initially, Vera Miles (who played Manny's wife in *The Man Who Knew Too Much*) was cast as Madeleine/Judy, but pregnancy forced her to withdraw in March 1957 to be replaced by Kim Novak. Barbara Bel Geddes, now probably best known for her part as Miss Ellie in the long-running television soap opera *Dallas*, was suggested for the role of Midge by Samuel Taylor, who was an admirer of her work. According to Auiler, Bel Geddes and Novak never met each other during the production.[11]

The filming of production 10344, still provisionally titled *From Among the Dead*, took place between February and December 1957, the first six months being occupied with second-unit photography in which shots that did not involve the main actors were taken. When first-unit filming began, Novak caused some consternation, first by her decision to take a holiday and then by her withdrawal of labour because of a dispute with Columbia, who were being paid $250,000 for the two Paramount films but whom she claimed were underpaying her salary. Having successfully negotiated more than a doubling of her salary (by January 1958 it was more than $3,000 a week), she finally arrived on the set in September 1957. Location shooting took place between and 30 September and 15 October in San Francisco, San Juan Bautista, Cypress Point and the Big Basin Redwoods State Park, and the cast and crew returned to the Paramount studios in Los Angeles for a further two months of work on the soundstage from 16 October. Filming was completed on 19 December, 1957.

POSTPRODUCTION

After taking a Christmas holiday in Jamaica, Hitchcock returned to the postproduction of the film. Although discussions had taken place between the director and Herrmann before production began, the composer was actually put on contract on 6 January, 1958 with a fee of $17,500.[12] As the cutting of Hitchcock's films was planned in great detail in advance, the film editor, George Tomasini, was able to starting piecing together a rough cut while the director was on vacation. Herrmann's holograph score is dated 3 January to 19 February, so he must have seen a screening of Tomasini's rough cut in Los Angeles at least ten days before those held for the director in New York on 13–14 January. Hitchcock made a number of suggestions for changes to the film during these sessions. His meticulous consideration of sound design in the film is illustrated by the fourteen pages of dubbing notes that detail many subtle instances of the use of spot effects and ambiences, a subject that is considered again in chapter 4. The discussion of the first scene is characteristic:

Over the opening scene we should hear some shouts and the metallic sound of feet climbing the rungs of a steel ladder. These sounds come while the screen is empty and before the first hand comes over to grip the railing. Naturally, these sounds will increase in volume as the three reach the top. Over all, we could have faint sounds of the city, mostly automobile horns and truck noises. Perhaps even the faint clang of a cable car bell. These faint sounds will continue, but should be dominated by the running feet of the three men across the rooftops.

Now we come to the leaping part of the chase. Naturally, of course, the sounds we now have in the picture should be eliminated entirely and fresh ones substituted. In addition to the feet leaping onto the tiles, we should hear the clatter of a few broken ones as they fall into the alleyway below. It is very important that the timing of the broken tiles reaching the alleyway below should correctly indicate the depth they have fallen. They should also have an echo quality. We must also bear in mind the quality of the running feet, both on the part of pursued (whose footsteps should be heard running into the faint distance) and the policeman and the detective (whose feet will be heard approaching), because all of these are off-screen sounds but very important for the continuity.

When the policeman falls, we should consider a long cry which dies away as he falls to his death. After he has reached the ground we should hear faint sounds of alarm and the patter of running feet to his rescue.[13]

On Hitchcock's return from New York on 3 February, the composer and director met to discuss the score after a further screening. There appear to be only three brief notes from Hitchcock to Herrmann about music in the film and these are discussed in the relevant places in chapters 4, 5 and 6.

Herrmann's normal practice was to conduct his own film scores, but he was prevented on this occasion by a strike by the musicians' union. In March, recording was moved to London where the Scottish conductor Muir Mathieson, a stalwart of the British film music industry from the 1930s and conductor of the scores of many of its most important and influential films, was to direct the orchestra. More than half of the score was recorded in London in sessions on 10–11 March, before the orchestra came out on strike in sympathy with the Los Angeles musicians under orders from International Musicians, Zurich. Paramount London then quickly set about finding a replacement ensemble, several Viennese orchestras proving willing to accept the job. Recordings made in London were done in stereo, whereas those from Vienna were monophonic. Ridge Walker from the Paramount Music Department has provided the following information about the recordings:

I do not find the name of any particular orchestra in London. There is mention of individual vouchers for each musician whereas for Vienna, there are contracts with two orchestras. In a letter dated May 16, 1958, Max Kimental (Germany) mentions scoring at Wien-Film Studios in Vienna with members of Vienna Symphonic Orchestra [sic]. I find a memo which forwarded contracts with I.G. Veiner Symphonika [sic] and one with Wiener Film Orchestra (The Fehring Dance Orchestra). The other interesting fact is that, by contracting individually with the London musicians, a buyout was obtained for the use of their performances for phonograph records. This is not true for the Vienna orchestras — because of their Trade Union contract, they would have had to be paid for records. And, indeed, you will not find any of the cues recorded in Vienna on the album.[14]

The recording venues of the cues are summarised in Table 3.1.

Table 3.1
Summary of the Sources of the Recordings of the Diegetic and Nondiegetic Cues in *Vertigo*.[15]

Cue	Title	Recording	Mono/Stereo	Orchestration
1A	Prelude	London	Stereo (ABC)	Tutti
1B	Roof-Top	London	Stereo (ABC)	Tutti
1C	J.C. Bach	Vienna	Mono	Strings
1D/2A	The Window	Vienna	Mono	3 cl, 2 bass cl, 3 trpts, 3 trbn, Hammond organ or novachord
2B	Madeline	London	Stereo (AC)	Hrp, strings
2C/3A	Madeline's Car	Vienna	Mono	Ob, 3 cl, 2 bass cl, hrn, strings
3AI	The Flowershop	Vienna	Mono	4 cl, vlns

Table 3.1 (cont.)

Cue	Title	Recording	Mono/Stereo	Orchestration
3B	The Alleyway	Vienna	Mono	3 cl, hrp, strings
3BI	The Mission	Vienna	Mono	4 cl, hrp, strings, Hammond organ or novachord
3C	Mission Organ	Vienna	Mono	Organ
3D	Graveyard	Vienna	Mono	2 bass cl and vlns
3DI	Tombstone	Vienna	Mono	2 cl, 2 bass cl, hrp, 3 cb
3E	Carlotta's Portrait	London	Stereo (ABC)	2 fl, 2 cl, 2 hrns, hrp, vibes, vlns
3F/4A	The Hotel	Vienna	Mono	3 trpts, 3 trbns, vibes, strings
4B	The Hallway	Vienna	Mono	3 trpts, 3 hrns, 3 trbns
4C	The Nosegay	Vienna	Mono	Strings
4D	NO CUE			
4E/5A	The Catalogue	Vienna	Mono	2 cl, hrp, vibes, vlas, vlcs
5B	The Gallery	Vienna	Mono	2 fl, 2 hrns, hrp, vibes, strings
5C	The Bay	London	Stereo (ABC)	Tutti
5D	Sleep	Vienna	Mono	Strings (no basses)
5E/6A	By The Fireside	Vienna	Mono	Strings
6B	Exit	Vienna	Mono	Strings
6C	The Streets	Vienna	Mono	2 fl, ob, 3 cl, 2 bass cl, 2 hrns, strings
6D/7A/7B	The Outing	Vienna	Mono	5 cl, strings

Cue	Title	Recording	Mono/Stereo	Orchestration
7C	The Forest	London	Stereo (ABC)	Woodwind (incl 3 cor anglais), brass, Hammond organ, 2 vibes, 2 susp cymbs, 3 cb.
7D	The Beach	London	Stereo (ABC)	Tutti
8A	3. AM	Vienna	Mono	Strings (no basses)
8B	The Dream	Vienna	Mono	2 fl, alto fl, 2 cl, vibes, vlns, vlas
8C/8D/8-E/9A	Farewell	London	Stereo (ABC)	3 fl, 2 ob, E. hr, 3 clar, 2 bass clar, 4 hrns, 2 hrps, vibes, strings
9AI	The Tower	London	Stereo (ABC)	Tutti
9B/10A	The Nightmare	London	Stereo (ABC)	Tutti
10B	Mozart	London	Mono	Strings and bassoons
10C/10D	Dawn	London	Stereo (ABC)	Tutti
10E	The Past	London	Stereo (ABC)	3 eng hrns, 3 cl, 2 bass cl, strings
10F/11A	The Girl	Vienna	Mono	strings (no basses)
11B	The Letter	London	Stereo (ABC)	3 fl, 3 cl, 2 b cl, 4 horns, 3 trbs, tuba, 2 timp, cymb, tam tam, 2 hrps, Hammond organ, strings
12A	NO CUE USED			
12B	Good Night	Vienna	Mono	Strings
12C	The Park	London	Stereo (ABC)	2 fl, 3 cl, 2 bass cl, 2 hrps, strings
12D	Sardis #4	Vienna	Mono	Saxes, strings
12E/13A	The Hair Color	London	Stereo (ABC)	Strings

Table 3.1 (cont.)

Cue	Title	Recording	Mono/Stereo	Orchestration
13AI	Beauty Parlor	London	Stereo (ABC)	2 vibes, 2 hrps, celeste
13B	Scene d'amour	London	Stereo (ABC)	Tutti
13C/13D-/14A	The Necklace	London	Stereo (ABC)	Picc, 2 fl, 2 ob, eng hrn, 4 cl, bass cl, 2 bsns, contra, 4 hrns, strings
14B	The Return	London	Stereo (ABC)	3 fl, 3 cl, 2 bass cl, 2 bsns, contra, 4 hrns, 3 trpts, timp, 2 hrps, strings
14BI	Finale	London	Stereo (ABC)	Tutti

In an attempt to emulate the success of "Che Séra Séra" sung by Doris Day in *The Man Who Knew Too Much*, Hitchcock contacted songwriters Jay Livingstone and Ray Evans, asking them for an appropriate song for *Vertigo*. A song was written and recorded by Billy Eckstein but, fortunately (because we would have thus lost Herrmann's magnificent prelude), was rejected for use in the film by Hitchcock.

Vertigo was premiered on 9 May, 1958, at San Francisco's Stage Door Theater, almost two years after Maxwell Anderson was commissioned to write the first draft of the screenplay and it went on general release at the end of the month. Critical response was initially rather lukewarm — the film was seen to be technically brilliant, but overlong and with a confusing plot. For a detailed consideration of the early reviews, the reader is advised to refer to Auiler's excellent discussion in *Vertigo: The Making of a Hitchcock Classic*.

READING *VERTIGO*

In complexity and subtlety, in emotional depth, in its power to disturb, in the centrality of its concerns, *Vertigo* can as well as any film be taken to represent the cinema's claims to be treated with the same respect accorded to the longer established art forms.[16]

Robin Wood's estimation reveals the privileged position held by *Vertigo* in the cinematic canon according to much contemporary film scholarship. Wood sees *Vertigo* as "a perfect organism" and "of all Hitchcock's films the one nearest to perfection."[17] In Donald Spoto's estimation, it is Hitchcock's "richest, most obsessive and least compromising film"[18] and "remains a work of authentic beauty and grandeur, a film of astonishing purity and formal perfection in every element."[19]

In line with Boileau and Narcejac's novella, and for musical reasons, I have divided the film into two sections, the second of which begins with the nightmare sequence, a counterpart prelude to the rooftops sequence of the first half. Wood prefers to see *Vertigo* as being formed thematically from a prologue and three acts or, in the musical sense, movements. His first movement concerns Scottie's trailing of Madeleine; the second takes us from her apparent suicide attempt in the San Francisco Bay to her "death" at the San Juan Bautista tower and Scottie's nervous breakdown; and the third Scottie's relationship with Judy.[20] Spoto notes the change in direction of camerawork after Madeleine's death, the prominent right to left motion established in the rooftop sequence at the start of the film being transformed to left–right in the shot preceding the scene in the courthouse and in subsequent shots. Thus, he implies, the mirror-image second part of the film should be seen to begin at this point.

Sterritt, adopting another piece of musical terminology, describes the film as a "symphony of attraction-repulsion feelings projected by Hitchcock onto his characters," and notes that the director was simultaneously fascinated and horrified by evil behaviour.[21] Such antinomies are found in most critical responses and Sterritt indicates that other such oppositions underlying both the narrative structure and the technical apparatus of the film include authenticity–performance—Madeleine as the fictional creation of both Elster and Scottie, and Judy as the performer of Madeleine, Carlotta *and* Judy as she presents herself to Scottie; and reality–illusion—in the latter part of the film, Scottie tries to substitute his illusion of Madeleine for the reality of Judy.[22] Perhaps the most important duality, however, is that of life and death, for as Spoto remarks, the condition of vertigo is "described as the fear of falling and the desire to fall; the longing for risk and the fear of loss; the desire to die and the terror of death; the fear of losing balance and control and the concomitant desire to swoon, to pass away, to lose life itself in the pursuit of love."[23] Scottie takes Elster's case because he already has a fascination with death that may have been brought about by his own close call with mortality or may be symptomatic of a deeper malaise reflected in his inability to connect in an emotional sense with the down-to-earth, motherly Midge. The fascination Madeleine exerts is, in Wood's terms, the "fascination of death, a drawing towards oblivion and final release; the yearning for the dream, for the Ideal, for the Infinite, become logically a yearning for death."[24] In Act 2, Scene 2 of Wagner's *Tristan und Isolde*, Tristan sings to Isolde:

> So should we die no more to part,
> Ever one in endless joy,
> Never waking, never fearing,
> Nameless aye by love enfolded,
> Each to each then given,
> In love for ever living![25]

In the oblivion of death, the two lovers will be united forever, each possessed only by the other. As several critics have noted, Scottie becomes one with the dead Madeleine in a comparable way in the nightmare sequence of *Vertigo*, by falling first into the open grave that she told him she had dreamed about, and then onto the roof of the Mission where her life had ended. Thus, for Spoto, "the vertigo has logically become his own attraction towards death as release, and death as union with Madeleine."[26]

Moving to the symbolic level, Brill in particular has catalogued many of the emblematic devices employed by Hitchcock in *Vertigo*. The opening passage of the film, he suggests, is about downwardness and descent and of dark passageways that are entries to the underworld, and later he describes the Golden Gate Bridge as looming "like a thoroughfare across the Styx," an image which evokes the Orpheus legend.[27] Interestingly, Scottie invariably seems to be driving downhill in his car when following Madeleine. Principal among the geometric shapes that Brill identifies is the spiral, which appears explicitly in Saul Bass's opening images for the titles sequence, by implication in the falls of the policeman and Madeleine, in Carlotta's hairstyle, in the "roundy-roundy" shot in the recognition scene and in Scottie's final stance at the top of the tower at the end of the film. The spiral, found in the opening titles and the stairway sequences in the tower, represents for Brill, as an "unstable alternative to the circle...the tendency to fall apart emotionally."[28] Mirrors, likewise, "warn us of the incompleteness of what we can see directly" for, particularly in the broken and shattered form described by Madeleine in her dream they present only a partial reflection of reality.[29] Judy is the mirror image of Madeleine, who in turn mirrors Carlotta; Scottie sees reflections of Madeleine after her death in several women before he discovers Judy. All is reflection. Where is truth?

In the end, then, the film's subject is illusion and fraud, what Spoto calls the "haunted and hopeless pursuit of an empty ideal."[30] As such, it is a study of the cinema itself, the purveyor of romantic fantasy, whose trade is illusion. Scottie is unable to distinguish the dream world played by Madeleine and directed by Elster from reality as embodied by Judy, and he too must become a director and mould Judy back to the Madeleine who never existed before he can be satisfied. We too are seduced by Judy's Madeleine and want the dream she inhabits to continue, and it is for this reason as much as any that the revelation of her true identity is so crucial, for in the second half of the film we are able see our responses through Scottie's because of the detachment it confers. In *Vertigo*, Elster exploits Judy, Judy exploits Scottie, Scottie exploits Judy, and Hitchcock, through the medium of film, exploits us but at the same time warns us that what is really important is reality itself.

NOTES

1. Ovid, *Metamorphoses*, book 10, translated by John Dryden et al.
2. Perhaps it is fanciful to suggest that Scottie's final pose in the tower at the end of the film alludes to this transformation into a tree.

3. The French expression *ressuscité d'entre les morts* means "risen from the dead."

4. Pierre Boileau and Thomas Narcejac, *D'entre Les Morts*, first translated by Geoffrey Sainsbury as *The Living and the Dead* (London: Bloomsbury Publishing Plc, 1997), p. 128.

5. Ibid., p. 169.

6. Ibid., p. 170

7. Dan Auiler, *Vertigo: The Making of a Hitchcock Classic* (New York: St Martin's Press, 1998), p. 28.

8. Ibid., p. 34.

9. This and much of the following information is taken from Auiler, *Vertigo*, pp. 27– 62.

10. Donald Spoto, *The Art of Alfred Hitchcock: Fifty Years of His Motion Pictures*, second edition (New York: Doubleday, 1992), pp. 266–67. John Russell Taylor, *Hitch: The Life and Times of Alfred Hitchcock* (New York: Da Capo Press, 1996), p. 240. Auiler, *Vertigo*, p. 49.

11. Auiler, Vertigo, p. 52.

12. Auiler, Vertigo, p. 128, Smith, *The Heart at Fire's Center*, p. 220.

13. Hitchcock's dubbing notes from 15 January, 1958. See Auiler, *Vertigo*, pp. 132–33.

14. Ridge Walker, personal communication.

15. I would like to thank Mr Walker for a copy of the recording notes which give deatils of venue and number of tracks. Tracks marked ABC involved 3 head stereo recordings. Track 2B was a two-head recording and track 10B a single head recording. All Viennese recordings were recorded on track A.

16. Robin Wood, *Hitchcock's Films Revisited* (New York: Columbia University Press, 1989), p. 130.

17. Ibid., p. 129.

18. Donald Spoto, *The Dark Side of Genius: The Life of Alfred Hitchcock* (London: Plexus,1994), p. 393.

19. Spoto, *The Art of Alfred Hitchcock*, p. 299.

20. Wood, *Hitchcock's Films Revisited*, p. 109.

21. Sterritt, *The Films of Alfred Hitchcock*, p. 83.

22. In terms of technique, the use of animation in the nightmare scene is an example of the disparity between illusion and reality.

23. Spoto, *The Art of Alfred Hitchcock*, p. 277.

24. Wood, *Hitchcock's Films Revisited*, p. 114.

25. Richard Wagner, *Tristan und Isolde*, translated Frederick Jameson, vocal score by Karl Klindworth (London: Schott & Co, 1906), pp. 226–27.

26. Spoto, *The Art of Alfred Hitchcock*, p. 288. See also Wood, p. 118 and Brill, *The Hitchcock Romance*, p. 218.

27. Brill, *The Hitchcock Romance*, p. 209.

28. Ibid., p. 205.

29. Ibid., p. 213.

30. Spoto, *The Art of Alfred Hitchcock*, p. 298.

CHAPTER 4

APPROACHING *VERTIGO* AS A
MUSICAL AND SONIC TEXT

> Music on the screen can seek out and intensify the inner thoughts of
> the characters. It can invest a scene with terror, grandeur, gaiety, or
> misery. It can propel narrative swiftly forward or slow it down. It
> often lifts mere dialogue into the realm of poetry. Finally it is the
> communicating link between the screen and the audience, reaching out
> and enveloping all into one single experience.[1]

THE SEMIOTICS AND SEMANTICS OF FILM MUSIC

Before the score for *Vertigo* can be considered in detail in chapters 5 and 6, the
means by which film music functions in the context of the soundtrack must be
examined. It is hoped that this offers a "toolkit" for the subsequent analysis of the
score. The "text" of *Vertigo* is the aggregate of a very large number of visual and
sonic elements comprising among others the screenplay, the action (including the
actors' body language and gesture), the lighting and set design, the sound design,
and the musical score. For some of these elements, there is a widely accepted set of
(often socially and culturally constructed) meanings from which the audience is
able to decode the narrative. Although composers, performers and musicologists
have ascribed the power of signification to music for many centuries, it has remained at the best inexact as a means of communication. Nietzsche considered
music to be intrinsically inexpressive, noting in *Human, All Too Human* that:

Dramatic music becomes possible only when the tonal art has conquered an enormous
domain of symbolic means, through song, opera and a hundred experiments in tone-painting.
"Absolute" music is either form in itself, at a primitive stage of music in which sounds made
in tempo and at a varying volume gave pleasure as such, or symbolism of form speaking to
the understanding without poetry after both arts had been united over a long course of
evolution and the musical form had finally become entirely enmeshed in threads of feeling
and concepts … In itself, no music is profound or significant, it does not speak of the "will"

or the "thing in itself."[2]

Such a view is taken to its extreme formulation in Stravinsky's dictum that "music is, by its very nature, essentially powerless to *express* anything at all ... *Expression* has never been an inherent property of music."[3]

In fact, the generally arbitrary relationship between the signifier and the signified in natural languages implies that there is nothing that *should* prevent music from encoding concepts in a similar way, and thereby becoming a fully communicative language. A lexicon of "words" built from "musemes" equivalent to phonemes might be assembled and "sentences" constructed which could parallel, and thus be as meaningful as, those of conventional speech, at least to those who have learnt the "language." Although such a fully functioning musical language has never evolved, there are some who have suggested that a basic *expressive* vocabulary can be found, at least in the repertoire of western art music. In *The Language of Music*, Deryck Cooke attempts to define what he regards as some of the fundamental terms, by considering musical phrases that share similar underlying melodic shapes.[4] For Cooke, these elementary musical shapes (such as a rise from the tonic, through the mediant to the dominant, or $1-3-5$) *express* emotional states such as joy, anguish, grief or happiness. In some cases, these formulae can have a mimetic quality — for instance, the falling 6th to 5th in a minor key ($6-5$) may be heard to approximate the contour of a brief sigh, and a rising and falling tone from the dominant to the submediant and back in a major key ($5-6-5$) to emulate a gasp of satisfaction.

The concept of communication implied by the word "express" is ambiguous, however: does music *convey* an emotional state to the listener, as a tear or a smile might in another nonverbal form of human interaction, or does it *stimulate* the emotional state in the listener? It might be argued that it does both, for, like the photographic image of a tear rolling down a cheek, it simultaneously objectively articulates the pain of the character while subjectively inviting the listener to share the sensation empathetically. Manfred Clynes proposed a neurological basis for Cooke's hypothesis, noting that "Common brain programs of biological time forms of expression called 'essentic forms' underlie specific dynamic expressive communication in various sensory modes, it is suggested, both in production and recognition of these elements of language."[5] According to Clynes, these essentic forms can be transformed into sounds or melodic structures which carry the emotions of anger, hate, grief, reverence, love, sex or joy in a universal way. Susanne Langer rejects this notion of emotional communication, remarking that:

If music has any significance, it is semantic, not symptomatic. Its "meaning" is evidently not that of a stimulus to evoke emotions, nor that of a signal to announce them; if it has an emotional content, it "has" it in the same sense that language "has" its conceptual content — *symbolically* ... Music is not the cause or cure of feelings, but their *logical expression*.[6]

Whatever form of communication music is, it clearly does not function like a natural language in its common usage. Although it has a strong syntactic component, its syntax and grammar operate in very different ways from those of spoken languages, and it does not seem feasible to deduce a deep grammar for music of all cultures of the kind that Chomsky has proposed for language.

However, if music was not widely *construed* as being able to function as an effective communicator or stimulant of emotion, it is unlikely that it would have found such a ready place in the sound film. For the film composer Frank Skinner, the author of the technical manual for film composers *Underscore*, which was first published in 1950, the relationship between musical ideas and "moods" is self-evident.[7] He suggests that the three fundamental elements common to all storylines are love, menace and comedy and distinguishes themes appropriate for such supposedly similar emotions as sincere love, puppy love, sophisticated love and dramatic love by their musical characteristics.[8] Although Skinner provides phrases and melodies which apparently exemplify these moods, he does not in general explain how or why they do so, though we are told that "menace" themes are "more effective in the lower register" and that comedy themes may involve phrases with "odd intervals."[9] The influential French critic Michel Chion used the term *empathic* for the kind of music Skinner describes, which "directly expresses its participation in the feeling of the scene, by taking on the scene's rhythm, tone and phrasing; obviously such music participates in cultural codes for things like sadness, happiness, and movement."[10] Chion notes that music can also operate in an apparently contradictory role to the narrative, and offers the term 'anempathic' for music which appears to be indifferent to the action "by progressing in a steady, undaunted and ineluctable manner." This kind of music reminds the listener of "mechanical nature" of the cinema itself, for the life displayed on the screen is an elaborately manufactured illusion.

Claudia Gorbman emphasises that music can also behave as a signifier of *emotion itself* in film.[11] Given the association of Herrmann's music with the irrational, this statement is clearly of considerable interest, for the "irrationality" of emotion-stimulating music is embedded in the highly rational techniques of musical composition, orchestration and reproduction. When a motif that Cooke might consider an encoding of, for example, "a passionate outburst of painful emotion" appears, it is likely to be subjected to manipulations such as repetition, sequence, transposition or inversion, all of which lie within the domain of "compositional logic," albeit that in a film score individual cues seldom have the opportunity to achieve fully rounded forms, given the exigencies of the film's narrative. This dual quality of music as both a "communicative language" in its use of rational form and process, and a "mimetic language" in its imitation of nature and of inner feelings is, at least according to Adorno, contradictory, and it is this contradiction which is a source of music's "expressive power."[12]

THEORISING MUSIC AND MEANING IN FILM SCORES

The use of music in film provides an opportunity to consider the relationship between a composer's "musical language" and the visible or implied action, possibly allowing us to infer something of its semantic content, though given Stravinsky's assertion discussed previously, this clearly must be approached with some caution. Two aspects of the formation of the *associations* between the music and the rest of the narrative can be considered: their location and the means by which they are made. In the case of location, this is relatively straightforward — the musical event may be simultaneous or synchronous with the action, or it may be proximate with it, either anticipating or closely following it. Crudely speaking, the musical signifier is thus established in an analogous way to that used by a parent or teacher introducing the elements of linguistic competence to a young child by using flashcards that illustrate an object while simultaneously calling out the object's name. The associations between the score and the rest of the text (the dialogue, the camerawork, the lighting, the set, etc.) may result in multiple simultaneous symbolic encodings — one should perhaps think of a *semantic web*. Once a symbolic association has been established, the composer is able to reuse it in a different context: (e.g., a musical idea that accompanies a lovers' kiss on its first appearance can take on an ironic or poignant quality when it subsequently accompanies the death of one of the lovers).

There are a number of ways in which the associations between music and the rest of the narrative can be formed and meaning thereby established, and some of these are identified next according to the categories of context-derived associations, cultural referents, intracultural semantics, isomorphisms and intertextuality. These are not always independent of each other, and for instance, a figure may simultaneously function as a sonic isomorphism and be an example of a culturally established semantic.

Context-Derived Associations

The musical symbol is formed simply by happening at the same time as another event or complex of events (from a single shot to a group of scenes). The music may not have any intrinsic characteristics that obviously relate it to the narrative (other than, perhaps, the pace of editing) and thus an arbitrary relationship between signifier and signified is established. Such associations can be both the loosest and the most powerful types of association because of the absence of supporting, or alternatively competing, meanings.

Cultural Referents

These associations are usually dependent on gross or stereotypical features of musical genre, style or instrumentation rather than specific details and are contingent the cultural awareness of the audience. The uilleann pipes instantly invoke Ireland or the Irish, the sitar India, and the gamelan South East Asia for anyone familiar with the sounds of these instruments and their sources, such 'cultural awareness' often being developed through the medium of film in the first place. In both *White Witch Doctor* and *The Snows of Kilimanjaro*, Herrmann makes extensive use of percussion and pentatonic scale forms, elements of the indigenous cultures that for the casual Westerner can symbolise the entire continent of Africa. The sleigh ride from *The Devil and Daniel Webster*, which is redolent of both

Copland and Ives, suggests backwoods America by employing folk-like material (which is itself destabilised by the "diabolical" descending four-note chromatic ostinato figure — a culturally established meaning). Moroccan music is signified in the restaurant scene in *The Man Who Knew Too Much* by the use of a portamento string technique and an appropriately Arab-sounding mode. In *Vertigo*, the apparently diegetic use of the organ in the Mission Dolores underlines the religious character of the place, and Carlotta Valdez's Spanish origins are alluded to by means of the Spanish American *habanera* rhythm and flamenco modal characteristics.

Intracultural Semantics

Meanings have also accrued to melodic, rhythmic and harmonic formulae *within* cultural practices (and therefore may not transfer so easily between cultures). In the Western art-music tradition some of these musical figures have been labelled *topics* (forms and musical practices such as marches, fanfares, *ombra* music, specific dance styles and so on).[13] Thus, for example, performances on brass instruments of musical patterns based on the lower overtones of the harmonic series, with considerable repetition of pitches such as the tonic and dominant will suggest fanfares, which in their turn can symbolise power and particularly the power and authority of the state. In *The Day the Earth Stood Still*, Herrmann uses a slow, harmonised reveille call as Bobby and Klatu visit the Arlington National Cemetery to see Bobby's father's grave, and the musical idea crosses through the next scene as the two sit on the bench discussing the concept of war, into a third as they stand in front of the Lincoln Monument. The figure thus coalesces symbolic representations of the casualties of war, and Lincoln the leader and peacemaker. Similarly, the interval of the tritone (a diminished fifth or augmented fourth) has become linked with concepts of evil, danger and mystery in Western art-music, attributes which may relate to the medieval nomenclature for the interval, *diabolus in musica* (the devil in music), a marker of its instability. In a tonal context, particularly when used as part of a diminished triad, the interval tends to have an unsettling and destabilising effect because of its harmonic ambiguity. As noted in chapter 1, in *Hangover Square* Herrmann uses the tritone as an important motif in the *Concerto Macabre*.

Isomorphism

The term *isomorphism* indicates a structural identity or correspondence between different elements. In its biological usage, it implies similarity in the morphology of organisms of different classes, and more loosely it denotes a kind of coding, remodelling or mapping from one domain to another. Some of the many possible types of isomorphism are detailed here in a section that is not intended to be exhaustive.

Isomorphisms Between the Musical and the Visual or Conceptual. These are most obviously found in the "word painting" of art-music, where the shapes formed by the pitches of musical ideas on the grid of manuscript paper relate graphically to objects or properties referred to in the text. In the air "Every Valley Shall be Exalted" from Handel's oratorio *Messiah*, for example, the words "the crooked straight" are set initially so that "crooked" falls on the oscillation of two notes a tone apart, while "straight" lies on a longer held single note. Word painting has been in wide scale use in Western art-music since as early as the thirteenth century, and while it is normally found in vocal music, film offers an analogous text to be set by the composer. Such isomorphisms are regularly found in the "Mickey Mousing" technique in which action and music are tightly synchronised, though as has been noted before, Herrmann was not particularly fond of this as a device and tended to avoid it. The arpeggiated figures that accompany the opening titles of *Vertigo* can perhaps be seen as being musically equivalent to the spiral shapes that emerge on screen.

Isomorphisms Between the Musical and the Sonic (imitation of, or allusion to, sounds emanating from a physical source). Also found in word painting, the members of this set of isomorphisms can be compared to the vocalisation of young children when they imitate, for example, the sound of a train, by repeating the sounds "choo-choo," and subsequently use the phonemes choo-choo as a signifier for the train itself. In linguistic terms, the relationship between the signifier and signified for these signs is *not* arbitrary. Such "sound words" often transcend the normal boundaries between languages and can be comprehended across many cultures. Some of Cooke's basic terms discussed previously are actually of this type. For instance, a falling two-note figure such as C–A, sung portamento, with a diminuendo and with a longer first note, can sound rather like a prolonged sigh. Examples in Herrmann's oeuvre are to be found in the string "shrieks" (or bird cries) in the shower scene from *Psycho*, in the steam train music from *The Ghost and Mrs. Muir* and in the bass clarinet "moans" in the cue "Tombstone" from *Vertigo*.

Physical or Sensory Isomorphisms. These include rhythmic gestures that are imitative of physiological states or conditions, such as respiration, heart beat, motion (including shivering and shuddering), and perhaps even physical pain. A very familiar use of this class appears in the heartbeat rhythm played in the timpani towards the end of Tchaikovsky's fantasy overture *Romeo and Juliet*. The music associated with Scottie's vertigo might also be included in this category.

Isomorphisms of the Structural or Architectural. The musical form of a passage, movement or even an entire work can in some cases be seen, at least metaphorically, as a remapping in musical terms of a structure or an architecture. An example of this deep symbolism can be found in the "cruciform" structure that has been observed in the Crucifixus of Bach's B Minor Mass. However, narrative constraints generally preclude such isomorphisms from film music.

Typographical Isomorphisms (or Partial Isomorphisms) of Musical Notation and

Literary Notation. Musical cryptographs encoding names or words (such as BACH — in German notation, the pitches B flat – A – C – B natural) have been used by composers such as Bach, Schumann, Brahms, Schoenberg, Shostakovich and Berg. Like structural or architectural isomorphisms discussed earlier, such hidden and arcane isomorphisms are part of the private fantasy of the composer and are unlikely to be recognised by the listener.

"Punning" or Literary Isomorphisms Between a Musical Device or Theoretical Concept and the Commonplace Use of a Word. An example of this type of isomorphism is the "closure" implied by the perfect cadence that might accompany the image of a closing door, or the use of a perfect interval (fourth, fifth or octave) to signify perfection. In Barrington Pheloung's score for the British TV drama series Morse, a punning reference is made to the eponymous hero of the series in the title music by means of a morse-code rhythm.[14]

Intertextuality

References to, or quotation from, other scores and styles of musical composition abound in the film music repertoire.

Extraopus Intertextuality. Here the association has already been established by another composer or creative artist, and thus brings with it not merely the sonic character of the quotation, but something of the original context (e.g., John Williams's themes for *Indiana Jones* or *ET* in the contemporary film world, Beethoven's Fifth Symphony or Moonlight Sonata, or Tchaikovsky's *Symphonie Pathétique* in the field of art-music). The intertextuality may simply be stylistic (such as Straussian orchestration) or may be motivic (the Empire's theme from *Star Wars* or Parsifal's motif from Wagner's opera). In *The Ghost and Mrs. Muir*, the "sea music" is clearly redolent of the "Dawn" Sea Interlude from Britten's opera *Peter Grimes* which received its American premiere in 1946, a year before the film score's composition. In *Vertigo*, Herrmann widely draws on intertextual references to Wagner's opera *Tristan und Isolde*, not usually by direct quotation, but through stylistic similarities. He also references the plainsong melody of the *Dies Irae* from the Requiem mass.

Intraopus Intertextuality. This is similar to the previous category, but intertextual references are drawn from within the composer's own repertoire. Herrmann's so-called "Hitchcock chord," the minor triad with a major seventh is found in both the preludes to *Vertigo* and *Psycho*, and the sea music from *The Ghost and Mrs. Muir* closely prefigures that of *Vertigo*.

As suggested previously, once a musical signifier has been created (either within or outside a film) it can be subject to transformations that may subvert or even invert its established "meaning," often for humorous or ironic effect. These transformations will generally involve changes to one or more of the following parameters: tempo, rhythm, dynamics, register, tonality, modality, harmony, melodic contour and instrumentation (bass instruments like the bassoon or tuba are commonly used as comic signifiers). They may also involve the juxtaposition or superimposition of elements that do not normally appear together for their effect. A composer or director may deliberately place an apparently contradictory musical symbol in counterpoint with the picture. For instance, in David Lynch's 1986 film, *Blue Velvet*, the violent climactic scenes are ironically played out against a performance by Ketty Lester of Edward Heyman and Victor Young's romantic number "Love Letters." Equally, sound and image may be contrapuntally related in the Eisensteinian sense, "a dissonant sound-image concatenation, where tensions remain unresolved" as Stam puts it.[15] Whether the association between picture and sound is established by their "consonant" or "dissonant" conjunction, however, the composite audiovisual symbol formed overrides the autonomy of sight or sound, the two becoming inextricably intertwined.

Of course, a debate has surrounded the functional relationship between music and the on-screen action since the early days of sound film. By 1937, the composer Maurice Jaubert was complaining about the twin techniques adopted, in particular, by Max Steiner, of "annotating" and closely synchronising to the drama.[16] For Jaubert, the latter procedure was both childish and ignorant, for it:

displays a total lack of understanding of the very essence of film music. Music is by nature continuous, organised rhythmically in time. If you compel it to follow slavishly events or gestures which are themselves discontinuous, not rhythmically ordered but the outcome simply of physiological or psychological reactions, you destroy in it the very quality by virtue of which it is music, reducing it to its primary condition of crude sound. Used for these purposes, music will never, I am convinced, prove to be a satisfactory substitute for natural sounds, justified by their authenticity.[17]

Instead, Jaubert suggests that music can support those parts of the drama that lie outside the linear narrative of the film ("the strict representation of reality"),[18] in dream sequences, flashbacks and so on. Most importantly, he feels that music should be *decorative* rather than *expressive*, by supporting "the plastic substance of the image with an *impersonal* texture of sound," and making "physically perceptible to us the inner rhythm of the image, without struggling to provide a translation of its content."[19]

Herrmann's score for *Vertigo* takes an intermediate position between the decorative and the expressive. He tends to avoid the close synchronisation of music and image deprecated by Jaubert, but clearly does personalise his "texture of sound." While musical characterisation in a leitmotivic sense (for example, in the themes associated with Judy's portrayal of Madeleine and of Carlotta) *is* an important element of the score, and it does draw, to a considerable extent, on standard means of signification, it is usually loosely and flexibly connected to the rest of the narrative rather than tightly bound to it. Within each cue, and each sequence of cues, a continuity is generated in which the diachronic is prioritised over the synchronic and in which allusion rather than imitation or translation predominates.

MUSICAL "POINT OF VIEW"

The notion of a musical "point of view" is well established in film music criticism.[20] In the visual domain, certain camera angles can suggest or imply that we are seeing the action through the eyes of one or more of the protagonists. As an example of this technique, consider the opening scene of *The Snows of Kilimanjaro* (1952) where we initially see birds of prey gliding down and landing on a tree apparently from the point of view of Harry Street. However, it is often difficult to identify precisely whose eyes we are looking through and in the subsequent shots in which Harry draws his wife Helen's attention to the birds, we could equally be seeing from her subjective point of view or that of both of them. If we, as viewers, are privileged with the ability to see through the eyes of the characters on the screen, is it also possible for us to share their emotions and sensations? As we have already noted, music does offer the opportunity, through a set of culturally established codes, to suggest or encode emotional or physiological states, and in extended scenes shot entirely from a single viewpoint it is relatively simple to provide a score that appears to present and amplify a character's psychology. However, in a scene such as the one just described from *The Snows of Kilimanjaro*, where there are several characters, and the subjective shots are short, sometimes ambiguous and interspersed with objective shots, the situation is often much more complicated.

Music has a range of possible functions in these circumstances, including the following:

1. It can provide a continuity that overrides the subjective and objective shots and represents the point of view or internal state of one of the characters;

2. As in Function 1, but representing the shared point of view of several or many characters;

3. It can represent the point of view of the protagonist(s) only during the subjective shots. It is quite possible that this approach will generate musical discontinuities that draw attention to the fragmentary nature of the editing, but this may also set a character's psychological state into even starker relief;

4. It can be independent of any of the characters' points of view.

An analysis of the music of the initial scene of *The Snows of Kilimanjaro* demonstrates Herrmann's approach on this particular occasion. The opening shot is an aerial view of the summit of Mount Kilimanjaro with a voice-over representing the authorial voice of Ernest Hemingway. Against this, we hear a high, isolated, oscillating figure in the violins. As the camera settles on Harry Street, a slow-moving chordal figure in a lower register is heard, which is musically distinct from the first idea, but which smoothly connects with it. On the reappearance of the oscillating violin melody, the descending vultures are now seen from Harry's subjective viewpoint. At this stage, a visual isomorphism between the musical line and the flight of the bird becomes apparent (the oscillations can be compared to the motion of the bird's wings), and, in retrospect, we might infer that the opening was actually filmed from the point of view of the vulture.[21] Much of the rest of this scene involves interplay between the two elements, each subjective shot being accompanied by the oscillating high violin music.

As the music that accompanies the subjective shots was established before we were even aware of the existence of either Harry or Helen, can it really be held to represent their inner states? The answer is not clear-cut, and depends on our personal interpretation. We are never certain whether the music is simply Mickey-Mousing the flight of the bird, creating a disturbing and somewhat tense atmosphere or providing an insight into Harry's psychology and parlous physical state. Undoubtedly, the theme helps to make explicit the link between the summit of Kilimanjaro seen in the opening shots and Harry Street's predicament. Some may hold that music's ambiguity in such situations is a weakness; but is also possible to see it as a source of richness, for the narrative is thus allowed to become more open and more susceptible to individual interpretation.

THE SOUNDTRACK AND SOUND DESIGN

In his earlier writings, critic Michel Chion theorised a tripartite organisation of the auditory space recorded on the film soundtrack rather different to the conventional division into dialogue, music and effects. For Chion, the three segments correspond to on-screen sound (the so-called "visualised" zone), off-screen sound and nondiegetic sound, the latter two elements forming what he calls *acousmatic* zones. The term *acousmatic* describes those sounds for which there is no visible source in the diegesis, and in the context of the film soundtrack, Chion notes two common scenarios for the sound source: "either it is visualised first, and subsequently acousmatised, or it is acousmatic to start with, and is visualised only afterward."[22] A sound can, of course, remain acousmatic — we might hear the sound of a knife being sharpened off-screen, an effect which could be used to heighten suspense in a horror film. If the sound source were never revealed, directly or by implication, we would be left with an unsolved mystery, potentially infuriating or provocative, depending on the context.

In the light of criticism, Chion adapted this somewhat crude model to deal with three ambiguous conditions: internalised sound that represents the physiological or psychological state of a character; ambient or territory sound — the characteristic "noises" of a locale; and "on-the-air" sound, apparently produced by a CD player, tape recorder, telephone, radio, TV or some other audio device usually visible on set. In his revised model, the category of internalised sound (usually a voiceover) lies at the intersection of on-screen and off-screen areas, for the protagonist may be a visible or implied presence (we may be seeing the scene apparently unfolding through her or his eyes). Similarly, ambient sounds lie on the boundary between on-screen, off-screen and nondiegetic sound. As far as "on-the-air" sound is concerned, Chion comments that, "depending on the particular weight given by such factors as mixing, levels, use of filters, and conditions of music recording ... [it] can transcend or blur the zones of onscreen, offscreen, and nondiegetic."[23]

The transgression of the boundaries between these categories is by no means a recent development. It has been a commonplace effect since the earliest days of sound films, for music which begins as part of the diegesis (with an on- or off-screen, or on-the-air source) to be transformed to nondiegetic music at a scene boundary. A familiar, if somewhat ambiguous example of this can be found in Hal B. Wallis's *Now Voyager* (1942), where the second subject of the exposition of the first movement of Tchaikovsky's *Symphonie Pathétique* is initially heard as on-the-air music, apparently reproduced by an on-set radio, before seemingly moving out of the diegesis. Similarly, spot effects can shift on or off screen, as the objects to which they give sonic weight move in and out of the frame. An interesting example of ambiguity between sound effects and non-diegetic music can be found in Herrmann's score to *The Ghost and Mrs. Muir*, where conventional "train music" terminates with a pair of chords in the woodwinds which mimic the Doppler effect produced when a steam engine's whistle is blown as the locomotive moves away from the listener. In fact, in this case, the sound is heard as the scene changes to the exterior of the estate agent's office, so that the music acousmatises the sound effect.

Although the term "sound design" may seem to embody a concept that only became possible in the more recent age of high-fidelity theatre sound, as has already been noted, Herrmann became aware of the potential of a well-constructed sound track in his early radio days. Lucille Fletcher's 1936 *Screen and Radio Weekly* article discusses some of the many and varied musical effects which he was called on to create, including the innovative use of sound technology.[24] By the time he was invited by Orson Welles to write the score for *Citizen Kane* in 1939, he was already extremely sensitive to the interrelation between dialogue, effects and music. He noted in a 25 May, 1941 article in *The New York Times* that sound-effects were intermingled with music in order to intensify certain scenes, and at times music even supplanted sound-effects (Herrmann cites the musical imitation of the ticking of a clock during the jigsaw puzzle scenes).[25]

The power of sound effects, not merely to add realism to a film, but psychological depth, was well understood by Hitchcock. In *The Wrong Man*, for instance, the off-screen train sounds and prison noises match John Balestrero's increasing sense of anxiety and despair. Elisabeth Weis sensitively summarises Hitchcock's attitude to the soundtrack:

Despite the studio tradition of separating the three sound tracks, Hitchcock did not conceive of them as separate entities. One distinctive element of his aural style is a continuity in his use of language, music and sound effects that reflects his ability to conceive of their combined impact before he actually hears them together. Hitchcock does not take for granted the conventional functions of a given track; there is an intermingling of their functions in many instances.

. . .

However, if one distinctive attribute of Hitchcock's sound track is the frequent intersection of the functions of the sound effects, music and dialogue tracks, his sound track is also distinctively contrapuntal to the visuals. That is to say, the sounds and images rarely duplicate and often contrast with one another. During a Hitchcock film we are typically looking at one thing or person while listening to another. By separating sound and image Hitchcock can thus achieve variety, denseness, tension, and, on occasion, irony.[26]

In *Vertigo*, effects and music are extremely carefully balanced and interlaced so that there is an almost seamless flow between them. The rooftop scene after the opening titles sequence presents an interesting example of this interaction (see also the excerpt from Hitchcock's dubbing notes in chapter 3). Here, a series of Foley and spot effects, which include the metallic clang of the ladder, gunshots and the thud of footfalls on the roof tiles, is carefully and almost seamlessly blended with the music so that there are no awkward discontinuities. Samuel Taylor's final version of the screenplay for *Vertigo* includes a number of indications of effects, such as the Foley boot scrapes on the metal rungs of the ladder leading to the parapet, the spot effects of telephones ringing, off- and on-screen doors and gates opening and shutting and the chimes of clocks. Perhaps the most interesting of his suggestions appears in Scottie's dream sequence, where the sound of a fog horn in the distance is intended to echo the sound of his scream.[27] In fact, Scottie does not scream at all in the sequence as cut; instead, the vocalisation is imitated orchestrally and nondiegetic music traverses the boundary with the succeeding scene, terminating in a long held low D played by bass clarinets, bassoons, contrabassoon, tuba, timpani, Hammond organ, cellos and basses. The sound of the fog horn does takes on a motivic quality, though it is explicitly mentioned in scene 218 outside Scottie's apartment and appears on a number of occasions in the film, either literally in the effects track, or figuratively in the score, perhaps as an aural link with Gavin Elster's shipbuilding yard. Of the sound effects provided in the final cut, but not suggested by Taylor, the eerie use of wind noise in "The Forest," which accompanies Scottie and Madeleine as they walk through the Big Basin Redwoods State Park, is particularly interesting, for the sound is used almost as if it was another colour in the instrumental palette and is carefully and perceptively balanced with the orchestra.

DIEGETIC MUSIC IN THE SCORE FOR *VERTIGO*

Diegetic or "source" music, which has an observable or implied source in the narrative, such as a band, gramophone or radio, plays a relatively insignificant part in the soundtrack for *Vertigo*, unlike earlier films such as *Citizen Kane* or *Hangover Square*. Taylor's screenplay does include a number of indications for music, however, and it is revealing how few of his suggestions were precisely adopted in the film. After the opening sequence on the rooftops that establishes the origins of Scottie's vertigo, the scene shifts to Midge's apartment. Taylor's script calls for music by Scarlatti to be played on the gramophone:

15 (P. 3) EXT. SAN FRANCISCO ROOF TOPS — (DUSK) — LONG SHOT

Up to this moment the background music has had an excitement to match the scene, and now it cuts off abruptly, leaving only the echo of the police whistle as the DISSOLVE begins. Then, in the dissolve, we hear the soft insistence of Scarlatti played by a chamber orchestra.

The diegetic source is made clear in the next scene:

16 (P. 3) INT. AN APARTMENT ON RUSSIAN HILL — (LATE AFTERNOON)

The music comes from a gramophone.

In "Mr Hitchcock's Additional Music Notes," Herrmann was given the following advice by the director:

REEL 1

1. Midge's Apartment. An important factor is the contrast between the dramatic music over the Rooftops and the soft, totally different quality of the background music in Midge's apartment.

Remember that the Rooftop's music is background music and Midge's apartment music is coming from the phonograph and is, therefore, quite small and reduced in volume: it is small, concentrated music coming out of a box.[28]

The music, which is actually heard from Midge's phonograph in the final cut of the film, is not in fact by Scarlatti at all, but by the so-called "English Bach," J. C. Bach. This has been a source of confusion to some critics, and the work it comes from does not seem to have been correctly identified in print hitherto. It is the second movement, *Andante con Sordini*, of the Sinfonia in E♭ Major first published as Op. 9 No. 2, which Bruce gives as Op. 2 No. 2. Fritz Stein, the editor of the Eulenberg score, remarks that "A truly 'Italian' Bach, however, is the *Andante con Sordini*, of classical pregnancy in its form, and in expression and sound a cabinet piece of the most gracile rococo art, the chant of the last violin fleeting in faint *piccicati* [sic] of soft sensuality and sweet melancholy."[29]

Elisabeth Weis presents an intriguing thesis partly based on the misapprehension that the music is by Mozart:

One of the hallmarks of Hitchcock's treatment of music in his classical style is his use of familiar music to define a character or his social milieu. He does so either by linking a character with a given tune or by implying something about the character's expressed attitude towards a piece of music. In the latter case there is usually a dichotomy in Hitchcock's use of music as motif: classical compositions are usually treated as a product of cultural refinement — often overrefinement — whereas popular music is treated as a more natural expression of emotion. The implication that classical music is less in touch with genuine feelings reaches its extreme with the reference to Mozart in *Vertigo*. As Robin Wood has argued, Mozart's music is "clearly identified with the superficial externality of Midge's world." In Scottie's opening scene with Midge, he asks her to turn off a Mozart recording.[30]

It may be that Weis's suggestion holds true whether or not the movement is actually by Mozart, but it should be noted that J. C. Bach's music is of a rather different order to Mozart's in terms of its musical characteristics. When I asked a number of very experienced academic and professional musicians to identify the composer and the work, none managed to do so, several feeling that it was probably pastiche because of its apparent stylistic inconsistencies. The one thing all the respondents were clear about was that it was certainly *not* by Mozart. When Midge asks Scottie "Have you had any dizzy spells this week?" and he responds "I'm having one now … From that music," he could be drawing attention to its stylistic instabilities, for at one moment it suggests Mozart, but at the next it looks forward to post revolutionary music. It is very likely that Herrmann was responsible for the choice of this somewhat recherché piece; indeed, in Hitchcock's dubbing notes of 15 January, 1958, the director remarks that "The music to be played on the phonograph in this scene should be discussed with Mr Herrman [*sic*]."[31]

"Source" music is also called for as Scottie prepares to follow Madeleine in his car for the first time:

24 (P. 19) EXT. BROCKLEBANK APARTMENTS — (DAY) — SEMI-CLOSEUP

Scottie, seated in his car, a light gray sedan, is reading the morning paper. The car radio is going and we hear conventional disc jockey music.

Rather than following Taylor's suggestion here, Herrmann begins the cue "Madeline's Car" immediately after the previous one, "Madeline," creating a continuity between this scene and the one in Ernie's restaurant, where Scottie saw Madeleine for the first time.

The second specific diegetic cue called for in Taylor's script is found in the scene in Midge's apartment subsequent to his first day tracking Madeleine's movements from Brocklebank Apartments and back, through the streets of San Francisco, by way of the flower shop, the Dolores Mission and graveyard, the art gallery and the McKittrick Hotel:

119 (P. 35) INT. MIDGE'S APARTMENT — (DAY)

Midge is at work on a nightgown ad. The phonograph is playing softly: probably Bach, probably harpsichord, probably Landowska.

Polish musician Wanda Landowska was influential in the twentieth-century renaissance of the harpsichord, and her performances and recordings of Bach (particularly *The Well-Tempered Clavier* and the *Goldberg Variations*), though far from "authentic" by modern standards, were popularly successful. Performances by Landowska of Bach certainly *could* have provided the opportunity to further establish Midge's high-art taste and perhaps reinforce her incapacity to connect emotionally to Scottie (whom she clearly loves) if this was Hitchcock's intention. In fact, no music, diegetic or otherwise, is used in this scene in the final cut, though the cue numbers in the holograph score (see below) jump from 4C to 4E, and it is thus quite possible that the missing 4D was originally a diegetic cue.

Midge's apartment again forms the focus for Taylor's next suggested piece of source music, in a scene that immediately proceeds Scottie's and Madeleine's passionate kiss on the shore at Cypress Point:

186 (P. 74) INT. MIDGE'S APARTMENT — (NIGHT)

In Midge's apartment the lights are on and soft music comes from the radio (possibly "progressive jazz" of the gentle George Shearing kind).

The nondiegetic accompaniment to the previous scene ends with an emphatic cadential closure, and it may have been felt that the use of music in the subsequent scene would have undermined this powerful effect. However, the opportunity to characterise Midge's musical taste is again sidestepped, and no music is used.

The most important of the diegetic cues appears in the scene in the Sanatorium after Madeleine's "death." Scottie is in an expressionless, near-catatonic state, and as part of his treatment is having music therapy:

216 (P. 98) INT. SANITARIUM [*sic*]BEDROOM — (DAY)

We see a portable phonograph with a record on, and we hear Mozart at his gayest, most incisive, most sparkling ...

MIDGE
(*brightly*)
It's Mozart. Wolfgang Amadeus. I had a long talk with the lady in musical therapy, and she said Mozart's the boy for you, Johnny. The broom that sweeps the cobwebs away. That's what the lady said. You know, it's wonderful how they've got it all taped now, John. They've got music for melancholiacs, and music for dipsomaniacs, and music for nympho-maniacs* ... I wonder what would happen if somebody mixed up their files? [*In the cinematic release "hypochondriacs" replaces "nymphomaniacs."]

The Mozart used in this scene is taken from the second movement, *Andante di molto*, of the Symphony No. 34 in C major, K 338. Given Taylor's suggestion for "Mozart at his gayest, most incisive, most sparkling," the movement is, perhaps, a slightly odd choice. The obvious selection would have been one of the brilliant overtures (perhaps to *The Marriage of Figaro*) or the symphonic finales. Instead, we hear a *empfindsamkeit* slow movement that is more ambiguous in tone, with many subtle rhythmic and harmonic details, irregular phrase lengths, and sudden flirtatious changes of pace and dynamics. Wood comments that

The point of the music, its total inability to reach Scottie, lost as he is in the abyss that he has fallen into, is defined by its context, and in fact the very superficial and shallow interpretation of the andante of the 34th Symphony (taken at a ridiculously brisk tempo) that Midge plays him fulfills its function admirably. The music as played suggests both a poise and an artificiality that admirably epitomizes for us the fragile shell.[32]

In fact, the screenplay does not relate this music to Midge's character at all — after all the files were supplied by the music therapist and Midge makes it clear to the doctor in the subsequent scene (217) that she feels that Mozart will not help

Scottie in his recovery. For Wood and for Weis, however, Midge's line "I don't think Mozart's going to help at all" is an admission of personal defeat and of her inadequacy, as much as Mozart's.[33]

232 (P. 117) INT. DANCE HALL FLOOR, FAIRMONT HOTEL—(NIGHT)

The lighting in the room is low, the orchestra is playing "Isn't It Romantic," there are many couples on the floor, dancing romantically.

The music used to this very brief cue is Victor Young's "Poochie," which originally appeared in the film *Skylark* (1941) and was reused in *Forever Female* (1953). This is the only piece of popular music in the entire film, but beyond that, it seems to have little significance.

Overall, the comparatively minor position assigned to diegetic music in *Vertigo* compared to, say, *The Man Who Knew Too Much*, is clearly of interest. While diegetic music tends to reinforce the "grounding" of the narrative (consider, for instance, the scene in the Albert Hall from the latter film), the prioritisation of the non-diegetic element of *Vertigo* literally underscores Scottie's detachment from reality which is one of its narrative premises. Much of the drama of *Vertigo* unfolds through his eyes and he is either intolerant of (J. C. Bach) or insensitive to (Mozart and Poochie) music. However, almost more than anything else, his musings and sensations are encoded by Herrmann's score, and his inability to face reality of which his vertigo is a symptom, is mirrored by his rejection of music in the real world.

HERRMANN'S SCORE FOR *VERTIGO* — AN OVERVIEW

A microfilm of the holograph of Bernard Herrmann's full score for *Vertigo* is held by the Paramount Studio Music Library, and a photocopy made from this, generously supplied by Famous Music, has been used in this study. The Prelude (Cue 1A) is dated 3 January through 19 February 1958, implying that the composition of the entire score took just 48 days. The music is mainly written on 18 and 24 stave paper marked "EDIZIONI DE SANTIS — Roma, Via del Corso, 133." Each segment of the score is titled and labelled with a descriptor containing a number referring to the reel of film (1 to 14) and a letter identifying the constituent cue or cues. Thus, for example, the first scene "Roof-Top," after the title and opening credits, is marked 1B. Many of the cues are subdivided at scene changes and some cross over reels, in which case they are given two labels (e.g. 8E/9A). A case in point is the cue entitled "Farewell" and labelled "{8C 8D 8E 9A}" which precedes Madeleine's fall from the tower: section 8C accompanies scenes 190–191 as Scottie and Madeleine drive down the highway south of San Francisco towards the Mission San Juan Bautista; section 8D (from the Habanera) supports scenes 195–198 in the Mission grounds; and section 8E/9A begins immediately after Scottie says "Madeleine, try … for me …" in the middle of scene 199. The positions at which cues are divided are normally marked with the letter O in the score. Herrmann identifies places that are to be synchronised to a specific event by using a barline that cuts through all the systems with a circled timing marked at the top of the system and an arrow pointing to the barline. It is not clear from the holograph whether Herrmann or the music editor was the originator of the descriptive titles given to the individual cues, though they are most likely to have been the composer's. In some cases, these are helpful, for they do help to clarify the composer's intention. For instance, knowing that cue 2B is labelled "Madeline" as opposed to "Carlotta" or "Judy" (and in fact Judy's appearance is first marked by a cue merely called "The Girl") is of value in elucidating the music's function in the narrative.

All bars are individually numbered, generally towards the middle of each system, but sometimes at the bottom of the score. There are very few metronome markings anywhere; only the cues "Prelude," "Madeline" [*sic*], "The Flowershop" and "Beauty Parlor" have explicit tempi in beats per minute. However, there are detailed timings indicated throughout the score, the total lengths of cues being calculated at the end of each one, and from this timing information it is simple to calculate back to the tempo of a cue using a click book. A conductor's short score and parts were prepared from the holograph score, and on these, ironically, the name of the composer is misspelled throughout as Bernard Hermann — one version that his father hadn't experimented with! The limited information about timing is perhaps not surprising given that Herrmann was renowned for not relying on technical assistance in the recording process. Len Engel, a music editor at Fox notes that:

Benny ... hardly used any cue marks on a film. When I first started working with him I found this hard to believe — how could he catch cues with nothing on the screen? No click tracks, nothing.[34]

Engel also notes that Herrmann demonstrated his prowess in a complex two-and- a-half-minute cue which involved a number of transitions and hit points. Engel was flabbergasted when he discovered that Herrmann required nothing more than lines at the start and end of the cue and contacted him to confirm that this was really all he wanted. Herrmann replied that it was fine and apparently went on to faultlessly conduct the scene with only the barest minimum of visual aids.

Herrmann's orchestra is substantial: three flutes (with piccolo and alto flute doublings), two oboes and a cor anglais (the oboes also doubling cor anglais), three clarinets and two bass clarinets, two bassoons and contrabassoon, four horns, three trumpets, three trombones and tuba, timpani and percussion, two harps, celeste, Hammond organ and strings. The percussion section includes two vibraphones, small, medium and large suspended cymbals, tam tam, castanets, tambourine, and triangle, but the majority of these are used sparingly, the most characteristic sound from this section being that of the vibraphone. Herrmann specifies that the string section should have eight to ten each of first and second violins and six to eight each of violas and cellos. It is not clear from the autograph of the "Prelude" how many contrabasses are required, though the cue "The Hotel" explicitly asks for three.[35] The individual numbers are scored for ensembles of varying sizes, only ten out of the forty-odd cues being scored for full orchestra. Table 4.1 provides a summary of all the diegetic and non-diegetic cues indicating metre and, where obvious, tonality. In some cases an arrow is used to show that the

Table 4.1
The Diegetic and Nondiegetic Cues in *Vertigo*.

Cue	Title	Motifs	Duration	Metre	Tempo	Tonality	Orchestration
1A	Prelude	"Mirror"	2.56 1/3	2/2	Moderato assi [sic]	D	Tutti
1B	Roof-Top	"Vertigo"	1.36 2/3	6/8 / 2/4	Allegro con brio	C	Tutti
1C	DIEGETIC - J C Bach, Sinfonia Op 9/2, 2nd Movement		2.25	C	Andante con sordini	C min	Ob, hrns, strings
1D/2A	The Window	"Vertigo"	0.15	3/2	Lento	?	3 cl, 2 bass cl, 3 trpts, 3 trmbns, hammond organ or novachord
2B	Madeline	"Madeleine"	1.12 1/3	6/8	Lento amoroso	→D	Hrp, strings
2C/3A	Madeline's Car		2.32	C	Molto moderato	D→	Ob, 3 cl, 2 bass cl, horn, strings
3AI	The Flowershop	"Madeleine"	0.34 2/3	6/8	Lento amoroso		4 cl, vlns
3B	The Alleyway		0.39 2/3	3/4	Lento	B♭7/D aug	3 cl, hrp, strings
3BI	The Mission		0.34	3/2	Moderato	B♭7	4 cl, hrp, strings, Hammond organ or novachord
3C	Mission Organ		0.32	4/2	Lento	A min	Organ
3D	Graveyard	"Madeleine"	1.56 2/3	6/4	Lento (molto tranquillo)	min	2 bass cl and vlns
3DI	Tombstone		0.12	C	Moderato	B♭7	2 cl, 2 bass cl, hrp, 3 cb
3E	Carlotta's Portrait	"Carlotta"	2.23	2/4	Lento (Mouvt. d'Habanera)	D	2 fl, 2 cl, 2 hrns, hrp, vibes, vlns
3F/4A	The Hotel		1.23	2/4	Lento (Habanera Timpo)	B♭7 → F	3 trpts, 3 trmbns, vibes, strings
4B	The Hallway		1.01 2/3	C	Lento (Molto tranquillo)	→A	3 trpts, 3 hrns, 3 trmbns
4C	The Nosegay	"Madeleine"	0.14	3/8	Lento amoroso	G →	Strings
4D	NO CUE						
4E/5A	The Catalogue	"Madeleine" "Carlotta"	0.29	3/4 – 2/4	Lento amoroso	G → D	2 cl, hrp, vibes, vlas, vlcs

Cue	Title	Motifs	Duration	Metre	Tempo	Tonality	Orchestration
5B	The Gallery	"Carlotta"	0.35	2/4	Lento (Habanera tempo)	B♭7 ⇀ D ⇀	2 fl, 2 hrns, hrp, vibes, strings
5C	The Bay	"Madeleine"	2.46	C	Moderato	E min ⇀	Tutti
5D	Sleep	"Sleep"	0.48	C	Lento	C min	Strings (no basses)
5E/6A	By The Fireside ("The Fireplace" is scratched out)	"Sleep" "Madeleine"	2.5	6/8	Lento amoroso	C min ⇀ D major ⇀ B♭7 ⇀ D	Strings
6B	Exit	"Sleep" "Madeleine"	0.42	C – 3/4 – C	Lento (Molto intenso)	C min	Strings
6C	The Streets		2.2	C	Molto moderato	⇀	2 fl, ob, 3 cl, 2 bass cl, 2 hrns, strings
6D/7A/7B	The Outing	"Madeleine" "Love"	1.25	6/8	Lento amoroso	D♭ ⇀	5 cl, strings
7C	The Forest		3.42	C	Largo	⇀ B♭ maj (closure)	Woodwind (incl 3 cor anglais), brass, Hammond organ, 2 vibes, 2 susp cymbs, 3 double basses.
7D	The Beach	"Madeleine"	3.26 ½	C – 3/2 – C – 2/2 – 6/4 – 3/2	Lento	⇀ C maj (closure)	Tutti
8A	3. AM	"Love"	0.2	3/4	Lento	C	Strings (no basses)
8B	The Dream	"Carlotta"	2.38	C – 2/4	Lento	G♭ (?) ⇀ D min ⇀ G♭7	2 fl, alto fl, 2 cl, vibes, vlns, vlas
8C/8D/8E/ 9A	Farewell	"Carlotta" "Love"	4.18	C – 2/4 – 3/4	Molto moderato — Lento (Habanera) — Molto Largamente	E min ⇀ D min ⇀ C	3 fl, 2 ob, E. hr, 3 clar, 2 bass clar, 4 hrns, 2 hrps, vibes, strings
9AI	The Tower	"Vertigo"	2.29	2/2 – 6/8 (2/4) – C –2/4 – C – 6/8 (2/4) – C	Allegro Furioso	C ⇀	Tutti
9B/10A	The Nightmare	"Carlotta" "Love"	2.22	Variable	Lento e mesto — Habanera (Lento) — Allegro	⇀ D	Tutti

Table 4.1 (cont.)

Cue	Title	Motifs	Duration	Metre	Tempo	Tonality	Orchestration
5B	The Gallery	"Carlotta"	0.35	2/4	Lento (Habanera tempo)	$B\flat^7 \to D$ $\to$	2 fl, 2 hrns, hrp, vibes, strings
5C	The Bay	"Madeleine"	2.46	C	Moderato	E min $\to$	Tutti
5D	Sleep	"Sleep"	0.48	C	Lento	C min	Strings (no basses)
5E/6A	By The Fireside ("The Fireplace" is scratched out)	"Sleep" "Madeleine"	2.5	6/8	Lento amoroso	C min $\to$ D major $\to$ $B\flat^7 \to D$	Strings
6B	Exit	"Sleep" "Madeleine"	0.42	C – 3/4 – C	Lento (Molto intenso)	C min	Strings
6C	The Streets		2.2	C	Molto moderato	$\to$	2 fl, ob, 3 cl, 2 bass cl, 2 hrns, strings
6D/7A/7B	The Outing	"Madeleine" "Love"	1.25	6/8	Lento amoroso	$D\flat \to$	5 cl, strings
7C	The Forest		3.42	C	Largo	$\to B\flat$ maj (closure)	Woodwind (incl 3 cor anglais), brass, Hammond organ, 2 vibes, 2 susp cymbs, 3 double basses.
7D	The Beach	"Madeleine"	3.26 ½	C – 3/2 – C – 2/2 – 6/4 – 3/2	Lento	$\to$ C maj (closure)	Tutti
8A	3. AM	"Love"	0.2	3/4	Lento	C	Strings (no basses)
8B	The Dream	"Carlotta"	2.38	C – 2/4	Lento	$G\flat$ (?) $\to$ D min $\to$ $G\flat^7$	2 fl, alto fl, 2 cl, vibes, vlns, vlas
8C/8D/8E/ 9A	Farewell	"Carlotta" "Love"	4.18	C – 2/4 – 3/4	Molto moderato – Lento (Habanera) – Molto Largamente	E min $\to$ D min $\to$ C	3 fl, 2 ob, E. hr, 3 clar, 2 bass clar, 4 hrns, 2 hrps, vibes, strings
9AI	The Tower	"Vertigo"	2.29	2/2 – 6/8 (2/4) – C – 2/4 – C – 6/8 (2/4) – C	Allegro Furioso	C $\to$	Tutti
9B/10A	The Nightmare	"Carlotta" "Love"	2.22	Variable	Lento e mesto — Habanera (Lento) — Allegro	$\to$ D	Tutti

Cue	Title	Motifs	Duration	Metre	Tempo	Tonality	Orchestration
13C/13D/-14A	The Necklace	"Carlotta"	2.33	2/4 // 5/4 // 3/2	Lento (Habanera)	D min →	Picc, 2 fl, 2 ob, eng hrn, 4 cl, bass cl, 2 bsn, contra, 4 horns, strings
14B	The Return	"Love"	2.4	3/4	Moderato assi [sic] – Largo	G	3 fl, 3 cl, 2 bass cl, 2 fags, contra, 4 hrns, 3 trpts, timp, 2 hrps, strings
14BI	Finale	"Love"	2.21	C	Allegro pesante — Moderato — Molto appassionato — Molto sost e appassionata	C	Tutti

Note: Durations are taken from the score, except in the case of "Prelude" which was timed from the video.

tonality may be ambiguous before or after a stable area has been established. Where a key name is used without a major or minor qualifier, the modality is usually indeterminate, but the pitch is felt to be a tonal centre.

The titles of motifs in Table 4.1 relate to the musical examples as follows:

Mirror   Chapter 2, Example 2.6.
Vertigo   Chapter 2, Example 2.12.
Madeleine   Chapter 2, Example 2.1.
Carlotta   Chapter 2, Example 2.3.
Sleep   Chapter 5, Example 5.10.
Love   Chapter 2, Examples 2.5, 2.9 and 2.16.

A detailed analysis of all the cues from *Vertigo* follows in chapters 5 and 6. A possible strategy for approaching the study of Herrmann's score might be first to locate the points where a cue begins and ends by reference to the brief descriptions of the action that open each section of the analysis. Before the analytic discussion is read, it is suggested that the appropriate segment of the film should be watched without any particular focus on the music. In the light of the score analysis, it may prove fruitful to review the scene again, but this time concentrating as much as possible on the musical elements alone. Repeated viewings of a scene are, in my experience, crucial to gaining an understanding of the effectiveness of the music and an awareness of how it supports the development of the narrative. Of course, no piece of musical analysis can hope to be remotely "complete," and my intention is to offer basic information about the scoring, thematic material and harmonic characteristics of the cue, which will help in its aural contextualisation, as well as indicating some of the forms of signification the score employs. It is hoped that readers may discover many more connections, links and correspondences of their own, and thereby their personal experience of the film may be enriched.

NOTES

1. Bernard Herrmann, "Music in Films — A Rebuttal," *The New York Times*, June 24, 1945.

2. Friedrich Nietzsche, *Human, All Too Human: A Book for Free Spirits*, transl. R. J. Hollingdale (Cambridge: CUP, 1986), p. 99.

3. Igor Stravinsky, *An Autobiography* (London: Calder & Boyars, 1975), p. 53.

4. Deryck Cooke, *The Language of Music* (Oxford: OUP, 1959).

5. Manfred Clynes and Nigel Nettheim, "The Living Quality of Music: Neurobiologic Patterns of Communicating Feeling" in ed. Clynes, *Music, Mind and Brain: The Neuropsychology of Music* (New York, London: Plenum Press, 1982), p. 80.

6. Susanne Langer, *Philosophy in a New Key* (Cambridge, MA: Harvard University Press, 1942), p. 218. Author's emphasis.

7. Frank Skinner, *Underscore* (New York: Criterion Music Corp, 1950). The endorsements on the rear cover include statements from Miklós Rózsa and Henry Mancini.

8. Ibid., p. 9.

9. Ibid., pp. 9–10.

10. Chion, *Audio-Vision*, p. 8.

11. Gorbman, *Unheard Melodies*, p. 73.

12. See Max Paddison, *Adorno's Aesthetics of Music* (Cambridge: CUP, 1993), pp. 143–144.

13. See Leonard Ratner, *Classic Music: Expression, Form and Style* (New York: Schirmer Books, 1980), pp. 9–29.

14. Though this can equally be seen as an isomorphism of the musical and the sonic.

15. Robert Stam, *Film Music: An Introduction* (Oxford: Blackwell, 2000), p. 42.

16. Maurice Jaubert, "Music on the Screen" from ed. Davy, Charles, *Footnotes to the Film* (London: Lovat Dickson Ltd, 1937), p. 107.

17. Jaubert, p. 108.

18. Ibid.

19. Ibid., p. 112.

20. See Gorbman, *Unheard Melodies*, pp. 83–84.

21. This is an example of the musical component of an association *anticipating* the visual component.

22. Chion, *Audio Vision*, p. 72.

23. Ibid., p. 77.

24. See Palmer, *The Composer in Hollywood*, 245–49.

25. Herrmann, "Score for a Film."

26. Elisabeth Weis, *The Silent Scream: Alfred Hitchcock's Sound Track* (Rutherford, Madison, Teaneck: Fairleigh Dickinson University Press, 1982), pp. 16–19.

27. Alex Coppel and Samuel Taylor, *From among the Dead* (screenplay) p. 98 (215).

28. Auiler, *Vertigo*, pp. 140–41.

29. Stein, Fritz, foreword to Bach, Johann Christian, *Sinfonia in Eb Major Op. 9 No. 2* (London: Ernst Eulenberg, n.d.), p. III. Stein's foreword is dated 1935.

30. Weis, *The Silent Scream*, pp. 90–91.

31. Auiler, *Vertigo*, pp. 131–32.

32. Wood, *Hitchcock's Films Revisited*, p. 119.

33. Weis, *The Silent Scream*, p. 91. Weis cites Robin Wood's *Hitchcock's Films* (London: A. Zwemmer, 1965, rev. 1969, p. 84.

34. Smith, *The Heart at Fire's Center*, p. 180.

35. Unfortunately, the Paramount Music Library was not able to provide the holograph of "Prelude"; however, the first page is reprinted in Kalinak's *Settling the Score*, p. 18. I thank John Waxman and the BBC Music Library for permission to see the printed score for this cue.

CHAPTER 5

ANALYSIS AND READINGS OF THE SCORE: MADELEINE

1A PRELUDE

See the discussion in chapter 2 on musical form.

1B "ROOF-TOP"

The opening shots of the film, after the title and credits, establish the origin of Scottie's vertigo. The scene is set on the rooftops above San Francisco, as Detective Scottie (John Ferguson) and an unnamed, uniformed policeman pursue a criminal. As they jump from one roof to another, Scottie lands badly, injuring himself, and is overcome with nausea as he swings in mid-air from the guttering that has detached itself from the wall. Overpowered by panic, he is unable to move. The policeman reaches out his hand to offer assistance, misses his footing, slips and falls to his death.

Watching this sequence without sound is revealing, for despite the motion of the three protagonists, the tempo of the camerawork and editing is almost leisurely, with a series of static or slowly panning shots. The function of the nondiegetic music is, therefore, to establish a tension and a pacing that is not present in the visuals and effects alone. There are a number of places where Herrmann might, in the classical Hollywood mode, have chosen to "Mickey Mouse" the on-screen action. For example, he could have musically tracked the hand movements of the men as they climb the fire escape; the gun shots might have been supported by orchestral stabs; and the Foley effects of the men's feet clattering against the sloping roof could have been reinforced by musical hit points. Characteristically, however, he avoids close synchronisation between the action and music, rejecting any further articulation of these features and employing a fairly regular tempo (marked *Allegro con brio* in the holograph score).

The musical texture is constructed from three basic elements that are related by
an effective 1:2:8 tempo ratio: an ostinato based on an undulating six-semiquaver
chromatic figure spanning a minor third in the strings and upper woodwinds (Example 5.1), which is subject to changes of register and pitch; a slowed-down version
of this pattern in quavers; and a sustained idea in a four-bar hypermetre played by
the lower brass, woodwinds and strings that rises and falls by an octave (Example
5.2). The use of several simultaneous tempi to generate excitement or tension was
by no means uncommon in nineteenth century Western art-music. Herrmann's
hero, Charles Ives, and a number of other radical U.S. composers such as Charles
Seeger, Conlan Nancarrow and Ruth Crawford had experimented widely with the
possibilities of polyrhythms in the earlier decades of the twentieth century, and
Herrmann was clearly aware of such developments, though his application of the
technique here is not particularly radical. The polyrhythmic process he employs
here could be likened, metaphorically, to a clockwork device, in which individual
cogs and gears trace out their own discrete pulses, but are meshed together to
output a single impulse every unit of time. It may seem odd that he should choose
such an apparently rational means to generate anxiety in his audience. One's initial
expectation might be for a music that somehow invokes the irrational by making use
of rhythmic irregularity, acceleration and retardation of tempo, dynamic variation
and so forth. Yet, by remaining rhythmically highly ordered and regular, Herrmann's
music does appropriately suggest that Scottie is caught up in a mechanism over
which he has no control, an inexorable process.

Example 5.1
The Semiquaver Ostinato Figure from "Roof-Top."

Example 5.2
The Bass Figure from "Roof-Top."

Herrmann's skill (or perhaps even audacity) as an orchestrator is illustrated near
the beginning of the cue. Here, the ostinato figure established by the violins and
violas is taken up by flutes (doubled by clarinets), oboes and cor anglais (in the six-
quaver version of the chromatic figure) all playing towards the bottom of their

registers. This produces an abrasive and grating sound that effectively comple-ments the image and sound design.[1] The use of chromaticism to suggest terror, menace or fear is, of course, very well established in Western art music (and is thus an example of an intracultural semantic), and the reiteration of the undulating figure, which might be taken as the sonic isomorphism of a moan or a shudder, amplifies the sense of anxiety. When the cellos, basses, bass clarinets, bassoons and contra-bassoons introduce the first sustained pitches, it is significant that they form the interval of an augmented fourth, or tritone, from C to F♯; as was noted in chapter 4, the tritone is a conventional signifier of malevolence as well as being a means of tonal destabilisation. The curves of the individual semiquaver figures are matched on the larger scale by an analogous process in much longer note values (the third textural element mentioned previously). The octave patterns played by the trom-bones and tuba (Example 5.2) follow the pattern F♯–B–C–D–E♭, the bass clarinets, bassoons and cellos returning the idea chromatically down to B♭. An important feature of this slowly moving idea is the use of syncopation such that an accent falls on the second hyperbeat of each hypermeasure (the minim in the second bar is tied over to the third bar), subtly eliciting a sense of anticipation.

Immediately before Scottie suffers his first bout of vertigo, the music settles on the pitches C and G (implying a return to a potential C major or C minor) and the hypermetre switches to a three-bar grouping as bass instruments hammer out D♭ and B♭ on the second and third bars of each hypermeasure. By confounding the expectation of the continuation of the quadruple hypermetre, Herrmann further disorientates the listener. Musically speaking, the bareness of the fifths at this point mirrors Scottie's vulnerability as he hangs suspended from the guttering. Simultaneously, the pitches D♭ and B♭ both undermine the tonicity of C by being dissonant to it and stabilise it by suggesting a kind of cadential closure.[2] Like the C–G dyad, Scottie is rooted to the spot, unable to move upwards or downwards.

The sonority Herrmann conjures up for Scottie's vertigo is remarkable in its simplicity and its appearance in the score belies its powerful effect. Three trumpets using hard mutes, supported by piccolos, oboes, cor anglais and a vibraphone sustain a D major triad, while clarinets and a second vibraphone play an E♭ minor triad. At the same time, the two harps perform freely rising and falling glissandi of D and D♭ major (the latter between E♭$_4$ and B♭$_7$ suggesting the E♭ Dorian mode) and a shimmering roll is played on a large suspended cymbal.[3] The tonal and harmonic instability of this event is all the greater because of the relative stability of the C–G dyad that preceded it. Why this sound is so apposite is hard to quantify precisely, but it has both the quality of a scream (for which it may be taken as a sonic isomor-phism) and, in the harp arpeggios, a physical isomorphism of the sensation of shivers passing up and down the spine. Perhaps this figure can be regarded as an externalisation of Scottie's internal response to the sensation of vertigo.

Each of the first two statements of the "vertigo sonority" is followed by a further chord fashioned from the superimposition of A♭ minor (stopped horns, Hammond organ and violins) and G minor triads (trombones, tuba, Hammond organ, violas and cellos) in a lower register, as Scottie, frozen with terror, looks upward to the uniformed policeman. The synchronisation of the final sequence, as the policeman falls to his death, is again loose and no attempt is made to musically track the plummeting officer. Instead a non-diatonic cadential figure in which F♮, functioning as a substitute-dominant, restores a unison C as tonic, the pedal tone C_2 in the four horns offering powerful support. This point of musical closure forcefully demarcates the opening episode from the events that ensue.

1C J. C. BACH, SINFONIA OP 9/2, 2ND MOVEMENT

The scene shifts to Midge's apartment on Russian Hill, though it is never explained how Scottie was rescued from his precarious position suspended from the guttering. As the recording of a movement from a J. C. Bach Sinfonia plays on the phonograph, Scottie and Midge discuss his future plans now that he has retired from the police force. The dialogue establishes the fact that an old college friend named Gavin Elster has contacted him, suggesting they meet. Scottie climbs onto a chair in an attempt to begin a program of self-therapy to overcome his acrophobia, but suffers another bout of vertigo when he looks out the picture window.

Example 5.3
The Opening Four Bars of the Second Movement of J. C. Bach's Sinfonia Op. 9 No. 2.

The diegetic use of the second movement, *Andante con Sordini*, of J. C. Bach's Sinfonia in E♭ Major was considered in detail in chapter 4. Several additional points are worthy of comment, however. First, the tonality of the movement is C minor, allowing a seamless connection with "Roof-Top," which ended on a low C. Second, an element of thematic continuity is also achieved with the previous cue. The opening line of the *Andante con Sordini* is characterised by two main melodic features: the encircling of the tonic C by its neighbours D and B in the first bar, and a rising perfect fifth from C to G in the second bar (Example 5.3). Both of these elements were anticipated in the closing section of "Roof-Top" from bar 51 (50 seconds in), when Scottie was seen hanging from the guttering; the music was dominated at this point by the repeated perfect 5th C–G and the D♭ and B♭ neighbour notes surrounding it.

1D/2A "THE WINDOW"

Herrmann supplies a slow, atonal, four-bar cue labelled "The Window" to accompany Scottie's vertigo attack. Scored for three trumpets and three trombones (all with hard mutes), three clarinets, two bass clarinets and a Hammond organ, it presents new versions of the dissonant vertigo chords first heard in "Roof-Top." The brass superimpose A♭ minor and G minor triads in a resonant voicing (played *sfp* with a crescendo to *fff*) that places the constituent pitches in a chain of thirds (suggesting A♭m^9 with sharpened seventh and eleventh), and the Hammond organ responds, *pp*, with simultaneous F minor and F♯ minor triads whose roots are separated by an augmented octave. The open (and therefore rather less dissonant) voicing of these chords suggest a weaker attack of acrophobia and the entry of the Hammond organ at a much lower dynamic level and in an even wider spacing signifies Scottie's slide into unconsciousness. Clarinets complete the cue by intoning a four-note fragment ending on E that intimates uncertainty by its tonal ambiguity.

2B "MADELINE"

During Scottie's meeting with Elster, he arranges to go to Ernie's Restaurant that evening to identify Madeleine in preparation for his surveillance duties. The scene in Ernie's follows immediately and is played without dialogue, the only aural diegetic components being wild sound and ambient effects.[4] In his screenplay, Taylor provided a long speech for Elster that was intended to be carried over from the previous scene in his office, through the dissolve, into the restaurant, where it would become a voice-over. This monologue gave detailed information about the effect on Madeleine of coming to San Francisco, the intensity of her excitement and Elster's increasing uneasiness about her mental state. In the film, this explanation has been eliminated and replaced entirely by Herrmann's music.

As Madeleine's theme (see chapter 2, Example 2.1), marked *Lento amoroso* (slow and amorous), begins, we do not initially see her from Scottie's point of view. Although the screenplay notes that "The CAMERA SEARCHES with him," in the final cut the camera tracks across the restaurant and zooms in to Madeleine before we see her explicitly from his point of view framed in the doorway. Spoto notes that "there is something statuesque about her, something eminently desirable and infinitely remote, the quintessence of the mystery of Woman," and Herrmann's music plays its part in the construction of Madeleine's otherness.[5]

The cue presents one of the primary musical ideas of the film and it has a number of characteristics that contribute to its yearning and mysterious quality:

1. It is scored for muted strings supported by a harp arpeggio at the climax.

2. It is in a unhurried tempo of seventy quaver beats per minute — one of the very few explicit tempo markings Herrmann gives in the holograph score — slightly below the mean resting heart rate for an adult, which helps make it feel serene without being ponderous. The harmonic rhythm is also slow — generally one chord change per bar.

3. It has a single unbroken melodic line in the first violins with an extended range of two-and-a-half octaves that progresses by means of "circular" phrases, each roughly a bar in length, which snake their way up to the climax at bar 10, the point at which Scottie and Madeleine's faces are seen in profile. (The tendency to associate circularity of melodic configuration with the feminine and linearity with the masculine is well established in art-music.) Dissonances are found on almost every downbeat, including the climax, and although these generally resolve on the next (weak) part of the beat, subsequent notes are often themselves dissonant to the prevailing harmony.

4. Like the "Romantic fragments" of Schumann, it begins off-centre with no clear tonal orientation initially. In fact, it has a particularly close similarity with the opening phrase of the fourth of Schumann's fantasies *Kreisleriana* (Example 5.4).

Example 5.4
The Opening Melody of Schumann's *Kreisleriana* IV.

5. The opening motif (F♯–G–B–A) also has a loose correspondence with the figure which begins Isolde's "Liebestod" at the end of act 3 of *Tristan und Isolde* (setting the text "Mild und leise" — "softly and gently"), though Wagner's phrase involves a rising perfect fourth and falling minor second (E♭–A♭–A♭–G). Like Wagner's, much of Herrmann's melodic writing involves stepwise motion and sequences or decorated sequences. When larger melodic leaps do appear— for example, the rising major seventh at the climax — their impact seems all the greater. The rhythm at the climax (quaver, dotted quaver and semiquaver) is identical to that used throughout the Prelude to *Tristan und Isolde.*

6. The cue has an element of tonal ambiguity. Although it cadences on C major and C minor triads respectively in bars 4 and 8, the attempted closure in D major in bar 12 is undercut by the introduction of A♯ in the violas, and the final D is left unsupported harmonically.

It is this latter aspect, dissonance treatment, which is perhaps the most interesting facet of the cue. It is instructive to compare the Prelude to act 1 of Wagner's *Tristan und Isolde* (Example 5.5) with "Madeline." Wagner's melodic line, which is in 6/8 and has a tempo marking of Langsam und schmachtend (slow and yearning), initially consists of short phrases which place rising major or minor sixths against chromatic continuations. The accompaniment has a leisurely harmonic rhythm and for the first eighteen bars, on every downbeat with an explicit harmonisation, there is a dissonant melodic note. By avoiding the resolution of such dissonances on strong beats and by shunning obvious and predictable harmonic progressions both composers manage to suggest an almost palpable feeling of desire, though Herrmann has only thirteen bars rather than Wagner's 111 to do so. As an example of Herrmann's treatment of dissonance, consider the second main phrase (see chapter 2, Example 2.1). Here the melody moves from C_4 through D_4 to $E♭_4$ (or more properly, its enharmonic equivalent, D♯ as the underlying harmony is F♯[6]) that will eventually resolve to an E_4 over a C major triad. However, Herrmann takes a rather convoluted route to this resolution, by first letting the melody rise to A_4, and then spiral down through G_4, $D\sharp_4$ and $F\sharp_4$ before finally arriving on E_4 over a C major triad. Thus, the expected fulfilment is initially frustrated, but the gratification engendered at the point of final resolution is greater than it would have been had the dissonance been resolved immediately.

Example 5.5
The Opening Section of the Prelude to *Tristan und Isolde*.

The progression employed at the climax of "Madeline" corresponds interestingly with that found at the first of the two great highpoints of the "Liebestod" from the end of *Tristan und Isolde*, on the word "klinget" (Example 5.6), where Wagner's harmonic sequence is A♯⁷–F♯⁷–E (in B major). In "Madeline," the progression from bars 9 to 10 is D♭–A⁷–G, the same underlying sequence transposed to the cue's implied tonic, D major. The final pages of *Tristan und Isolde* involve a massive modified plagal cadence, moving from the minor subdominant (E minor) to the tonic (B major). Similarly, Herrmann's final cadence moves from the subdominant minor to tonic. By leaving the final tonic (D) unaccompanied, too strong a sense of closure is avoided, and more pragmatically, a seamless connection is made with the subsequent cue, for D is immediately taken up as the middle note of the opening chord of B♭⁷. Although the Orpheus legend rather than *Tristan und Isolde* was the starting point for Boileau and Narcejac's novella, the former has at least one important narrative link to *Vertigo*, for, like Tristan, Scottie is given the task of looking after his employer's wife, but ends up falling in love with her. Undoubtedly, Herrmann's occasional references to Wagnerian harmonic or melodic usages in his score (e.g. in "Farewell") bring with them this further intertextual layer that adds to the richness of the film.

Example 5.6
The First Climax of the Liebestod from *Tristan und Isolde*.

2C/3A "MADELINE'S CAR"

It is now daytime. Scottie tails Madeleine's car from Brocklebank Apartments through the streets of San Francisco to an alleyway behind Podesta's flower shop.

This cue gives prominence to the bass clarinet, one of Herrmann's favourite and most characteristic instruments, and reinforces the perception of Scottie's feelings of unease and anticipation as he follows Madeleine. No attempt is made to musically track the motion of the car, but the narrative continuity is supported by the use of a Spanish-American tinged ostinato that is in essence a mixture of tango and cha-cha-cha rhythms played at a rather slow tempo (chapter 2, Example 2.14), the appropriateness of which is linked to Madeleine's alter ego, Carlotta Valdes. However, at this stage, all that we and Scottie know about Madeleine is that she has been acting strangely, and there has been, as yet, no revelation of the nature of her supposed possession. The music prepares us, at least on a subconscious level, for the scene in the graveyard when Carlotta's name will be explicitly introduced. As is so often the case in Herrmann's film music, process and continuity are more important here than any attempt to tightly synchronise the music to the action.

The ostinato figure, which is organised in ten-bar units, is passed from clarinets (three B♭ and two bass clarinets) to muted strings and then back again. Above this, starting on the third bar of the figure, lies a melodic idea which is subdivided into two-bar phrases and treated in an imitative fashion (chapter 2, Example 2.2). Although the holograph indicates crotchets and minims throughout, in Muir Mathieson's recording of the score the first crotchet of a number of these phrases is shortened to a quaver, further insinuating the Spanish-American rhythm, which will be made fully explicit in the habanera rhythm of "Carlotta's Portrait." In terms of harmony, the opening material initially suggests a fifth-less $B♭^7$, though the subsequent addition of a sustained E_2 in the second bass clarinet produces a tonally ambiguous chord (E_2–$B♭_2$–D_3–$A♭_3$–D_4) whose pitches can be found in a wholetone scale on D. Although this can be analysed as an augmented (French) sixth chord (B♭–D–E–G♯) in the key of D, Herrmann certainly does not attempt to resolve it to D, merely transposing it upward by a semitone step at the beginning of each new ten-bar passage. The effect of these whole-tone chords from the standpoint of diatonic harmony is one of suspension and irresolution, conventionally lending them an air of mystery. Until the final four bars of the cue, Herrmann emphasises the second of each pair of bars by using sustained notes, and this promotes a certain edginess because of the subtle syncopation of the duple hypermetre as well as faintly evoking the sound of the foghorns that feature so importantly in the effects track throughout the film.

The vaguely troubling quality of this gently throbbing rhythmic figure is intensified by the melodic lines it accompanies. Herrmann's use of an imitative technique, in which each two-bar melodic phrase is echoed an augmented fourth higher or diminished fifth lower, could be construed as an example of a punning isomorphism. Certainly, the transposed version played by the violas follows the original version in the violins in a way that corresponds to Scottie's tailing of Madeleine. The relationship that develops between pairs of two-bar melodic phrases is also of interest, a figure showing a greater tendency towards expansion being balanced by one that maintains a steady state. As an example of this, consider the first two violin phrases which expand from A♭–B♭–C♭–B♭–A♭ (a figure embodying mirror symmetry) to A♭–B♭–C♭–A♭–G♭–F, in response to which the viola tersely repeats the phrase D–E–F–E–D. An association between Madeleine and the material of the first of these phrases (in the violins) is formed by its synchronicity with Scottie's point of view shot of Brocklebank Apartments (from which Madeleine will soon emerge). Similarly, the second phrase (in the violas) accompanies an objective shot of Scottie in his car. The connection between this musical process and the development of the narrative can be analysed in several ways:

1. If the role of music is to objectively support the narrative, the process can simply be seen to underline the relationship between the two characters. Madeleine, whom we understand from Gavin Elster is suffering from a delusional state and whose behaviour is erratic, might quite reasonably be represented by an idea that is more subject to development. Scottie's function, as the private eye in pursuit, is to remain impassive and detached, and thus the musical material that symbolises him could be expected to be more regular and less subject to change.

2. Equally, it could symbolise Scottie's confused feelings for Madeleine. He has already found himself attracted to her, and yet she is the wife of a client and a friend. This would imply a subjective role for the music as an encoding of Scottie's state of mind.

The melody is initially constrained, moving only by tone or semitone steps, apparently getting nowhere in particular. According to Bruce, the material finds its source in the final arching melodic phrase of "Madeline" (D_4–E_4–$F\sharp_4$–E_4–$B\flat_3$–D_4), and there is certainly merit in this suggestion if only the basic contour is considered, and the change of modality is ignored.[6]

On the first upward transposition of the ten-bar passage up by one semitone (sounding rather as if the car has shifted up a gear), Herrmann reverses the texture by placing the ostinato in the muted strings and the melodic lines in solo clarinet and oboe. The melody is now more intense, particularly in the second and fourth phrases where the boundaries between bars are marked by larger intervals. A second transposition restores the original instrumentation, but the imitative relationship is inverted: the viola line, which originally echoed the violins' phrase, now precedes it, as if the connection between the pursuer and the pursued had been reversed. The melodic intensification noted in the previous section persists, the first violins moving into a very high register and the contour being adapted so that it closely anticipates the configuration of "Madeline" that will open the next cue: in "Carlotta's Car" the first violins play E_6–$F\sharp_6$–G_6–$B\flat_6$–A_6; and "The Flowershop" they open with the figure $F\sharp_6$–G_6–B_6–A_6.

The final ten bars accompany the arrival of Madeleine and Scottie in the alleyway and Scottie's progress through the dark passage that leads to the flower shop. The change to *pizzicato*, the slight thickening of the harmony, and the removal of just one quaver from the second bar of the figure creates a more incisive texture and assertive rhythm which promotes a mood of increasing uncertainty. The expectation of a further appearance of the imitative melodic lines is not realised this time and the ostinato, reduced to two bars, is passed rapidly between strings and winds. The cue ends mysteriously and ambiguously, a parallel sequence of slow, quiet, major triads with flattened sevenths and sharpened ninths in second inversion (a harmonic précis of the succession over the previous six bars) being heard in the clarinets as Scottie crosses the passageway. A reiteration of the first pair of chords of this latter sequence by bowed strings leaves the cue unresolved as Scottie opens the door.

In Herrmann's holograph score, four bars were deleted from the final section, before the bar numbers were added. It is not clear whether these were removed on musical or dramatic grounds. It is possible that the scene was shortened by seven and a half seconds between spotting and recording, or that the cut was made during the process of composition. However, the rest of the holograph has relatively few amendments of this sort.

3AI "THE FLOWERSHOP"

Opening the door from the passageway, Scottie is surprised to find that he is looking into a flower shop (Podesta, Baldocchi) and he observes Madeleine talking to an assistant, who briefly leaves, returning with a nosegay of flowers. The screenplay notes that Madeleine "approaches camera until she is again in profile — just as she was in Ernie's Restaurant when Scottie first saw her."[7] In a beautifully constructed shot we see her reflection in the mirrored surface of the door that Scottie is standing behind and we are thus able, simultaneously, to view both characters *and* observe Madeleine's profile from Scottie's point of view.

Material from the first six bars of "Madeline" is reused in this cue, which is scored for four clarinets and muted violins.[8] The melody begins stratospherically in the first violins, two octaves higher than it originally appeared, the second violins picking out the unprepared suspensions and their resolutions an octave lower across the barlines. This is in very marked contrast to the low and sombre register of the end of "Madeline's Car," the move to a high "bright" sound complementing the dramatic change of lighting between the passageway and the flower shop. However, as noted previously, we have been prepared for the move into this register by the violin material of the third section of "Madeline's Car." Soaring above the accompanying harmonies with no bass instruments to ground it, the music suggests that Madeleine exists as an inaccessible figure, detached from everyday reality, for Scottie.

For the final three bars of the cue, the melody drops into a lower register and the second violins join the firsts an octave below. The effect of this very slight change in instrumentation is an increase in richness and strength of tone, which can perhaps be taken as an intimation of Madeleine's materiality. Of course, at this stage, we have no inkling that she is a counterfeit or an accomplice to murder — she has not, so far, even been invested with speech by Hitchcock.

3B "THE ALLEYWAY"

Scottie slips back to the alleyway and surreptitiously waits for Madeleine to return from the flower shop to her car.

"The Alleyway" follows immediately after "The Flowershop" and varies material from "Madeline's Car," returning to its harmonic area if not its surface detail and maintaining its edgy uncertainty. It is in triple time and scored for solo clarinet, harp and muted strings. Three harp arpeggios of B♭⁷ are loosely synchronised with the crossing of thresholds: the first is at the beginning of the cue as Scottie shuts the flower shop door; and the second and third as, in turn, he and Madeleine emerge from the exit into the alleyway. By catching these irregularly placed visual events, the phrase lengths become asymmetrical, and are constrained to fall into three-, five- and four-bar units, respectively. This may seem to be an inconsequential point, but since "Roof-Top" most of the cues have been characterised by regular phrase lengths usually organised in multiples of two bars: the combination of an irregular hypermetre with a surface rhythm which, sarabande-like, emphasises the second beat of most of the bars, is disorientating.

Example 5.7
The Clarinet Figure from "The Alleyway" and Its Derivatives.

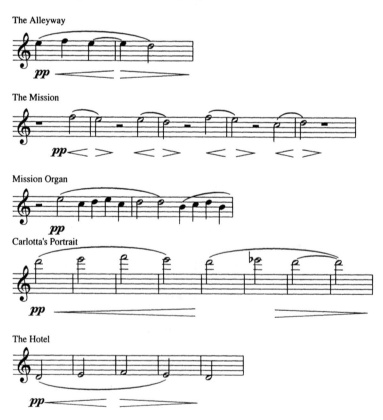

Harmonically, the cue is entirely founded on three chords: Bb^7 and augmented triads on D and Eb. These tonally ambiguous augmented chords, which for much of the time simply slither into each other by parallel motion, reinforce the air of obscurity and confusion. Madeleine's theme, as it appeared in "The Flowershop," particularly the last few notes of its final phrase $(G_4-F\sharp_4-E_4-D_4)$, seems to be the source of the melodic material, though a fragment in the clarinet $(E_5-F_5-E_5-D_5)$ that starts as Madeleine reappears (Example 5.7), is a variant of the figure played by the violas in bars 5 and 6 of "Madeline's Car" (D–E–F–E–D). Two bars have been removed before or during recording; these were originally the penultimate bars and involved the pitches $C_5-D_5-E_5-D_5$ played by the solo clarinet. By the deletion of these, the balance of the final phase is somewhat compromised and the connection with the subsequent cues weakened (see the derivatives of the figure illustrated in Example 5.7).

3BI "THE MISSION"

Scottie follows Madeleine's car from the flower shop along Dolores Avenue, to the Dolores Mission.

Like "The Alleyway," which it follows without a break, "The Mission" also varies material first heard in "Madeline's Car." The Bb^7 chord is now compressed to a vestigial form as the interval of a major 2nd from Ab–Bb, doubled in octaves and played by clarinets, harp and Hammond organ. Against this, muted violins present an expressive idea which is based on the clarinet figure heard in "The Alleyway" (Example 5.7). Herrmann prepares us for the arrival at the mission by his use of conventional codes for the religious, the dyads in the clarinets, harp and organ seeming to represent in a stylised and slightly unsettling way, the repeated chiming of a bell, and the Dorian modality and general contour of the fragmented melody being redolent of plainsong. In particular, this idea can be compared to the plainsong melody associated with the "Dies Irae" from the Latin Requiem Mass (F–E–F–D–E–C–D–D), which has been used by composers such as Liszt, Berlioz and Rachmaninov to signify both death and the supernatural. Each minim couplet of the melody is articulated so that it imitates a sigh, the crescendo and diminuendo recalling the vocal technique of *messa di voce.*[9]

The cue is structured in three short sections, the second and third parts involving successive octave transpositions of the first, moving downward through the string section from first violins to cellos. The close synchronisation between the action and the metre of the music in the first eight bars of this cue is unlikely to be fortuitous. While the changes of shot rarely land exactly on a barline (and for the listener without the luxury of a score it is difficult to detect exactly where a barline is anyway), the relative uniformity of the tempo of the picture editing and the music is extremely striking and helps draw us into the Mission with Scottie.

Section	Bar(s)	Action and editing
1	1	Lap dissolve from the previous scene into a close-up of Scottie at the steering wheel.
	2	Lap dissolve to Madeleine's green Jaguar from Scottie's point of view.
	3	Objective shot of Madeleine's car parking outside the Mission Dolores.
	4	Close-up of Scottie at the steering wheel.
2	5	Madeleine emerges from her car from Scottie's point of view.
	6	Close-up of Scottie
	7	Madeleine goes towards the Mission from Scottie's point of view.
	8	Objective shot of Scottie getting out of his car.
3	9 – 12	Objective shot of Scottie walking towards the mission and entering it

3C "MISSION ORGAN"

Scottie follows Madeleine into the Mission Dolores. The camera follows him as he walks up to the east end of the church and out a door on his right-hand side.

Although the screenplay does not indicate the use of diegetic music at this point, we hear a pipe organ playing, apparently from within the mission, though we are never shown its source. Herrmann's archaic notation of the cue in 4/2 time, redolent as it is of early organ voluntaries, seems to be an "in joke" for the performer, and the piece recalls the vacuous improvisation of a competent, if uninspired, organist with its chain of melodic and harmonic sequences. Its function in the narrative is simply to cover Scottie's movement from one end of the building to the other and to add a little local colour. The melodic material, while rather thin, clearly derives from the final three pitches of the previous cue (E–C–D) which are repeated to make one basic melodic unit, before being submitted to eight sequential repetitions and a suitably ecclesiastical-sounding perfect cadence (see Example 5.7).

David Raksin comments amusingly on Herrmann's use of repetition and sequence in his scores in an interview with Royal Brown:

When I was showing *Vertigo* to a bunch of my students at UCLA, a kid said to me, "Listen. When Kim Novak walks through the church on the way to the graveyard, there's an organ playing. Do you know the name of that piece?" I said, "No, it's something by Benny Herrmann. But I know the name of the church. It's called Our Lady of Perpetual Sequences!"[10]

3D "GRAVEYARD"

In a scene that parallels the movement from the dark passageway into Podesta's flower shop, Scottie emerges into bright daylight in the graveyard. He notices Madeleine in the distance looking at a headstone and hides behind a grotto from where he observes her until she leaves. After she departs through a gate at the side of the graveyard (Hitchcock taking a further opportunity to show her in profile as he did in both Ernie's Restaurant and the flower shop), Scottie goes to the grave she has been staring at.

The correspondence between this scene and the one in the flower shop is made more obvious by the reuse of Madeleine's theme, now extended to twenty-six bars and reorchestrated so that the violins play the melody in high register, doubled in thirds throughout, while two bass clarinets, *quasi subtone*, play perfect fifths in the main. This yields a texture with an enormous gap of almost three octaves between the two instrumental colours, an effect that recalls one described by Berlioz in his treatise on orchestration. Berlioz discusses the combination of trombones in low register with flutes in high register in the "hostias" section of his Requiem,[11] where his intention was for the flutes to apparently supply "the extreme high harmonic resonance" of the trombone pedal notes.[12] In Herrmann's orchestration, a similar outcome is achieved, though unlike Berlioz, he does not employ static chords and the texture he creates has a simultaneous radiance and hollowness that beautifully complements the hazy luminosity of the photography.

A subtle difference apparent at the beginning of the cue is the addition of just one note to the melody of "Madeline" so that it now begins on an E. This may simply be to achieve continuity with the A minor chord at the end of "Mission Organ" from which it seamlessly emerges, but in this form it bears a striking similarity to the slow section (rehearsal numbers 15–20) of Delius's English Rhapsody *Brigg Fair.* Otherwise. Herrmann maintains the melody as it appeared in "The Flowershop" for six bars before elaborating it by means of varied repetition and sequential writing. The cue moves to much flatter tonal regions than have been explored hitherto in the score and it ends on an implied E♭ minor chord, though the tonic in the second bass clarinet is silenced before the final interval of G♭–B♭ is played in the violins. Two bars (14–15) have been omitted from the film soundtrack, the cut being marked in the holograph score by circled crosses.

It is interesting to note how often Scottie appears in shot at points at which the bass clarinets are heard prominently. One might almost submit that the duality of the instrumentation reflects the actions of the two characters, Madeleine radiantly wafting through the graveyard while Scottie waits in the shadows, hiding behind the grotto and quietly observing. Like the bass clarinets and violins, they are currently separated by a chasm.

3DI "TOMBSTONE"

Scottie notes the inscription on the headstone "Carlotta Valdes. Born 3 December, 1831. Died 5 March, 1857." He then exits the graveyard by a side gate.

Herrmann writes a very short three-bar cue scored for two clarinets, two bass clarinets, harp and three double basses to accompany the chiming of the bell (the sound of which was recorded from the actual Dolores Mission bells on 30 September, 1957). There is an almost tongue-in-cheek quality about Hitchcock's decision to use this sound effect (which Taylor's screenplay does not ask for), insinuating, as it does, that the connection between Madeleine and Carlotta suddenly "rings a bell" for Scottie. Of course, the effect also prepares us for the scene in the bell tower at the end of the first part of the film in which Madeleine apparently jumps to her death. Herrmann again draws on the arpeggiation of a $B\flat^7$ chord (which was previously used to synchronise the closing of doors in "The Alleyway") and a fragmentary reminiscence of the clarinet figure from "The Alleyway," now reduced to a repeated sighing couplet (F_2-E_2) in the second bass clarinet. A final sustained D prepares for the tonal centre of the subsequent cue.

3E "CARLOTTA'S PORTRAIT"

Scottie returns to his car and drives towards Lincoln Park in a short sequence that does not have any nondiegetic music (the previous eight cues followed each other without any breaks at all). He enters the art gallery of the Palace of the Legion of Honor and sees Madeleine gazing at a painting. From Scottie's point of view, Hitchcock draws our attention to two features shared by Madeleine and the woman in the painting: the distinctive coiffure with spirally organised bun and the nosegay of flowers. The camera also settles on the woman's necklace, which will play an important role later in the film. Questioning an attendant, Scottie discovers that the painting is titled "Portrait of Carlotta."[13]

In the discussion of "Madeline's Car," it was noted that the music alluded to a Spanish-American association that had not yet been made clear by other means. In the scene in the graveyard, we were introduced to the name of Carlotta Valdes (the first reference to this character), but we still know no more about her ethnicity or background. The visual components of this sequence have the important narrative function of implying either that Madeleine was, in some obsessional way, modelling herself on Carlotta, or that she was really possessed by her, and it seems to me that Herrmann's music encourages the latter reading.[14] The most conspicuous musical feature is the use of the habanera rhythm played by the harp (perhaps as a surrogate guitar) on a repeated D_4 throughout the cue (see chapter 2, Example 2.3).[15] The dance associated with the habanera, which takes its name from Havana and which achieved popularity, particularly in Spain, in the early part of the nineteenth century, is both restrained and erotic. Perhaps the most familiar use of its rhythm in art-music is in "L'amour est un oiseau rebelle" from Bizet's opera *Carmen* of 1875. Bizet's Gypsy Carmen espouses sexual freedom and radiates eroticism, and her death in the opera effectively results from the inability of her former lover Don

José, whom she ditches in favour of the Toreador Escamillo, to cope with her libertine lifestyle. By choosing the habanera rhythm, Herrmann inevitably draws on these intertextual references. Carlotta, the music implies, is also mysterious, exotic and erotic.

Herrmann had used the habanera rhythm in another film written only a few years before *Vertigo*, in the cue "Siesta" from *Garden of Evil* (1954), a film set in Mexico. "Carlotta's Portrait" is a very different kind of habanera to either this cue or Bizet's "L'amour est un oiseau rebelle," however, for it is a wraithlike dance, the life sucked out of it, trapped in cyclic repetition, without development or progress.

The image of Carlotta presented in the visuals is amplified and supported by a number of musical features:

1. The cue is scored for two flutes, two clarinets, two horns, harp, vibraphone and violins, an instrumentation that avoids the use of bass instruments. The tessitura of the ensemble is, figuratively speaking, a female one, only the clarinets bringing the register below C_4 at any point and the effect of this is to make it sound as if it is suspended and ungrounded.

2. The orchestration is characterised by styles of playing that are notable for their avoidance of the conventions of expressivity, whether through the nonvibrato of the flutes, the *quasi subtone* of the clarinets or the *sur la touche* (on the fingerboard) of the muted violins. This combines to create a "ghostly" sound that is thin, cold and distant.

3. Although a Spanish-American rhythm is used as an ostinato, it is reduced to a simple but insistent reiterating rhythm, without the vitality of the extravagantly arpeggiated bass lines commonly found in art-music habaneras such as those of Bizet, Ravel and Debussy.

4. Structurally, the cue has something of the character of the baroque passacaglia, with a repeating harmonic sequence supporting gradual textural variation rather than teleological development. Unlike "Madeline," there is no sense of forward movement towards a climax but of continuing stasis.

5. While the melody played by the wind instruments is loosely derived from the opening of "Madeline," its rising semitone and major third is reworked in a figure that contains a minor third instead (see chapter 2). The restrained regularity of "Carlotta's Portrait" is in marked contrast to the melodic irregularity of the earlier cue, with its complex dissonance treatment.

6. A notable feature, that is entirely absent from "Madeline," is the use of the pitch that lies an augmented fourth above the modal final as a lower neighbour note (G♯). The augmented fourth between tonic and subdominant is found in some flamenco modes and may be seen as a further reference to the cultural practices of Spanish America.[16]

7. In "Graveyard," the melody was also doubled a third lower, but there the choice of major or minor version of the interval was determined by the local diatonic context. Here, the constancy of the interval of a major third is unsettling because of the "foreign" tones it introduces.

8. At the beginning of the cue, muted violins present a figure that involves the fall of an octave. Such rising and falling octaves were an important element of "Roof-Top," but have

not been heard since and their presence here, albeit in a much higher register, may be a subtle reminiscence of Scottie's first vertigo attack. Further on, the violins present a countermelody in high register, doubled an octave lower, which opens with the pitches D–E–F–E–D–E♭–D (see Example 5.7). This is derived from material first played by the violins and violas near the start of "Madeline's Car," and offers a musical link between Madeleine and Carlotta.

9. The vibraphone plays a sustained D_5 on the first bar of each group of four, which helps to articulate a four-bar hypermetre and recalls the chiming of the bell in "Tombstone," but now as a distant echo.

10. The B♭[7] chord, which was such a prominent harmonic feature of the cues "Madeline's Car," "The Alleyway," "The Mission" and "Tombstone" is significantly absent. In each of these cues, Scottie was pursuing and observing Madeleine, but now the focus is on Carlotta.

As well as suggesting Carlotta's ethnicity, her erotic nature, and perhaps even, on a subconscious level, her untimely death, these characteristics help to signify unease, frailty, otherworldliness and even neurosis.

An interesting feature of the holograph score is the existence of a number of unrecorded extra bars. The bar at which the recorded version of the cue finishes is marked with the Roman numeral I, twenty-two further bars being prefaced with the numeral II. At the bottom of the score, apparently in Herrmann's hand, is the remark "Note 1st and 2nd Endings!" It is not clear where or how these extra bars were intended to be used.

3F/4A "THE HOTEL"

In a short unaccompanied sequence, Scottie follows Madeleine's car from the Legion of Honor, through poorer streets of San Francisco, to the McKittrick Hotel. The cue begins as, from Scottie's viewpoint through his windscreen, we see Madeleine emerging from her car and walking up the steps to the hotel. Scottie steps out of his sedan and, looking up, sees Madeleine opening the blind of a first-floor room and taking off her jacket. He then enters the hotel lobby.

The underlying B♭[7] sonority is reasserted in this cue scored for three muted trumpets, three muted trombones, vibraphone and strings. In the same basic tempo as "Carlotta's Portrait," the habanera rhythm is played *mf* by muted cellos and basses while violins and violas reiterate, *pp*, the by now familiar motif D–E–F–E in minims (see Example 5.7). The habanera rhythm has thus spilled out of the context of the art gallery and attached itself to Scottie's perception of Madeleine (the scene is shot largely from his point of view—and in fact, there have been none from her viewpoint in the film so far). As Scottie looks up to the window and sees Madeleine raise the blind and remove her jacket, the habanera rhythm is briefly suspended while the vibraphone plays the (D–E–F–E) motif in crotchet, a subtle change of texture that helps to articulate the narrative without simply redundantly duplicating the action in another medium. The pairs of A minor and F minor triads which end the cue are startling, partly because of the muted brass tone colour, which is in such marked contrast to the string and vibraphone tone of the rest of the cue, but also for the reason that they represent a kind of harmonic succession (parallel root-position triads) which has not been used in the score hitherto. Most certainly, the effect of the last two chords is not one of closure.

4B "THE HALLWAY"

Scottie asks the hotel manageress to check if the woman she knows as Carlotta Valdes is in her room. She goes upstairs and calls down to Scottie to follow her up. He looks around the empty room and, as he stares out of the window, is amazed to see that Madeleine's car has vanished. This scene has no rational explanation later in the movie and we never discover how Madeleine entered or exited the hotel, or whether the manageress was colluding with her and Gavin Elster.

The brass timbre and parallel harmony that marked Scottie's entrance into the hotel lobby returns in this cue which is scored for trios of muted trumpets, horns and trombones.[17] Now the parallel motion is extended so that a succession of minor triads of A, F and G is established, the figure being passed antiphonally from trombones to trumpets and thence to horns.[18] The upper voice of this chord progression (E–C–D–E) is yet a further derivative of the clarinet melody from "The Alleyway," particularly as it was manifested in "Mission Organ" (see Example 5.5). The lack of tonal connection between the triads, the false relations caused by the flat and natural versions of the pitch A and the cyclic repetition of the figure combine to reinforce the sense of confusion established by the other narrative elements. As Scottie looks up to the ceiling, the motif is adjusted so that a second inversion D major chord appears for two beats, a brightening which mirrors the upward lift of his eyes and is perhaps suggestive of possible enlightenment that awaits upstairs. This modified motif is then passed between trios of trombones and horns. The process that was established at the start of the cue is now reinstated, so that parallel minor triads accompany Scottie as he walks to the door and enters Carlotta's room, and the figure containing the second inversion chord of D reappears just before he looks out of the window.

4C "THE NOSEGAY"

As Scottie pulls up his car outside Brocklebank Apartments, he sees Madeleine's green Jaguar in the car park, with the nosegay sitting on the dashboard.

Scored for divided and muted strings, the cue uses the falling segment from bars 5 and 6 of "Madeline" but now in 3/8 time, with the slightest suggestion of the waltz rhythm that will play such an important role later in the film. After the tonal obscurity of "The Hallway," the clear G major tonality and simple, linear melodic descent signifies a less ambiguous and more positive mood. The entry of the first violins above the resolution of the appoggiatura (E_4–D_4) in the upper divisions of second violins, violas and cellos, slightly diminishes the effect of this conventional device, which according to Cooke "produces the effect of a burst of pleasurable longing."[19] A rising seventh and falling second in the violins ($F\sharp_5$–E_6–D_6) as Scottie sees the nosegay brings the cue to its end, the octave displacement of the final two notes creating a brief assertive gesture that is undercut by the fall back to D over a diminished seventh chord, potential closure being averted.

4D NO CUE

This is almost certainly the missing cue that was discussed in the section on diegetic music in chapter 4. Taylor suggested that a recording of Wanda Landowska playing Bach should accompany the subsequent scene in Midge's apartment, in which Scottie seeks Midge's advice about finding a local historian. In the final cut, the scene is played without music.

4E/5A "THE CATALOGUE"

After their meeting with Pop Leibel, the owner of the Argosy Bookshop, Scottie drives Midge back to her apartment and her inquiries about Elster's wife seem to catch a raw nerve with Scottie. The music begins as Midge leaves Scottie "lost in thought" in the car.[20] Opening the catalogue he was given by the attendant at the art gallery, he looks at the portrait of Carlotta and from the point of view of his "mind's eye" he sees Madeleine's image superimposed on that of Carlotta.

It is revealing that the scene in Pop Leibel's bookshop should not have any non-diegetic music. This would have seemed the obvious place to reuse Carlotta's motif, and perhaps the absence of music may be taken as a concealed clue that Madeleine is not, in fact, possessed by the Carlotta that Pop Leibel describes. "The Catalogue" opens with yet another reworking of "Madeline" played by the upper divisions of divided violas and cellos in 3/4 time and beginning on E (as it did in "Graveyard"), but with the ascending minor seventh and falling major second figure heard at the end of "The Nosegay." Herrmann's orchestration is somewhat unconventional, for in his doubling of the melody in octaves, he reverses the normal arrangement by placing the cellos above the violas. Perhaps the fall of register can be read as an indicator of Scottie's increasing infatuation with Madeleine, for he is drawing her theme into his domain. His reverie is broken off as he opens the catalogue, the chromatically descending section of the opening phrase of "Carlotta's Portrait" resurfacing, played by clarinets, harp and vibraphone, the instrumentation balanced so that the harp predominates, sounding all the more guitar-like.

5B "THE GALLERY"

After a conversation between Scottie and Elster which clarifies information that has so far only been hinted at visually or musically, we see Scottie at the wheel of his car. The cue begins on the dissolve to the exterior of the Palace of the Legion of Honour, outside which is parked Madeleine's green Jaguar. A lap dissolve brings us inside the art gallery and once again we see Madeleine staring at the portrait of Carlotta in a scene which parallels her previous visit. Taylor's screenplay notes that "she rises and approaches the portrait and stands before it, the nosegay clasped in her two hands before her, and stares up almost as though in votive offering or in prayer."[21] A return to the exterior of the Palace ends the cue.

"The Gallery" involves no new material, but subtle modifications of previously heard music clarify and underline the visuals. The eight-bar sequence from "Carlotta's Portrait," played by two flutes, harp, vibraphone and violins, is expanded to ten bars and framed by forceful sustained $B\flat^7$ chords in the strings, now with the habanera rhythm played *mf* on $B\flat_3$ by two muted horns. Herrmann thus further accentuates the distinction between Scottie's pursuit music (which has hitherto been underpinned by the $B\flat^7$ chord) and Madeleine/Carlotta's triadic D minor material.

5C "THE BAY"

In one of the key scenes of the first part of the film, Scottie follows Madeleine's car along Sea Cliff Drive and Presidio Road to the Golden Gate Bridge. He watches her as she stands beside the dock, throwing petals from her nosegay into the water, and is startled as she throws herself in. He immediately jumps in after her, swims out and grabs hold of her, and after carrying her back up the steps, places her in her car. For a moment, Scottie is not sure if she is dead or alive and he desperately calls out her name. When she opens her eyes, she appears to be in a trance.

Herrmann scores this important cue for the full orchestra, the first tutti since "Roof-Top." The neurotic insistence on $B\flat^7$ disappears for the time being, and familiar material from previous cues is completely reworked and recontextualised. Harps and violins arpeggiate, simultaneously in quavers and semiquavers, a harmonic progression whose rate of change is one chord per bar. The glittering sound of this material recalls the title sequence of *The Ghost and Mrs. Muir,* where a not dissimilar passage accompanies shots of the sea.[22] It is also loosely evocative of textures found in Debussy's *La Mer,* for example in the passage shortly after Figure 54 of "Dialogue du vent et de la mer." The opening melody (Example 5.8) derives from Madeleine's theme, but has been opened out into a more linear shape, without the latter's convolutions of suspensions and appoggiaturas, and is subject to more rapid modulation. Herrmann takes advantage of the greater colouristic opportunities offered by the full orchestra to support the melody's evolution by passing it between two groups of instruments containing, respectively, violas, cellos and horns, and oboes and cor anglais (all of which tend to be characterised as particularly "expressive" instruments). A final ingredient in the texture is the rising and falling octave-based figure in the bass instruments, a type of motion was that was first used in "Roof-Top" and its reappearance here, albeit in a different configuration, prepares us for a connection between the two scenes. Herrmann's change of gear for the start of this cue may be perplexing initially. In retrospect, we might have expected music which was more explicitly threatening, as in "Roof-Top." However, the apparent catastrophe, when it comes, is doubly unexpected because we have not been prepared for it by the use of standard signifiers for impending disaster.

Example 5.8
Opening Melody of "The Bay."

As Scottie's car draws to a halt, the B♭⁷ chord in the strings is brought into prominence once again, suspending the previously established harmonic rhythm. This chord owes its effectiveness to the strength of its harmonic implications. In a tonal context, a dominant seventh chord normally demands either to be resolved to the chord lying a fifth below or a fourth above (in this case E♭), or treating it as an augmented sixth, to a second inversion chord of the tonic. The fact that Herrmann makes no attempt to resolve it at all, generates an almost palpable tension. As well as the vibraphone's gentle recall of the familiar motif D–E–F–E–D against the now static musical backdrop, the bass clarinet restates, *subtone,* the sighing couplet from "Tombstone" as Scottie looks at Madeleine's silhouette against the bridge in the distance. Immediately before Madeleine jumps from the dockside, the strings settle on a sonorous voicing of the B♭⁷ chord which moderates its dissonant seventh to the extent that it sounds stable, but this is dramatically undercut by the immediate change in every musical element. The move from tranquillity to hectic activity in the score sonically matches the shock of Madeleine's jump into the bay.

When Madeleine throws herself from the dockside, the hypermetre changes to three-bar groupings (it will be recalled that exactly the same thing happened at the climax of "Roof-Top") and a sequence of fundamentally whole-tone chords grinds its way down, descending by chromatic step. Against this, the two harps simultaneously play glissandi in the keys of D and C♭ major (a variation of the effect used to represent Scottie's vertigo earlier), and the horns and violins toss backwards and forwards an undulating shriek-like figure which is a distant relative of the opening contour of "Madeline" (see chapter 2, Example 2.15). As Scottie grabs hold of Madeleine in the water, the stormy music gradually subsides, the surging semiquavers shifting to quavers, and settles on a C♯ pedal in timpani and basses which supports a succession of vagrant harmonies involving nearest-neighbour and pivotal motion.

The character of the music changes completely as Scottie carries Madeleine back to her car, the muted and sustained string tone and the suggestion of the "Madeline" motif, now for the first time in common time, combining to signify considerable pathos. Although the initial pair of two-bar phrases offer the possibility of ascending sequential extension, this is stifled by the linear fall from G down to D, the final sighing couplet (E–D) rising upwards twice by octaves, mirroring Madeleine's apparent lapse into unconsciousness.

5D "SLEEP"

The subsequent scene is set in Scottie's apartment. From his living room, we can see Madeleine's clothes hanging on a line in the kitchen ("all of them" according to the screenplay).[23] We can also see, through an open door, into the bedroom where Madeleine lies sleeping, presumably naked, in Scottie's bed. She distractedly mumbles, "Where is my child?" At that moment, the telephone in the bedroom rings and he rushes to answer it; from Scottie's reply we presume that the caller must be Gavin Elster. Scottie quickly ends the call and for the first time we see Madeleine, literally, as a figure of flesh rather than a radiant apparition, her naked shoulders appearing above the bedclothes, and her face looking directly at Scottie's. He realises, with embarrassment, that she cannot get up because of her nakedness, and passes her a robe before leaving the room, closing the door behind him.

Scored for muted string orchestra, "Sleep" is musically continuous with "The Bay," beginning in the same high register that the solo violin had ascended to in its terminal gesture. It begins with a statement of what is probably the most analysed single harmony in Western music, the so-called "Tristan chord," a half diminished seventh chord on F (F–G♯–B–D♯). Although Herrmann enharmonically renotates most of its elements, he uses the same pitches in exactly the same voicing as Wagner famously did in *Tristan und Isolde*, albeit two octaves higher initially (F$_5$–C♭$_6$–E♭$_6$–A♭$_6$).[24] It is almost inconceivable that such a literate musician as Herrmann would not have been fully aware of this chord's identity, and in fact in 1962, he explicitly and extensively referenced *Tristan und Isolde* in his score for *Tender Is the Night*. However, his resolution of the chord is very different to Wagner's (Example 5.9). Rather than resolving chromatically upwards to a French sixth and thence to a dominant seventh as happens in *Tristan und Isolde* (see Example 5.5), he moves to a first inversion C minor triad.[25] This progression has two contradictory explanations. If the "Tristan chord" is regarded as a dominant thirteenth in C minor (G–B–D–F–A♭–C–E♭) with root, fifth and eleventh omitted, it becomes a kind of perfect cadence. Alternatively, if it is viewed as an altered subdominant seventh in C minor (F–A♭–C–E♭) with a flattened fifth (C♭), then the cadence can be seen as plagal. In fact, Herrmann's choice of voicing seems to place the first pair of chords in a plagal relationship and the second pair into a perfect relationship allowing him to draw on both readings.

Madeleine's apparent fall into unconsciousness in "The Bay" was supported by the use of a descending appoggiatura figure which rose by an octave on each repetition; her return to consciousness from sleep reverses the process with a gradually falling chain of chords. Alternate pairs of chords are revoiced so that a descending melodic line A♭–G–E♭–C in minims is passed down through three octaves between the sections of the string orchestra, and dynamically shaded so that they imitate the slow inspiration and exhalation of sleep. A final version augments the note lengths to semibreves, the last note (C_3) appearing austerely suspended over a bare fifth $(C-G)$.

Example 5.9
Motif from "Sleep." On Its First Presentation the Figure Is Played an Octave Higher.

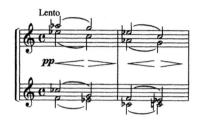

5E/6A "BY THE FIRESIDE"[26]

Scottie closes the bedroom door and brings a fresh cup and cream jug from the kitchen, placing them on the table next to the coffee pot. Madeleine emerges from the door of the bedroom dressed in the red robe, apparently confused and disconcerted, and embarrassed both by her nakedness beneath the robe and her awareness that Scottie must have undressed her. Scottie invites her to sit in front of the fire, and she asks him to explain how she came to be in his apartment. He describes her fall into the bay and how he fished her out, and she seems slowly to remember, suggesting that she must have had a fainting fit. The cue ends as she describes his questioning as "direct."

The music, marked *Lento Amoroso*, and once again scored for string orchestra, begins like "Sleep," with four pairs of chords slowly sinking from the high register in multiply-divided violins (Example 5.10). As Madeleine opens the door, her theme is restated *sempre sotto voce* and *espr & dolce* (always quietly, expressive and sweet). Its configuration here is similar to its first appearance in Ernie's Restaurant, but it is an octave higher now and has an adapted upbeat figure (C–D–E♭) which facilitates the modulation from the C minor of "Sleep" to the G major of the next section. Whereas "Madeline" spiralled up to a powerful climax in high register, Herrmann adjusts the melodic contour so that its tessitura is reduced by an octave and its dynamic level is lowered. Now there is no longer the same sense of fulfilment when we reach the equivalent highpoint in this cue (as Scottie invites Madeleine to sit by the fire). The climax of "Madeline" was marked by a triumphant embellishment, a triplet figure (C♯ – E – D) which briefly deferred the resolution of C♯ to B. This has disappeared, and we are simply left with a five-note descending segment of a B minor scale ($F♯_5$–E_5–D_5–$C♯_5$–B_4).

The chromatically ascending bass line of the next section (as Madeleine asks "I fell into the bay and you fished me out?") takes up and develops the quaver—

dotted quaver—semiquaver rhythmic motif from the climax (which, as was noted previously, is a prominent feature throughout the Prelude to Wagner's *Tristan und Isolde*). This passage does have a practical function—to prepare the way for the

Example 5.10
Page 4 of Herrmann's Holograph Score of "By the Fireside."

next section in B♭. On the arrival on a chord of B♭ major, as Madeleine remarks that she must have had a dizzy spell, the music recalls cues associated with Scottie's tailing of Madeleine, and in particular the middle section of "The Bay," just before she jumped in to the sea. The first violins return to the high register of the opening and play, doubling in (mainly major) thirds, a variant of the (D–E–F–E) figure that has appeared on many occasions so far. Violas respond to this in a gently rocking lullaby-like rhythm. The doubled thirds here are a reminder both of the "Graveyard" and of "Carlotta's Portrait" and its variants, and the B♭ harmony, particularly in the second of each pair of bars where an additional E and A♭ produces a whole-tone sonority, is redolent of "Madeline's Car."

As Madeleine mentions how beautiful she finds Presidio Point and thanks Scottie for the fire, a series of appoggiaturas begin in the first violins that bring the tonality back towards D. The second violins echo and extended the figure a quaver later supported by the rest of the string orchestra, creating an accent on a weak beat, isomorphic with a sigh. The harmonic underpinning sets into relief the two central tonalities of the score so far, D ("Madeline") and B♭ (Scottie's pursuit), by alternating the tonic chords of both keys.[27] At the final cadence point, as Madeleine remarks to Scottie "You're terribly direct in your questions," the potential resolution in D is undermined by a half diminished seventh chord in closed voicing—the "Tristan chord" which began the cue—now transposed onto G♯.

6B "EXIT"

A phone call from Gavin Elster breaks into Scottie and Madeleine's conversation at a point of increasing intimacy. While taking the call in his bedroom Scottie hears the front door shutting, a sound effect which is not mentioned in the screenplay. Rushing out of the bedroom into the living room he discovers that she has gone, the robe he had lent her lying in the kitchen where her clothes had hung. We see Madeleine getting into her car just as Midge drives up. Surprised by what she sees, Midge stops her car and softly remarks to herself "Well, now, Johnny-O ...Was it a ghost? ...And was it fun?" before driving off.

The cue begins as Scottie enters the bedroom. It is marked *molto intenso* (very intense) and like the previous two, it is scored for muted strings. Once again, the Tristan-derived sleep motif dominates, but this time its first resolution in the top voice is upwards to C rather than downwards to G, stressing the narrative punctuation brought about by Madeleine's departure. The searing pairs of chords are loosely synchronised with the action, the first coinciding with Scottie's point of view shot of the empty living room and the second with a view of the kitchen and the robe lying on the work surface. Against three more repetitions of the sleep motif appears a brief variant of "Madeline," the change of mode to minor by convention lending it a more tragic air. The tremolo (literally trembling) descending chord sequence that accompanies Midge's arrival is perhaps intended to indicate her concealed agitation (Example 5.11). There is a very loose correspondence between this progression and the "Magic Fire" music from act 3, scene 3 of Wagner's opera *Die Walküre* in the sustained and nonarpeggiated version heard as Brünnhilde slips into a deep sleep behind the protection of the magic fire (Example 5.12).[28] At the same time, violas and cellos play a line that is remarkable for its unbroken linear ascent through a perfect eleventh, before falling back to E_4 and descending to the final A_3, supported by an augmented triad. This gesture (the ascending component of which is also a prominent feature of the bass line of the "Magic Fire" music) is suggestive of a heroic effort, which in the end proves futile.

Example 5.11
Harmonic Reduction of the Final Six Bars of "Exit."

Example 5.12
Harmonic Reduction of the Magic Fire Music from Wagner's *Die Walküre*.

6C "THE STREETS"

In a sequence which closely parallels Scottie's early surveillance of Madeleine, he follows her from Brocklebank Apartments, through the streets of San Francisco, ending up, to his surprise, outside his own front door.

It is entirely characteristic of Herrmann's approach that he is unwilling simply to reproduce material from earlier scenes, almost always making some significant modification. Although "The Streets" is in many respects similar to "Madeleine's Car," a number of small changes have been made. Two flutes and a second horn have been added to the ensemble, and the instrumentation of the first three sections reversed so that the phrases originally played by violins and violas are now taken by clarinets and solo oboe, and *vice versa*. A subtle, but perceptible change of harmony is introduced into the two-bar ostinato figure—now a full dominant seventh chord (e.g. B♭–D–F–A♭) alternates with a French sixth (E–B♭–D–G♯). The effect of this is to add a tiny frisson that reinforces Scottie's growing puzzlement, even irritation.

In the final section of "Madeleine's Car," the arrival in the alleyway was accompanied by increasingly menacing music, but the equivalent passage is completely rewritten for this scene. Now a succession (marked *molto sost* or very sustained) whose harmony changes every crotchet, and in which the pitches E– F♯–G–F♯ are harmonised with added sixth, seventh and ninth chords (G^6–F♯⁷–F⁹–F♯⁷), is passed antiphonally around the ensemble. The differences in this final part of the cue match the narrative changes, for Scottie is by now aware that he is arriving at a place that he is very familiar with—his own home.

In his "Additional Music Notes" for Reel 6, Hitchcock offered an explicit suggestion for the music for this scene:

The car ride from Exterior Brocklebank down to Exterior Scottie's Apartment. This music should start off quite dramatically and, by degrees, get more comic—developing when Scottie starts to throw up his hands.[29]

Herrmann clearly chose to ignore this advice, for the music of the final part of the cue does not seem to invoke the conventional codes for humour.

6D/7A/7B "THE OUTING"

We see Madeleine posting a letter through Scottie's letterbox. Scottie walks over to greet her, and after a short conversation, she bids farewell to him and sets off towards her car. Before she has time to drive away, Scottie rushes over to the car and suggests that he should join her on her excursion. Madeleine agrees, and we see them driving south along Skyline Drive. The screenplay originally provided dialogue for this sequence taking up a theme of some relevance to the later development of the plot, and of our understanding of Madeleine's apparent mental state:

SCOTTIE:
(*Finally*)
Do you know where you're going?

MADELEINE:
Of course not! I'm a wanderer!
(*Pause. Then brightly*)
I'd like to go somewhere I've never been!

SCOTTIE:
How can you be sure?

MADELEINE:
If I've been there? That's silly! Either you've been to a place or you haven't.

Hitchcock ends the sequence with a profile of Madeleine from Scottie's point of view, linking the shot with the series that began in Ernie's.

Scored for five clarinets and muted strings, the cue begins immediately as Madeleine sets off towards her Jaguar. Herrmann transposes "Madeline" so that it lies a semitone lower than it did on its first appearance and passes the melody between first and second violins and violas. The modification of the cue's tonality is of some interest, for in Western art-music it has long been held that major keys with key signatures of four or more flats are particularly well suited to represent or suggest profound emotions. Although in the modern equal-tempered system it is hard to justify the notion that any key can have a specific character *per se*, the flattening of pitch relative to the prevailing tonality of earlier cues may well have some subconscious effect.

Part way through the cue, just as Madeleine agrees to Scottie's suggestion that he should join her by saying, "You left your door open," Herrmann delicately steers the tonality back up a semitone in a passage that echoes "The Flowershop." This is the first stage in a gradual musical "brightening" that continues in the transfer of the melody in the violins to the upper register, synchronised with the start of the long shot of the car travelling along Skyline Drive. In the final two bars, as Scottie glances at Madeleine's face in profile, we hear a new figure that expands a phrase from "Madeline:"

1. "Madeline": $F\sharp_4-G_4-B_4-A_4-G_4-F\sharp_4-E_4-D_4$

2. "The Outing": $F\sharp_4-G_4-B_4-D_5-C_5-B_4-E_4$

The falling segment of this motif ($D_5-C_5-B_4-E_4$) was prefigured at the climax of the first section of "By The Fireside" (bars 15–16), the melody at this point being $F\sharp_5 -E_5-D_5-C\sharp_5-B_4-E_4$. This idea, which is echoed by a solo clarinet, is now harmonised by alternate A♭ and Am^9 chords and the effect of this is to place a strong dissonance on the melodic D. Perhaps this "love motif," which was first intimated in the prelude and will take on a primary role later in the score, can be taken to symbolise Scottie's feelings of desire for Madeleine rather than the idealised view of her represented by "Madeline."

7C "THE FOREST"

Scottie and Madeleine arrive at the Big Basin Redwoods State Park. We see them standing near the trunk of an ancient and enormous tree discussing its age. The mood becomes sombre and Madeleine's conversation returns to the issue of death, implying through her comments about the dated rings on the cross-section of a tree that she was born many years before. She walks away from Scottie, and for a moment we are led to believe that she has completely vanished, but Scottie discovers her leaning against a tree. He tries to question her about why she jumped into the bay, but she refuses to answer, asking him to take her away from the woods to "somewhere in the light."[30]

For this mysterious and sombre sequence, Herrmann produces the most extraordinary range of colours from an ensemble of woodwinds, brass, Hammond organ, percussion and double basses. While this is not, in the strict sense of the word, *Klangfarbenmelodie*, Schoenberg's technique of subtly modifying the tone colour of static or slowly changing harmonies, Herrmann's constant alteration of the instrumentation is certainly reminiscent of "Farben" from Schoenberg's *Five Or-chestral Pieces* (1909). Bruce notes that the slow-moving chord sequence has something of a chorale about it, drawing our attention to the trunks of the trees that stand like the pillars of a church.[31] Of course, we have come across this type of motion before, in "Carlotta's Portrait," at the end of "Madeline's Car" where similar slow-moving chords accompany Scottie's progress through the dark passage to the flower shop, and most recently in "Sleep."

The impression of weight is partly due to the "heavy" brass employed, in par-ticular muted trombones and tuba, but mainly to the general use of bass instru-ments. Most striking is the almost kaleidoscopic instrumentation. In the first six-teen bars, trombones, tubas and basses are supplanted firstly by horns, and then in turn by: bass clarinets; trombones and tubas; horns, bass clarinets and basses; oboes, bassoons and contrabassoons; trombones, tubas and basses; clarinets and bass clarinets; and finally three English horns, bassoons and contrabassoons. Slurred pairs of chords are grouped in two-bar units, like the lumbering tread of some massive prehistoric animal. The cue begins with a succession of parallel major seventh chords in second inversion (chapter 2, Example 2.11) and this type of motion dominates, even though the individual harmonies are subject to modifica-tion, for example to the minor triads with sharpened elevenths in the horns in the third and fourth bars. The use of such dissonant chords in a largely chromatic melodic context (inasmuch as one can talk of melody here) produces a tonal vague-ness verging on atonality that neatly complements the obscurity of the visuals.

As Madeleine points to the rings of on the cross section of the sequoia, she remarks mysteriously "Somewhere in here I was born ... and here I died ... and it was only a moment for you ... you took no notice." At the same time, the instrumen-tation changes to piccolo and flutes playing coldly, *senza vibrato*, in octaves above muted horns and trumpets. The chromatically inflected melodic line, which evokes both the bass clarinet's falling couplet (F–E) from "Tombstone," and the melody from "Carlotta's Portrait," in combination with the spectrally thin sound of the trumpets and horns sustaining static, dissonant and closely voiced chords, is intended no doubt intended to encourage apprehension in the listener. In the sub-sequent varied repeat, *quasi subtone* clarinets and muted horns repaint the material in muted colours. More remarkable still is the passage that follows. Madeleine, for a moment, seems to have completely and inexplicably disappeared, an illusion encouraged in the viewer by Hitchcock. Herrmann crafts a fantastic reworking of the cue "Tombstone," with Hammond organ eerily sustaining a B♭ minor chord with major seventh (the "Hitchcock chord") *ppp*, the two vibraphones thrice chiming out the same chord a semitone higher as a distant reminiscence of the Mission bell, and *subtone* bass clarinets and double basses reworking the couplet sighs as falling major sevenths.

The final section of the cue reverses the order of the material in the first part. As Madeleine, as if "slightly hypnotized," softly and distantly answers Scottie's ques-tions, the cold, remote music of the flutes, piccolo and muted trumpets, and clari-nets and horns returns.[32] This is followed by a brief reminiscence of the opening chromatic succession, a compressed fragment of "Madeline" and, most surprising of all, a solid chord of B♭ major to close the cue.

7D "THE BEACH"

A dissolve from the previous scene takes us to Cypress Point (or Point Lobos) later in the same day. Seeing Madeleine approaching the sea and fearing that she may try to jump in again, Scottie rushes across to her from the car. When she asks him why he ran he tells her "I'm responsible for you now, you know."[33] Madeleine attempts to explain how she feels, her fragmentary memories of an earlier life seeming to her like shards of broken mirror, and she talks about the fresh empty grave she believes is waiting for her. She tells him of her dream-like memory of a tower, a bell and a garden, apparently in Spain. Desperately, she remarks that the simple explanation is that she is mad and runs towards the edge of the land. Scottie dashes to her and embraces her. After a fervent kiss, Madeleine whispers "Don't leave me .... stay with me" to which Scottie responds "All the time."[34] The screen fades to black with a pause suggesting a major point of narrative closure.

The bright colours of Point Lobos replace the dark and sombre shades of the forest just as Podesta's flowershop succeeded the alleyway in the earlier sequence. In the first cue for full orchestra since "The Bay," Herrmann makes restrained use of the potential resources, reserving the tutti for the final few climactic bars as Scottie and Madeleine embrace. Out of the B♭ major triad that cadenced "The Forest" emerges a passionate melody (another variant of "Madeline") in the muted cellos (Example 5.13) which is reminiscent of parts of the score for *Jane Eyre* and of the opera *Wuthering Heights*.[35] Working its way up to the high register by means of varied sequential writing, the cello melody is accompanied in the first violin by a figure which initially mirrors the resolution of the cellos' dissonance on G♭ to F with a rising semitone from B♭ to C♭. Herrmann thus introduces into the music the concept of the mirror, and particularly the shattered mirror, which will be alluded to in Scottie and Madeleine's dialogue. The metaphor persists in the violin's immediate repeat of the first full bar in retrograde (B♭–C♭–B♭–C♭ ‖ C♭–B♭–C♭–B♭). Structurally, the opening passage of the cue divides into two asymmetrical-length sections, the seven-bar cello phrase being responded to by a five-bar phrase in the first violins which begins immediately after Madeleine's first line: "Why did you run?" and is closely related to a figure from the first section of "Madeline's Car."

Example 5.13
The Cello Theme from the Start of "The Beach."

As Madeleine describes her sense of walking down a corridor once lined with mirrors, but from which now hang only their shattered fragments, a new idea appears in the highest register in the first violins (doubled an octave lower by the seconds) that expands the opening minor-seconds motif. Again, it embodies mirror symmetry isomorphically, this time by presenting a musical motif that falls stepwise through a minor third and then returns to its starting point (B♭–A♭–G–A♭–B♭), an inversion of the motif from the beginning of "Madeline's Car" (A♭–B♭–C♭–B♭–A♭), though the symmetry is broken at the end of the figure by the addition of a final A♭. The pattern thus established is treated to an extended, descending series of sequential repetitions, the first four falling successively by a tone. From then on, the sequence continues, but the internal structure, phrase pattern and interval of the sequential step are altered. Sustained intervals of major or minor thirds, each of a full bar's length, support the violin line and these pass between woodwinds and strings, working their way down to the cue's nadir as Madeleine mentions the fresh and empty grave which lies waiting for her. The low brass now intone a first inversion chord of A♭ which resolves onto the very familiar chord of B♭⁷, and this cadence-like figure is repeated, followed by a variant of the opening melody of the cue whispered, subtone, by clarinets and bass clarinets.

Madeleine mentions a tower, a bell, and a garden below as she recalls what she claims to be the fragments of a dream, and the strings, *sul tasto*, briefly recollect the habanera rhythm from "Carlotta's Portrait" before playing a tremolo passage that leads into the passionate final section of the cue. Now, for only the second time since "Roof-Top," the string players are instructed to remove their mutes and to play with full tone. The passage is dominated by two fragments from "Madeline," the four-note motif from its opening (F♯–G–B–A) and the falling figure (C–B♭–B♭–A♭) derived from its climax. These, suitably transposed and modified, are tossed between strings and winds like the crashing waves behind the couple, leading to a massive climax as Scottie and Madeleine kiss (chapter 2, Example 2.5). An important feature of this final section is the cadential progression from A♭ major to C major – the closure here is so emphatic, that if one did not know otherwise, one might suspect that this was the end of the film.

8A "3 A.M."

We see a figure walking the streets in the half-light of early morning. Although it is too dark too see that this is Scottie, the screenplay makes it clear that it is him, that the time is around 3 a.m., and that he is restlessly wandering round Union Square.

At the end of "The Outing," as Scottie surreptitiously looked at Madeleine's profile while she was driving, Herrmann introduced what I have called the "love motif" as a variant of a figure from "Madeline." It was suggested above that this might be taken to symbolise Scottie's more intimate feelings for Madeleine. Now slightly adjusted (E_5–G_5–B_5–D_6–C_6–B_5–E_5), the figure is played by muted strings in a slow waltz-like rhythm. The falling cell (D–C–B–E) is subsequently passed down through a series of octave displacements and is underpinned by pseudo-cadential figures leading from A♭ major to E min⁶, to A min⁹ and to C major respectively (chapter 2, Example 2.9).[36] The rhythmic characterisation of this figure is worthy of note, its symmetrical organisation (minim – crotchet | crotchet – minim) stressing the second bar of each pair. The association with the earlier sequence in Madeleine's car allows the music to function as a reflection of Scottie's thoughts, the image of Madeleine, appearing repeatedly, preventing him from sleeping. In the second part of the film, this motif will take on an obsessive quality reflecting Scottie's desperate desire to rediscover Madeleine after her death.

8B "THE DREAM"

Madeleine arrives at Scottie's apartment early in the morning to tell him of the dream she has had. She remembers clearly now the Spanish village, the church, the cloister, and the livery stable. Scottie immediately recognises her description as that of the San Juan Bautista Mission, one hundred miles south of San Francisco, and promises to take her there that afternoon.

Herrmann contrives a symmetrical ternary form for this cue, and reworks material from both "Carlotta's Portrait" and from "3 A.M." Thus, Madeleine's discussion of her dream is framed by a prelude and a postlude, which accompany Scottie's attempts to comfort her and rationalise her situation. The cue begins as Scottie opens the door, woken by Madeleine's insistent ringing of the bell. Muted and divided violins commence with the double-thirds motif from "Carlotta's Portrait," initially played *sff* with a diminuendo to articulate the dramatic change of lighting as Scottie opens the door. It is now a semitone higher than before and in an adjusted rhythm (the same dragging dactyl-spondee rhythm that Beethoven uses in the slow movement of his Seventh Symphony). In the second to fourth bars, the love motif from "3 A.M." is adjusted by a change of mode and a filling-in of the falling perfect fifth with a third, so that $D_6 - C_6 - B_5 - E_5 - D_5 - C_5$ becomes $Db_6 - C_6 - Bb_5 - Gb_5 - Eb_5 - Db_5 - C_5$. By loosely synchronising the falling triadic figure ($Bb_5 - Gb_5 - Eb_5$) to Madeleine's reference to her dream, an association is formed which is reinforced by the repetition of the figure an octave lower as Scottie declares, "It was a dream. You're awake." When the figure reappears a third time, after the middle section, it is again linked with her dream, Scottie remarking that it will "finish your dream and destroy it" as it is played.

The middle section, which begins as Madeleine says, "It was the tower again," is scored for two flutes, alto flute, two clarinets, vibraphone, violins and violas. It reverts to the habanera rhythm of "Carlotta's Portrait," now played *arco* rather than *pizzicato* by the muted violas, and reproduces much of the earlier melodic material but with a completely revised orchestration. Herrmann manages to fit exactly five repetitions of the eight-bar figure into this section of the cue which deals with the substance of Madeleine's dream. This is a testament to the sophistication of his method of loose synchronisation and mood enhancement rather than Mickey-Mousing and constant adaptation of the musical fabric to narrative convenience; he manages to create a complex web of associations while maintaining musical integrity and coherence. The use of material from "Carlotta's Portrait," which was briefly evoked in "The Bay," needs little explanation at this point. As always,

Herrmann makes tiny and detailed changes to the texture, such as the addition of an extra note to the violins' countermelody in the third section; [37] use of the alto flute in the fourth; and complete removal of the habanera rhythm in the fifth, while Madeleine talks of the darkness closing in.

The reprise of the opening section subtly underscores the changes of camera position. The first four bars accompany medium close-up shots of Scottie and Madeleine and the second four complement the overhead shot as they walk towards the front door. In the last bar the major third dyad of F–A implies the dominant of B♭ minor, though this resolution is not forthcoming in the next cue, for it begins on a chord of E min[16].

8C/8D/8E/9A "FAREWELL"

A dissolve from the whiteness of Scottie's front door at the end of the previous scene leads into a long shot of the highway south of San Francisco as Scottie and Madeleine arrive at the San Juan Bautista Mission. The scene changes to the livery stable, where we find Madeleine sitting in a surrey. Scottie tries to persuade her that she has been there before recently, not in the distant past, but Madeleine's mind seems to return to far off times when she was a child. He draws her to him and kisses her, telling her that he loves her and she replies that she also loves him, but that it is too late. She runs across the grass towards the church with its imposing tower, and Scottie rapidly chases after and stops her. In a broken voice, she tells him that "It wasn't supposed to happen this way," and asks him not to follow her into the church.

Herrmann begins this elaborate cue by restating the opening section of "The Bay" that accompanied Scottie's tailing of Madeleine to the Golden Gate Bridge, with its rippling arpeggios in violins and harp, though now it is played at a tempo that is fifty percent faster. As Scottie and Madeleine arrive at the mission, violins take up the habanera rhythm in high register and this is echoed antiphonally by flutes at the very bottom of their register. Meanwhile, the vibraphone begins its regular, insistent chiming, initially every two bars and later every four bars. In the screenplay, Taylor notes that "The music of the Mission theme, mingled with Carlotta's theme, begins to drift in, an evocation of the past, a sighing that grows and seems to have behind it the echo of lost voices calling."[38] Herrmann does not seem to have taken this suggestion literally, and although some material derived from "Carlotta's Portrait" appears (most obviously the habanera rhythm), the Mission does not seem to have a specific theme clearly associated with it. Perhaps the brief succession of remotely related four-part chords in the horns (as the flutes start playing the habanera rhythm), the upper voice of which (A♭–G♭–A♭–B♭–A♭–G♭) is vaguely redolent of plainchant, is intended to suggest the "echo of lost voices."

The match of the next thirty-six bars to the visuals is fascinating. Although most viewers will probably not be consciously aware of it, the music helps articulate the camerawork and editing. Each four-bar phrase (see Example 5.14) is carefully timed and the beginnings of many of them are synchronised to specific events or changes of shot:

1. (Bars 24 – 27) The camera closes in on the outside of the livery stable. Violins play a high descending phrase in minims (F–E–D–B) against a dominant minor ninth chord on CI (C♯–E♯–G♯–B–D) in the lower strings, the harp arpeggiating this chord on the third bar. Flutes and muted horns alternate the habanera rhythm on D_4.

2. (Bars 28–31) The camera moves inside the stable and we see Madeleine sitting on the surrey with Scottie standing next to it. Two flutes and solo oboes play a descending line (C♯–B–B♭–A♭) against a dominant seventh chord on G in second inversion (D–F–G–B) in English horn, clarinets and bass clarinets. While this chord contains three notes in common with the previous chord, its root lies a diminished fifth away and it is harmonically remote from the G^7 chord. From this point on, horns alone repeat the habanera rhythm.

3. (Bars 32–35) A static two shot of Madeleine and Scottie. Violins play a figure formed from a pair of sighing appoggiaturas (F♯– F–A–G♯) against the dominant minor ninth chord on C♯ as before.

4. (Bars 36–39) The camera begins to slowly zoom into Madeleine. The flutes and an oboe intone a descending chromatic fragment (B–B♭–A–A♭) against the G^7 harmony.

5. (Bars 40– 43) The camera continues the slow zoom into Madeleine. Violins play a descending diatonic phrase (G–F–E–D) against a half-diminished chord of D in first in version (F–A♭–C–D).

6. (Bars 44–47) A close-up of Madeleine cuts halfway through the phrase to Scottie at the model of the horse. The flutes and an oboe play a rising fragment (E–F–G–A♭) against a B♭^{7} chord.

7. (Bars 48 –51) Scottie taps the horse. Violins repeat a rising couplet (A–B♭) against the dominant minor ninth chord on C♯.

8. (Bars 52–55) We look out of the livery stable towards the Mission church and tower, from Madeleine's point of view, and then return to Scottie. A falling phrase in the flutes and oboe (B–A–F–E) is accompanied again by third inversion of a G^7 chord.

9. Madeleine first still looks straight ahead, and then slowly moves forward. The rising couplet, now from D–E♭, is played over a C♯ dominant minor ninth chord, first by strings with mutes removed and then by winds.

Example 5.14
Harmonic Précis of Bars 24–59 of "Farewell."

A curious feature of the recording of this passage is to be found in the arpeggios played by the second harpist. According to the score, they should be played on the third bar of each phrase, as they are by the first harp in the alternating four-bar unit. However, they are consistently played one bar earlier than this from bar 37 onwards. This may have been caused by a copyist's error or a mistake in the performance that was not detected in recording, or it may possibly have been a creative decision made by Mathieson during the recording. In any event, it does break up the symmetry of the phrases somewhat, whether intentionally or not.

As Madeleine and Scottie kiss, Herrmann revisits and develops the love motif first heard at the end of "The Outing" (while Scottie lovingly gazed at Madeleine's profile), then later in "3 A.M." (as he aimlessly wandered through the streets of San Francisco). Now it is marked *poco a poco appassionato* (becoming gradually more impassioned) and is lavishly scored for strings (the first violins playing the melody with great "warmth" on the D string) and woodwinds. This can be surely be taken to represent Scottie's "musical point of view," that is, an idealised view of Madeleine. The subsequent section of the cue is derived directly, though in a lighter instrumentation, from the climax of "The Beach," as the couple embraced with the waves crashing behind them. At the equivalent point in "The Beach" (when full closure was achieved on a chord of C major), the tempo is increased dramatically and a one-in-the-bar waltz based on the first four notes of "Madeline" ($F\sharp$–G–B–A) is set into motion. After various sequentially repeated permutations of this cell, it stabilises on the figure D_5–C_5–B_4–C_5 in bar 87, and this works its way up to the first of the two major climaxes (see chapter 2, Example 2.5). Bruce interestingly compares this passage (in its restatement in the later cue "Scène d'amour") with the scene in act 2 of *Tristan und Isolde* in which Isolde impatiently awaits the return of Tristan.[39] Unlike Wagner's climax, Herrmann arranges the culmination of his ascending sequence, a decoration of the falling fifth from the end of "The Outing," so that it falls on a major ninth that resolves downward by a major second; like the highpoint of the Liebestod, it is attended by turns which impel it forward. The second climax is achieved more rapidly by way of a sequence that rises by a step in each successive bar (rather than every pair of bars). In the final moments, as Madeleine rushes towards the church, the love motif from "The Outing" (D_5–C_5–B_4–E_4) is given its head, emphatically playing the cadential figure linking $A\flat$ to A min^9. Horns articulate one last in-filled version of the figure, and the cue cadences by way of an $A\flat$ minor chord with added sixth (which, enharmonically renotated, is $G\sharp$–B–$D\sharp$–F —the "Tristan chord" in another inversion) leading to an irresolute dominant ninth chord of G in first inversion played tremolo and *fff* by the strings, with horns, harps and bass clarinets.

9AI "THE TOWER"

Scottie rushes into the church after Madeleine and in one of the most famous scenes of all cinema, he follows her up the staircase of the tower, but is repeatedly overcome with nausea and vertigo. He watches her climbing through the trap door into the loft, and looking out of a window sees a body falling onto the roof below. As he gingerly makes his way down the stairs, we see a priest arriving with a ladder accompanied by nuns, and making their way onto the roof. The scene changes to the view from the cloister through the arches that was used when Scottie and Madeleine first arrived at the Mission. From the Plaza Hall room is heard the voice of the coroner.

Three chords signify Scottie's feelings of vertigo as looks up to the tower. We have heard these species of dissonant harmonies on two occasions so far. The first time they appeared was in "Roof-Top," where they were fashioned from two super-imposed triads, a feature that has led writers such as Bruce to describe them as bitonal.[40] In "The Window," a less abrasive voicing was used in which the triads were placed above each other, and it was proposed that this might be taken to represent an attack that was not so overwhelming. Here, the chords are reduced to just four different pitches, one component being doubled at the octave. The first, as Scottie looks up, contains the pitches $G\flat_4$–$B\flat_4$–D_5–$F\sharp_5$–A_5 and is played by stopped horns, trumpets with hard mutes and two vibraphones. In effect, this is an augmented triad on $B\flat$ with a major seventh, an undoubtedly dissonant chord, but it is not clear that the term *bitonal* is entirely helpful to describe it. The next chord, as the camera returns to Scottie's face, is composed of the notes $A\sharp_3$–$C\sharp_4$–G_4–$B\flat_4$–D_5, the leading note ninth from D minor ($C\sharp$–E–G–$B\flat$–D) without a third, and is played by horns, trombones and harps. Madeleine's entry into the church is accompanied by the last of the three "vertigo" chords, an echo of the first two octaves lower, played by clarinets and bass clarinets.

The ostinato first heard in "Roof-Top" is now set into motion in a completely reworked version as Scottie rushes after Madeleine into the church. Herrmann thickens the texture by adding a low $B\flat$ in the horns to the sustained C and $F\sharp$ in bassoons, contrabassoons, cellos and basses. Given the general lightness of the orchestration and avoidance of the lowest register in many of the cues since "Roof-Top," the impact of this sonority is all the greater. Similarly, the hard synchronisation of the next three shots to versions of the "vertigo chord" is startling because of Herrmann's general avoidance of this technique. When Scottie looks, first to the altar at the front of the church, then right to the front, and finally left to the open door and stairway to the tower, the three vertigo chords reappear at the same pitch level as at the start of the cue, but more faintly.

The flow of the ostinato figure, which was briefly suspended by these three gestures, is now resumed with the addition of the rising and falling octave figure in the trombones and tuba. It will be recalled that Herrmann first used this motif (see Example 5.2) as Scottie pursued the criminal in the opening scene of the film. At that point, it was rhythmically symmetrical, but now the symmetry is disrupted and as a subtle but effective development, the third note of the figure appears a crotchet beat earlier than expected. Although the ostinato material used in this section is similar in outline to that of the equivalent passage of "Roof-Top," and the same underlying harmonic successions are maintained, there are many detailed changes and the individual figures are completely reorganised. Scottie's first attack of vertigo interrupts the bass figure, at the point at which the fourth bar of the pattern is expected. By placing this event on what is effectively an upbeat (the hypermetre is in four-bar units), the effect is all the more overpowering, like the sensation one has on a roller coaster ride when it begins going uphill after a steep descent, the sudden change of direction taking the body unawares. Herrmann's voicing and orchestration of the chord is radically different to that adopted in "Roof-Top." Now the E♭ minor and D major chords are superposed in a chain of thirds by trombones, horns and trumpets, and the penetrating timbre of the three piccolos is replaced by a sustained chord in the Hammond organ. Scottie's attempts to make his way up the stairway, fighting against his nausea, are accompanied by the resumption of the ostinato figures, the octaves motif being adapted to rising and falling tritones, and a triplet crotchet figure accenting the second of each pair of bars. For the second wave of vertigo, the chords appear in exactly the same configuration as they did previously, and are followed for a third time by the ostinato figures, a rising chromatic bass line and a repeated quaver figure in the horns and trumpets punctuating every bar (Example 5.15). At the climax, as Madeleine is seen to plummet from the tower from Scottie's point of view through the window, her fall is not Mickey Moused by a rapidly descending line, but by the addition of a series of sustained chords in successively lower octaves. The total pitch content of these chords (ignoring the harp arpeggios of D major and G♭ major) is C–D–E–F♯–G–A–B♭, the notes of the so-called acoustic or natural scale formed from the first thirteen harmonics of a harmonic series built on C. This same set of pitches will be heard later in the score in the cue "Good Night" (see chapter 2, Example 2.13).[41]

When Madeleine's body hits the roof below, the interval of the tritone from C–F♯, so prominent at the beginning of the cue, returns while horns, trombones and tuba evoke the appoggiaturas of "Tombstone," though the direction of the falling semitone figure is reversed to a rising one. In the earlier cue, this figure had seemed like a sigh, now it takes on an air of finality. The subsequent texture, accompanying the shattered and broken Scottie's laborious descent of the stairway, is fascinating. Like "The Forest," it is an exercise in *Klangfarbenmelodie*, the "vertigo chords" being continually rescored as they work their way down to the low register. The very high shot looking down on the tower and roof as the priest and workmen climb the ladder is articulated by a chromatic fall to a sustained low E in bass instruments and a peal of chords from the horns which ends on an unresolved D min[7] chord in second inversion. This passage is repeated as we see Scottie emerge from the church far below and stagger off.

The final section of the cue acts as a bridge to the second part of the film, the shots through the arches reminding us of the equivalent camera angles when Scottie and Madeleine arrived at the Mission. We are aware that time has passed and that we are listening to the words of an official in a coroner's inquest being held in the Mission. Strings and winds vacillate between the pitches E and B♭ — a tritone apart — and the narrative is left hanging in the air, the music functioning like a question mark.

Example 5.15
The Holograph Score of Page 4 of "The Tower."

NOTES

1. Although Herrmann uses the simultaneous time signatures of 6/8 and 2/4, he does not combine simple and compound groupings of quavers polyrhythmically.

2. The B♭ and D♭ might be regarded as the upper two pitches of a diminished triad on G functioning as an altered dominant.

3. Elsewhere in the score, Herrmann uses a key signature of six flats for this harp glissando. For example, in bar 64 of "The Nightmare" he explicitly notes six flats and writes "E♭ minor."

4. Auiler, *Vertigo*, notes that all the scenes in Ernie's (including the exteriors) were shot on the soundstage. Auiler pp. 106–7.

5. Spoto, *The Art of Alfred Hitchcock*, p. 282.

6. Bruce, *Bernard Herrmann*, p. 149.

7. Screenplay, p. 22, scene 56.

8. Although Herrmann marks this as quaver = 60 in the score, it is played in the film at a tempo which is closer to quaver = 70.

9. *Messa di voce* involves the swelling and diminishing of the tone on long-held notes.

10. Brown, *Overtones and Undertones*, p. 288.

11. Hector Berlioz, transl. Mary Cowden Clarke, *A Treatise on Modern Instrumentation and Orchestration* (London: Novello, Ewer and Co., 1882), pp. 154–55.

12. Ibid.

13. The painting was done by John Ferren for the film.

14. In the novel *Between the Dead* the painting was a self portrait by Pauline Lagerlac and kept in Madeleine's own home.

15. Herrmann explicitly marks the tempo as "Lento (Mouvt. d'Habanera)."

16. For example, D–E–F–G♯–A–B♭–C♯–D.

17. Unconventionally, Herrmann's score has the instruments in this order.

18. There is a minor error in the 3rd horn part in bars 6 and 9 of the cue where Herrmann has notated an A_4 rather than an the E_4 that he appears to have intended.

19. Cooke, *The Language of Music*, p. 146.

20. Screenplay, scenes 122 and 122A, p. 41.

21. Screenplay, scene 125, pp. 43–44.

22. Material from this cue from *The Ghost and Mrs. Muir* reappears during the sunrise in act 1 of *Wuthering Heights.* See the discussion in chapter 1.

23. Screenplay, scene 151, p. 47. Though, because of censorship, two versions of the shot were filmed, one with the bra hanging on the line, and one without it. It was the version without the bra that was printed. Auiler, p. 100.

24. In the prelude to act 1 of *Tristan und Isolde* it is notated as F–B–D♯–G♯.

25. In an alternative reading, the chord can be regarded as a VII[7] in G♭ major or minor.

26. The title "The Fireplace" is ruled out in the score.

27. A relationship between B♭[7] and D can be seen if the top note of the first chord is enharmonically renotated as G♯, creating a German sixth chord in D. The cadence is an elliptical ♭VI–V–I, where the middle chord is omitted.

28. Spoto, in *The Dark Side of Genius*, suggests that the score include references to the "Magic Fire" music (p. 400), a suggestion rejected by Bruce (p. 147). Bruce cites the first edition of Spoto's *The Art of Alfred Hitchcock* p. 317, in which he says that the end of the previous cue ("By the Fireside") was "a variation of the Magic Fire Music." Spoto may have confused the two cues, which are continuous in the film.

29. Auiler, *Vertigo*, p. 142.

30. Screenplay, p. 70.

31. Bruce, *Bernard Herrmann*, p. 152.

32. Screenplay, p. 68.

33. Screenplay, pp. 70–71.

34. Screenplay, p. 74.

35. For instance, Heathcliff's aria "I am the only being whose doom no tongue would ask" from act 1, scene 2 of the opera.

36. The progressions in each case involve nearest neighbour motion.

37. At the point that Scottie says, "It's no dream. You've been there before. You've seen it" the violins rise up to E_6 and fall back down to D_6.

38. Screenplay, p. 85.

39. Bruce, *Bernard Herrmann*, pp. 124–27.

40. Ibid., p. 139.

41. Piccolos play D_6–$F\sharp_6$–A_6, clarinets $F\sharp_5$–$B\flat_5$–D_6, trumpets C_5–E_5–G_5, horns $F\sharp_4$–$B\flat_4$, and strings $B\flat_5$–$F\sharp_6$–A_6.

CHAPTER 6

ANALYSIS AND READINGS OF THE SCORE:
EURYDICE RESSUSCITÉE

9B/10A "THE NIGHTMARE"

After the inquest, Scottie, obviously a broken man, visits the San Mateo cemetery south of San Francisco and stands in front of Madeleine's gravestone. A brief shot of the city shrouded in fog at night leads to the famous nightmare sequence designed by John Ferren, which mixes animation and live action with coloured lighting effects. We see Scottie lying in bed, a pulsation between the natural colour and indigo blue being established at a resting heart rate. As his nightmare progresses, the speed of the pulsing colour effect increases, matching his rising tachycardia. In a Disney-like animation, Scottie sees Carlotta's nosegay, the petals breaking up and scattering. He then recalls the scene after the inquest, but with Carlotta standing next to Elster, the camera focussing on her necklace. At this point the screenplay required Elster to say to Carlotta "Tell him he's not to blame," a line which is not used in the film.[1] A dissolve leads to the graveyard of the Mission Dolores, where Scottie walks down the corridor mentioned by Madeleine, towards an open grave. He falls: first apparently into an abyss, his head filling the screen; then towards the roof of the church of the San Juan Bautista mission; and finally into whiteness at the point of impact. Scottie wakes from the dream in a state of profound shock.

Although Ferren's sketch for the scene of 27 August 1957 makes it clear that, at least for the opening sequence of the nightmare, there should be no music, just silence or a heartbeat effect, this stipulation did not appear in the notes of a production meeting held on 4 September.[2] In fact, Herrmann chose to establish musical continuity between the previous two shots (the cemetery and the San Francisco skyline) and the beginning of the nightmare sequence. Scored for full orchestra, the cue begins with a variant of the love motif from "3 A.M." marked *lento e mesto* (slowly and sadly), descending through three octaves and employing a time signature that fluctuates between 3/4 and 4/4 tempo. By flattening the tonality of the passage by one semitone relative to its previous appearance, Herrmann recalls an earlier cue where this technique was used — "The Outing." Although the inquest scene intervened between the end of "The Tower" and the start of "The Nightmare," he could have used the terminal E of the former as the first note of this cue. Instead, he begins on E♭, the fall of a semitone signifying his depression by a kind of literary isomorphism (the tonality of the passage being figuratively depressed or pushed down). A final rendition of the fragment $B\flat_3 - D\flat_4 - C\flat_4 - B\flat_3$ heard in the violins as we see Scottie lying in his bed, prepares for an increasingly agitated section based around a rising sequence of *tremolando* arpeggiated triads played by the strings. Once established, this involves a succession of diminished triads on C and D, and minor triads of F♯ and D minor (Example 6.1) played against sustained F–A dyads in the bass clarinets, bassoons, cellos and basses. After the diatonicism of the opening bars, the chromaticism of this section, combined with the tension-building effect of the stretto entries, is all the more disturbing.[3] Both this and the subsequent section have been pruned, and bars 13 to 15, 19 to 23, 29 to 30 and 36 to 41 have been excised from the recording. There are no markings in the holograph score indicating that these bars should be removed; neither are there any obvious discontinuities between the segments suggesting that they have been cut and spliced in editing. Whatever the case, presumably the version Herrmann spotted was somewhat longer than the one that was released.

Example 6.1
The Tremolo Figure from "Nightmare."

Just as a nightmare is a distorted version of reality, Herrmann distorts and deforms material from cues that originally accompanied waking reality to suggest the hyper reality of the unconscious mind. The return of the habanera rhythm anticipates the beginning of the nosegay animation, implying, perhaps, that Scottie is already dreaming of Madeleine/Carlotta before we have been permitted to penetrate his mind and experience the nightmare from his point of view. This is the most powerful variant of "Carlotta's Portrait" heard so far, and there are many new details of orchestration, such as the low-register trills and flutter-tonguing in the flutes, the tremolo *sul ponticello* bowing in the violins, and the addition of castanets and tambourine—perhaps the most unmistakable signifier of Spanish music of all. Particularly dramatic is the modification of the habanera figure so that it ascends by two-octave leaps, and this is subsequently adjusted to a rising and falling minor ninth—an interval conventionally regarded as indicative of considerable pain or anguish. Throughout this passage, Herrmann maintains a regular tempo and no attempt is made to synchronise the pace of the music with the slowly accelerating pulses of colour.

In the middle of the Disneyesque nosegay sequence, a melody is played by woodwind and strings in doubled major thirds, counterpointed with a chromatically rising scale in the first violins and flutes. This is a simple variant of the opening figure from "Carlotta's Portrait" in shorter note values, the opening three pitches of which (C–B–B♭) are taken from the second half of the melody.[4] As the camera zooms in on Carlotta's necklace, the melody, split into two phrases played by oboes and cor anglais, and violins and violas respectively, is repeated in longer note values, and this has the effect of retarding the harmonic rhythm relative to the ever-accelerating colour pulses. The final two pitches of the Carlotta figure (B♭–A) are taken by bass clarinets, bassoons, tuba, harps, cellos and basses and extended by two further notes (A♭–E). As Bruce points out, the suspenseful motif formed by these four notes (B♭–A–A♭–E) is a common Herrmann gesture, found in a number of his other scores including *The Man Who Knew Too Much, North By Northwest* and *Obsession*.[5]

Scottie's fall into the open grave is accompanied by the reworking of the succession of arpeggiated triads that opened the nightmare sequence (Example 6.1) in a series of overlapping entries, and the climax is approached by the addition of the same idea in augmentation. When the highpoint arrives, it is marked by a texture formed from overlaid "vertigo chords"; E♭ minor, D major, G minor and A♭ Major triads, which were positioned contiguously in pairs in "Roof-Top" (E♭ min/D, G min/A♭), are now gradually superimposed and combined with harp glissandi of D major and E♭ minor.[6] In the discussion of sound design in chapter 4 it was noted that the screenplay indicates that Scottie should be woken from the nightmare by his scream and that this final section of the cue could be taken as a musical encoding of this sound. Thus, the nondiegetic scream, which takes place within Scottie's unconscious mind, and is therefore outside the normal narrative frame, is signified by the nondiegetic score. A final quasi-cadential figure descending from E♭ to D in the bass register recalls both the falling couplet from the end of "Roof-Top" and from "Tombstone," two figures that are strongly associated with death.

10B MOZART SYMPHONY NO 34 IN C K 338, 2ND MOVEMENT, ANDANTE DI MOLTO (PIU TOSTO ALLEGRETTO)

Scottie, having suffered a complete nervous breakdown, is now recuperating in a sanatorium and we find him sitting in an armchair in an almost catatonic state. Midge attempts to draw him out by chatting about the Mozart that is playing on the gramophone, but he doesn't respond to her, and remains inert and impassive. The depth of Midge's feelings, and her despair about his condition, find expression through several of her comments, in particular in her remarks "You're not lost. Mother's here" and her reference to him as "John."[7] Before leaving she leans over and kisses him maternally, saying "You don't know I'm here, do you? But I'm here."

This scene was considered in some detail in chapter 4, where the assumption that the music was associated with Midge was questioned. In its own right, Mozart's music (see Example 6.2) could be seen to signify a neurotic or obsessional state in its restless reiteration of pitches and motivic fragments, its quirky rhythmic changes and its forestalling of closure. To read the passage as a symbol of restraint and of Midge's inability to connect is to oversimplify, for its capriciousness is in marked contrast with Scottie's present unresponsive state.

Example 6.2
The Opening of the Second Movement of Mozart's Symphony No 34 in C K 338.

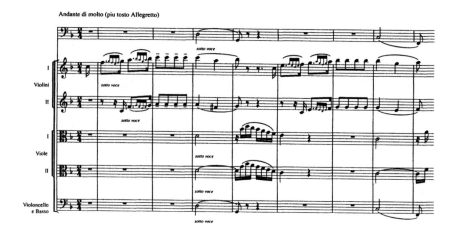

10C/10D "DAWN"

After leaving the sanatorium ward, Midge visits the psychiatrist to ask him how long he believes it will be before Scottie will recover. His prognosis is pessimistic and he indicates that it will probably take at least six months, perhaps even a year. Midge explains to him that Scottie was in love with Madeleine and, in fact, still is; moreover, it seems to her that the music therapy will be of no use to him at all. The cue begins as she leaves the doctor's office and begins to walk slowly down the corridor, in her last appearance in the film. There has been some adjustment to the action relative to the screenplay after this point, for Taylor did not specify the subsequent aerial view of San Francisco, but started the second half of the film in deep gloom with a foggy shot of San Francisco at night followed by an internal view of Scottie's empty apartment. The implication to be drawn from the bright panoramic shot which pans from left to right (and it will be remembered that the opening scene of the film involved prominent pans from right to left over the rooftops) is that some time has passed and Scottie has now recovered his mental health, at least to the extent that he has been released from the sanatorium. The scene changes to Brocklebank Apartments where we discover Scottie looking at Madeleine's green Jaguar and, in the distance, a woman dressed somewhat like Madeleine emerging from the apartments and walking towards the car. He rushes forwards, but as he approaches the car he realises that the woman is much older than Madeleine. It is clear from his behaviour that he has not yet accepted the fact that she is dead and cannot return, and that he still has not properly recovered.

The opening section of this cue, which like the previous one is scored for full orchestra, presents only the second segment of nondiegetic music associated with Midge, the first being in "Exit." The sombre melody (Example 6.3), which accompanies her exit from the sanatorium along a dark corridor, is in the Phrygian mode on F♯ (F♯–G–A–B–C♯–D–E–F♯) and is played by the muted cellos against a sustained tonic pedal in the double basses. Although this archaic mode is quite close to the modern minor scale, its flattened second seems to give it an even more piercingly painful quality. The melody is a variant of the violins' second phrase from "The Beach" where it accompanied Madeleine's enquiry of Scottie "Why did you run?" and his response "I'm responsible for you now, you know."[8] It falls from its apex through a chain of thirds (D–B–G–E), a dejected reversal of the upbeat figure from the love motif, ending with a variant of Madeleine's motif (D–E–G–F♯) and seems to supports a reading that Midge has accepted both that Scottie is seriously ill and that he will never love her in the way that he loved Madeleine.

Example 6.3
The Cello Melody Opening "Dawn."

Against the aerial view of the city, violins present a cantabile melody in octaves that is a near relative of the first phrase of both "The Bay" and "Farewell." A brightening of mood after the gloom of the previous scenes is signified by the changes of modality, from the Phrygian mode of the opening cello figure, to C♯ minor with the entry of the violins, and thence to D♭ major as the flutes double the melody. Once again, the details of the orchestration are fascinating. Beneath the unison melody in the violins, Herrmann initially employs a light and delicate accompaniment of three flutes and three clarinets playing a sustained half-diminished seventh chord on D♯ in final inversion (C♯$_4$–D♯$_4$–F♯$_4$–A$_4$) in low register, while the two harps arpeggiate the same harmony. This chord is another transposed version of the "Tristan chord" that made its first major appearance in "Sleep" and will become a major feature of the score of the rest of the film. Successive changes of harmony are attended by the gradual addition of instruments to the texture so that it is subtly thickened and made "warmer." The underlying progression (D♯^{ø7}–B^7–D♭ –G♭–E^6–Cmaj7), which is by no means remarkable in terms of late-Romantic practice, involves a mixture of: pivotal harmony in the move from D♯^{ø7} to B^7; parallel and nearest neighbour movement (B^7 to D♭ and G♭ to E^6); and movement by fifths (D♭– G♭). Taken as a whole, these melodic, harmonic and timbral characteristics suggest that, while the mood is more optimistic, Madeleine's presence is still felt, presumably by Scottie although we have not yet seen him in this sequence.

As Brocklebank Apartments come into view, the camera slowly tilts down and pans across from right to left to the gates where we see Scottie standing and looking at Madeleine's green Jaguar, against which the love motif is played by the horns. This seems to signify both the painful nature of Scottie's memory of Madeleine and his obsessional yearning for her by means of the emphatic treatment of the melody, the slower tempo, the expressive nuances and the repetition of the motif at the same pitch rather than falling through a series of octave descents.[9] Scottie's contemplation is interrupted abruptly as he sees emerging from the apartment block, a woman, who, from the distance, looks like Madeleine. An *agitato* passage played *sul ponticello* by the strings works its way upward by sequential repetition, supported by a succession of remotely related chords. The expectation built by this passage relies partly on the conventional effect of the *sul pont.* tremolos, but equally on the chord sequence it articulates. The middle three chords of the progression, F♭ major (enharmonically equivalent to E major), A♭ major and C major are tonally distant from each other but are connected by single common pivotal tones. Such progressions of major chords that rise by the interval of a major thirds seem to encode mounting anticipation and confidence because of their increasing tonal "brightness."[10] Herrmann brusquely terminates the cue on a suspenseful whole-tone chord founded on E with Scottie's realisation that the woman is clearly not Madeleine.

10E "THE PAST"

In a scene that was originally intended to precede his visit to Brocklebank Apartments according to the screenplay, Scottie visits Ernie's Restaurant. Much as he did before, he sits by the bar, but he now seems distracted. He is suddenly roused by the sight of a woman sitting in the same area of the restaurant that Madeleine had been seated with Gavin Elster when he first saw her and for a moment seems to imagine that it might really be her, but as she stands up and walks towards him he realises that he is mistaken. The scene shifts to the art gallery of the Palace of the Legion of Honor, where he stares at yet another young woman whom, from the distance, he again believes might be Madeleine. Finally, he stands outside Podesta's flower shop, looking in the window at a nosegay similar to the one bought by Madeleine.

Scored for three cor anglais, three clarinets, two bass clarinets and muted strings, the cue is marked *Adagio mesto e sost* (very slowly, sadly and sustained) and begins immediately before the lap dissolve to the street outside Ernie's Restaurant. Herrmann could have reused "Madeline" at this point to mislead us to believe that the woman was indeed Madeleine, but instead, the love motif is obsessively repeated. In a piece of orchestration redolent of Tchaikovsky, Herrmann draws the richest tone from the strings by having them play the melody in unison on the D string (the C string in the case of the violas). The entries of the sustained second inversion chords of A♭ major played by the woodwinds, which were previously played at the start of the bar, simultaneously with the melody, are now slightly retarded to heighten their expressive impact and to emphasise the unprepared melodic dissonance on D. Although the motion between the chords of Aʹ major and Cmaj7 could have been effected with the minimum of movement, Herrmann's voicing of the cor anglais parts maximises the distance travelled, and this has the effect of emphasising the oppressively descending perfect fifth harmonised by the second chord of each pair.

As Scottie becomes aware of the couple at the back of the restaurant, a very prominent and resonantly voiced 4-3 suspension (G–F♯), one of the crassest clichés of Western sacred music, is heard in the first violins and violas. The suspension (doubled by violas) strongly implies a subsequent perfect cadence in G minor, but this is briefly circumvented by the movement to the note A, one tone higher. The anticipation generated by this failure to resolve is both satisfied and intensified in the next passage, as Scottie stares at the couple. Although the expected resolution onto a chord of G minor does appear in the divided violins, it is in second inversion, the most unstable position, and it initiates a passage which is played *sul ponticello* with a crescendo from *pp* to *ff*, both conventional ways of encoding suspense. Scottie's disappointment is signified by the falling appoggiaturas in the violins, which are derived from the first bar of the love motif (D–C), and are widely separated from their supporting bass notes. A similar reiteration of the pitches D and C appeared in the passage leading to the climax of "The Beach," and their restatement now seems particularly poignant.

The scene in the art gallery restores the habanera rhythm in the first clarinet, the sighing couplet figure effectively continuing in the divided first violins, in a thin, ghostly, *sul tasto* tremolando supported by a slightly fuller accompaniment. Over this texture, the upper division of first violins introduces a brief expressive fragment (A_5–C_6–$B\flat_5$) as Scottie catches sight of the girl and goes forward to look at her more closely. The violin melody used for the final shot outside Podesta's flower shop (Example 6.4) is the logical continuation of the previous fragment and recalls in minor mode the falling motif heard at the end of "The Bay" as Scottie lifted Madeleine's unconscious body into her Jaguar. Now, tonally ambiguous chords (F aug and F°7) leave the cue suspended and unresolved, the voicing of the underlying harmony allowing the melody to float above it.

Example 6.4
The Last Three Bars of "The Past."

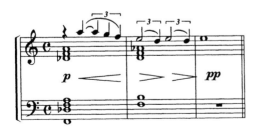

10F/11A "THE GIRL"

Scottie looks along Grant Street from Podesta's and sees a group of shop girls approaching. His eye is drawn to one wearing a green suit, and although her hair is darker, her profile is very similar to that of Madeleine. Scottie turns and follows her, "instinctively" according to the screenplay.[11] A dissolve leads to Sutter Street where he watches her going into the Hotel Empire, a rather shabby and inexpensive hotel. He stands on the pavement staring, and as he looks up (as he had done at the McKittrick Hotel) he notices a window opening on the second floor. He counts the number of floors, working out where the room must be, and crosses the road and enters the hotel. A further dissolve takes us to the door outside the girl's room, on which Scottie knocks.

Although we see the girl from Scottie's point of view for some seconds, Herrmann does not start the cue until she is seen in full profile (as Madeleine appeared in several key shots in the first part of the film). Again, the music is dominated by the descending phrase of the love motif, played in fourfold descent slowly and lingeringly by muted divided strings. The falling four-note figure (D – C – B – E) of the love motif can be seen to function as the counterpart of the opening phrase of "Madeline" (F♯ – G – B – A). Whereas "Madeline" seems to be tentative and part of a melodic shape tending towards circularity, the love motif is assured and essentially linear. It would be easy to suggest that Herrmann is drawing on a kind of gender-based musical characterisation that regards these figures as symbols of the female and male respectively. However, phallic symbolisation usually involves ascent (one thinks, for example, of the motif associated with Siegfried's sword from Wagner's *Ring* cycle), and the downward slope of the linear motif suggests a much less potent condition.

As Scottie stands opposite the hotel, the music settles on the pitches C♭ and E♭ in the cellos and violas, and the upper strings begin an ascent which loosely Mickey-Mouses his eye movements as he looks up the building. The ascending arpeggio is yet another unfolding of the "Tristan chord"—a half-diminished seventh chord on F now in third inversion (E♭–F–A♭–C♭) and a responding, descending chain of expressively articulated appoggiaturas harmonised by minor chords begins as the girl opens her window. Just before Scottie enters the hotel, we hear the subdued resumption of the love motif, now remaining at the same pitch when repeated, though with continually changing orchestration. The final few bars reduce the figure to three notes, the last note being deleted.

It is significant that this cue should simply be labelled "The Girl," for in the first part of the film, Madeleine and her *alter ego* Carlotta, were both explicitly identified in the titles of cues. Like Midge, however, Judy is not given an independent theme of her own, and Herrmann relies on the reworking of previously heard material. This reinforces the impression that Judy exists simply as the reanimation of Madeleine for Scottie and he has little interest in her as an individual.

11B "THE LETTER"

This scene follows the meeting between the girl we now know to be Judy Barton and Scottie. During a controversial flashback, the inclusion of which caused heated debate in postproduction, we discover what really happened in the tower.[12] Judy writes a letter to Scottie explaining that he was the victim of Elster's murder plan, but telling him that she still loves him and wishes that she had the nerve to stay and carry on with the lie. According to the screenplay "She pauses and looks up and thinks, and wonders, and tries to see the future, and as she does, the fear in her eyes dissolve[s] into anxious hope, and then resolve[s]."[13] She folds the letter, tears it up, and throws it away.

Example 6.5
The Opening Two Bars of "The Letter."

In a shot that is not described in the screenplay, we see Judy slowly turn round: First her head appears in close-up from the rear, then her profile and finally her full face looking straight into the camera. Herrmann begins with a falling chromatic fragment (D–C♯–C–B) harmonised by major seventh chords in second inversion played subtone by three clarinets and two bass clarinets (Example 6.5). A falling line was a feature of "Carlotta's Portrait" and its derivatives, and it took a prominent role in "The Nightmare." The chord sequence appeared in precisely the same configuration in "The Forest" as Madeleine and Scottie arrived at the cross-section of the ancient tree. Now it lends an air of mystery, encouraging us to ask ourselves if this really is Madeleine. The answer comes immediately with the flashback to the scene at the church in the San Juan Bautista Mission, where we see the proceedings from an objective perspective. We might have expected Herrmann to simply reuse the earlier cue—after all the action is very similar—but the material is substantially re-orchestrated and simplified. The ostinato figure, which starts on C in all voices, is now played *pp* by the three flutes and muted violins and cellos, and the rising and falling octave idea in the bass, reinforced by the harps, simply ascends by chromatic steps from F♯ up to A before returning to the F♯. A dyad of C–F♯ is eerily sustained by the Hammond organ and two timpani, with rolls on a tam tam and a large suspended cymbal. The lap dissolve from the final scene in the tower, as Elster covers Judy's mouth to stop her screaming, to her horrified face as she recalls the events is accompanied by a sustained tritone (F♯–C) in lower strings and clarinets.

Example 6.6
Opening the C Minor Waltz from "The Letter."

As Judy moves towards the wardrobe to collect her suitcase and clothes so that she can pack and leave the hotel, a new melody in a slow waltz time (Example 6.6) with a depressed and laboured air appears in the strings. This striking melody's unambiguous C minor modality, the heavy accentuation of its second beat, the reiterated rise and fall of its contour and the falling semitone in the bass all combine to signify dejection, and the addition of the hand-stopped notes in the first horn and *sul ponticello* tremolos in the violas intensifies the mood. A possible source of this new figure is Scottie's love motif from "3 A.M.," for it has a similar outline, though the constituent intervals have been subject to considerable modification. As Judy touches the grey suit she wore as Madeleine, the waltz is briefly and abruptly broken off with a stinging half-diminished chord on F♯ in first inversion in harps, flutes and clarinets, though it resumes immediately in B minor with a falling chromatic bass line. The first bar of this phrase ($C\sharp_5$–B_4–E_5–D_5) derives from a figure heard in "Farewell" during the one-in-the-bar waltz immediately after Madeleine and Scottie kissed (B_4–A_4–D_5–C_5). This idea and a second balancing one are repeated in an almost obsessional manner until the waltz finally peters out on an augmented triad on F as Judy begins writing her letter of explanation to Scottie.

Multiply-divided violins and violas accompany Judy's voice-over, and while the music remains quiet and subdued and does not impede the dialogue, it has a remarkable bloom and radiance. Static pedal tones of F in the cellos and basses support gently swaying chords to which further pitches are accreted every two bars. With Judy's remark that it was she who made the mistake—of falling in love with Scottie—the tonality moves to much flatter (and therefore conventionally more "expressive") regions, including G♭ major, E♭ minor and B♭ minor. This section ends on an augmented triad taken up by flutes and clarinets as Judy muses and tears up the letter, resolving to trust her luck with Scottie. Now the B minor version of the waltz recommences as Judy returns her suitcase and dresses to the wardrobe, moving the grey suit to the back where it is out of sight. The melodic line settles on the reiteration of the sighing couplet E_5 and D_5 corresponding to the end of "The Past" as Scottie stood outside the flower shop. It has become clear that Judy's feelings of yearning and desire for Scottie are the equal of Scottie's for Madeleine.

12A NO CUE

The previous cue was numbered 11B and the subsequent one 12B, indicating that a cue was originally intended for the scene in Ernie's Restaurant. While Scottie and Judy eat, a girl dressed like Madeleine catches Scottie's eye, and it is conceivable that a version of "Madeline" could have been used to indicate the parallel with the earlier scene. However, the narrative is probably strengthened by the absence of music, highlighting the point that Madeleine, as Scottie imagined her, never really existed.

12B "GOOD NIGHT"

The scene in Ernie's dissolves onto the neon sign of the Hotel Empire. The camera tilts down to the road as a car drives up and Scottie and Judy emerge from it. They enter the hotel and a second dissolve shows them in the corridor leading to Judy's room. Standing at the doorway, Judy thanks Scottie and he responds by asking her if she will go out with him the next morning. Judy reminds him that she has to work and, entering her room suggests that his offer to take care of her is a ruse to get into her bed, an implication that he adamantly denies. Her appearance in silhouette against the green neon light from the hotel sign electrifies Scottie. In Taylor's screenplay his behaviour is much more forceful, snapping the light switch off and telling her not to look at him so that he can take in her profile. After she agrees to meet him the next morning, Scottie leaves.

"Good Night" is scored for muted strings and begins in 5/4 time on the dissolve from Ernie's Restaurant. The opening sonority involves a harmony built largely from the first six odd-numbered members of a harmonic series on C_1 (C_2–G_2–E_3–$B\flat_3$–D_4–$F\sharp_4$), a resonant voicing of the "chord of nature" (chapter 2, Example 2.13).[14] Herrmann makes no further use of this chord in the cue, and it is not entirely clearly why he chose to employ it, though the same set of pitches was used when Madeleine fell to her death in "The Tower." The rising and falling minor sixths of the violin figure (D_5–$B\flat_5$–D_5) do not have any obvious source in earlier cues, but perhaps they can be seen as a reduced and interval-compressed version of the outline of Scottie's love motif (E–G–B–D–C–B–E). Similarly, in "The Letter," the C minor section after the flashback sequence involved a rise through a C minor triad to A♭ (C–E♭–G–A♭) as Judy recalled Madeleine's death. The motif, with its asymmetrical 5/4 metre and expressively articulated and prolonged B♭ seems to signify a certain uneasiness in the relationship between the pair. The melody that develops from this figure bears a relationship to "Madeline," with its falling seconds and involutions, but like the love motif, it is simply repeated dropping an octave lower, and does not display the tendency towards harmonic elaboration that "Madeline" exhibited.

As Judy opens the door, the lower division of second violins and the divided violas begin playing tremolando half-diminished seventh chords while the violins introduce a falling pattern (chapter 2, Example 2.10), which can be seen as a straightened-out version of the principal melodic notes of the first phrase of "Madeline." Transposed and adapted to the linear configuration of the love theme F♯–G–B–A–

G–E–F♯–E becomes E–D–C–B–A.[15] (The motif also appeared as a descending five note segment of a B minor scale at the climax of "By The Fireside," in which the ornamental pitches from "Madeline" were removed.) Similarly, other fragments of "Madeline" reappear in new guises: as Judy says, "I have to go to work. I've got a job" its closing phrase returns with a simplified rhythm; and just after she remarks "I've been understanding since I was seventeen" a segment of melody from the climax recurs in outline.

This latter melody is harmonised by alternate chords of F♯°⁷ and A♭⁷, an example of a particularly Wagnerian practice in which neighbouring chords are connected not by proximity in the tonal hierarchy, but by part-writing involving a mixture of common tones and movement by semitone step. Herrmann is able to place melodic ideas which are tonally remote from each other side-by-side by using harmony which simultaneously pulls in two different directions (G major and D♭ major) and the vacillation between the two chord species creates considerable tension, as neither achieves its expected resolution. It will be noticed that the move to the flat side is related to Scottie's desire to be with and look after Judy, and that the G major material is associated with Judy's uncertainty about how to proceed. The pleading effect of the interchange between the two chords is intensified by the fine details of orchestration, for the D♭ major material is supported by a thinner and more delicate texture.

A further three-bar unit on G♯°⁷ involving a linear melodic descent, answered by a bar of B♭⁷ and the reversal of the melodic direction leads to the climax. The expected resolution of B♭⁷ onto E♭ major is avoided, and the love theme, with its characteristic oscillation between A♭ and Am⁹, is invoked as Scottie gazes at Judy's arresting silhouette in the corona of fluorescent green light. There is a curiously restrained and even depressed quality about the sequence of falling sighing couplets that follows in the violas, its supporting bass line sinking gloomily downwards. As Scottie leaves the room Herrmann restates the floating violin melody from near the beginning of the cue—just after the opening minor sixths—and in combination with the abrupt departure it complements the sense of uncertainty, even distaste, which contends with desire in his mind. The cue ends on a triad of E major as the dominant of A minor.

12C "THE PARK"

The following morning, Scottie and Judy walk together through Golden Gate Park. We see a cascading fountain, the "Portals of the Past" behind the lake, and lovers lying on the grass kissing. Scottie and Judy do not hold each other's hands, and she looks at the lovers with "wistful envy," though he seems entirely unconscious of them, his mind apparently on other things.[16]

The stylistic model for the Italianate cavatina that Herrmann composes for "The Park" (chapter 2, Example 2.8) would seem to be Puccini, and one is particularly reminded of 'O mio babbino caro' ("Oh my beloved daddy") from *Gianni Schicci* (see Example 6.7). Both pieces are in 6/8 time, involve flat keys (A♭ major for the Puccini, G♭ major for the Herrmann), and have rippling arpeggiated accompaniments based on similar diatonic harmony. The extreme flatness of the tonality relative to the rest of the score and the absence of any connection to the final chord of "Good Night" (which it follows without any break) is conspicuous. It has already been suggested above that there has been a tendency in Western art-music to associate flat keys with deep pathos, yet here we have a rather lightweight and delicate intermezzo in G♭ major accompanying the two protagonists, who are obviously not yet passionately involved with each other. Undoubtedly the melody indicates a leavening of the mood and is consistent with the image of the fountain in the background.

Example 6.7
The First Eight Bars of the Melody of Lauretta's Aria "Oh! mio babbino caro" from Puccini's *Gianni Schicchi*.

Musically, the opening idea of "The Park" incorporates the rising minor sixths of the previous cue (B♭–G♭) into a figure which is the retrograde (and thus a kind of mirror image) of the opening phrase of Madeleine's theme as it appeared in "Graveyard" (E–F♯–G–B becomes B♭–G♭–F–E♭ — see chapter 2, Example 2.8).[17] This latter figure becomes particularly prominent as Judy looks over to see the lovers. It might be suggested that it symbolises Judy as the inverse of her *alter ego*, for Madeleine was remote, sophisticated, and yet somehow innocent, whereas Judy is ordinary, down to earth and clearly experienced in the ways of the world.

12D NONDIEGETIC CUE "POOCHIE" BY VICTOR YOUNG

The scene shifts to a dance floor in the Fairmont Hotel. Other couples are talking to each other while dancing, but there is no eye contact between Scottie and Judy though she rests her head against his chest and looks up to him. Scottie appears to be somewhat distracted.

Although the screenplay indicates that the music being played is "Isn't it Romantic," the music actually selected was "Poochie" by Victor Young, from the film *Skylark*, a Paramount film released in 1941. The cue was also used in *Forever Female* (1953) where it was titled "Sardis #4," and eight bars scored for saxophones and strings have been extracted from its middle.

12E/13A "THE HAIR COLOUR"

Scene 236 takes place in Scottie's apartment at night, presumably after the purchase of the replicas of Madeleine's clothes and shoes from Ransohoff's store. Judy has been crying and Scottie tries to comfort her by offering her a cognac and delivering almost the same line that he did to Madeleine when he rescued her from the bay—"Here Judy, take this straight down. It's like medicine." All the camera positions in this part of the scene provide objective viewpoints, the two protagonists spending most of the time looking away from each other. When Judy offers to wear the clothes if Scottie will to love her for herself rather than as a reflection of Madeleine, he notices her hair and persuades her that she must dye it to complete the makeover. Through the segment, the number of subjective reverse shots gradually increase as Scottie and Judy make eye contact. After Judy has acquiesced to Scottie's request, he offers her a cushion to sit on in front of the fire, just as he gave one to Madeleine after rescuing her from the bay.

"The Hair Colour" begins immediately after Judy says "If you'll just like me," is scored for muted string orchestra and has a tempo marking of *Andante appassionato.* Despite this, the passion is suppressed and restrained, reflecting Scottie's dissatisfaction with Judy's inability to measure up to his idealised Madeleine. The cue employs the love motif, now extended and in a completely revised orchestration. This motif is, and has been since its inception in "The Outing," a manifestation of Scottie's obsessional feelings for Madeleine and expresses *his* point of view; its function, to adopt Claudia Gorbman's term, is therefore *metadiegetic.* I have already argued that Judy does not have any distinct music of her own in the film, at least in the sense that it is "persistent." Although "The Letter" involved two novel ideas—the C minor slow waltz figure and the gently swaying chord sequence—neither of these returns and may be seen, to adopt computing terminology, as "local" rather than "global" variables. The rest of the material in that cue was adapted from, and in a sense "unmasked," music from the first part of the film.

Immediately after Judy asks Scottie, "If I let you change me will it do it?" the motif derived from "Madeline" that accompanied Madeleine and Scottie's passionate kiss at the the climactic moment of "The Beach" and later, towards the highpoint of "Farewell" recurs (chapter 2, Example 2.4). Now the effect is markedly different—Scottie pecks at Judy's cheek without any real involvement and this is reflected in the much more subdued dynamic and lighter instrumentation. Although the one-in-the-bar waltz attempts to lift off, it rapidly grinds to a halt and the threefold repetition of the falling segment of the love motif, descending by octaves, brings the cue to its end in a pale reflection of its earlier incarnations.

13AI "BEAUTY PARLOR"

Scottie arrives at the Elizabeth Arden Salon, where Judy is having her make over and asks the beauty operators to tell Judy that he will wait for her back at the hotel. With some concern, he checks that she fully understands the treatment he requires for Judy and we see brief glimpses of the transformation: the eyelash treatment, the application of makeup, the rinsing of shampoo from her hair and the varnishing of her fingernails.

Although at only six bars in length this is one of the shortest cues in the score, it is also one of the most significant. The motif which dominated the Prelude (chapter 2, Example 2.6) is heard, scored for the unusual ensemble of two vibraphones, two harps and celeste, beginning immediately after Scottie leaves the beauty parlour. The symmetrical properties of the arpeggiated figures, which are "to be played in a hard and brittle manner" according to the score, seem to symbolise the transformation taking place in the beauty parlour, by reminding us that Madeleine and Judy are the mirror images of each other. There is something magical about this transformation, which the hard-edged and crystalline musical-box sonority seems to underscore particularly aptly—Madeleine is being conjured up from the grave by the Elizabeth Arden beauticians.

13B "SCÉNE [*SIC*] D'AMOUR"

Scottie impatiently waits in Judy's hotel room for her return. He looks out of the window, and we are led to assume that he has seen her, though the point-of-view shot of her walking along the street indicated in the screenplay does not appear in the film. He opens the door and stands by the doorway anxiously surveying the corridor until she arrives. When she enters the room, he still appear dissatisfied with her appearance, telling her that her hair should be tied back in a bun; and with an air of resignation, Judy agrees to his request and goes into the bathroom. Scottie sits with his back turned to the door in a state of great agitation, and as he hears the bathroom door open, he slowly turns round and sees her emerge, like a spectre, illuminated with an extraordinary, otherworldly green glow. His face lights up as he recognises her as *Madeleine* and in a reverse shot we see Judy faintly smile, aware that he is finally content. In the kiss that follows, the scene from the stables at the San Juan Bautista Mission is evoked, from Scottie's mental "point of view," before the final dissolve. Sterritt makes a very pertinent comment about Scottie's perplexed expression in this famous "roundy-roundy" shot, namely that it occurs *after*, rather than at the same time as, the appearance of the image of the stable. The audacity of this, he suggests, is "less the event itself—although it is a stunning *coup de cinéma*—than the boldness of allowing Scottie a response that visibly acknowledges the filmmaker's active control over the moment, and stretches the concept of the classical Hollywood narrative to (and probably beyond) its breaking point."[18]

Herrmann brings the love motif to its apotheosis in this long and elaborate cue scored for the full orchestra that begins immediately after "Beauty Parlor," as we see Scottie standing expectantly in the hotel room, flicking through a newspaper. Initially prefaced by three upbeat crotchets (E_5–G_5–B_5), the love motif is played in high register by divided and muted violins and for the first time in the score it is subject to some development rather than simply being repeated in different octaves or in slightly varying instrumentation. As Scottie fiddles with the shoebox, the second violins play the figure a major third lower, the falling perfect fifth being replaced by a major second so that it becomes a segment of a minor scale. A third variant of the figure constructed from two expressive falling couplets separated by a rising fifth (B_5–A_5–E_6–D_6) appears as Scottie moves over to the chest of drawers with its prominent mirror—a significant narrative motif in the scene—and distractedly looks at the items on it. The levelling and subsequent extension of the motif, and the lengthening of the final note of each four-bar phrase, reflects Scottie's shifting emotions of fear and excitement, doubt and anticipation.

As Scottie looks out the window down to the street and (we presume) sees Judy, his action is loosely synchronised with a falling sequential passage, which, from the second bar, effectively forms a decorated scale of F minor linearly descending through two octaves in a slow waltz rhythm—a foil to the conclusion of "The Necklace." It is curious that this passage, which underscores what should be Scottie's mounting excitement, should make use of cultural codes for melancholy and desolation – Cooke notes that in the minor mode a descending 5–(4)–3–(2)–1 figure "has been much used to express an "incoming" painful emotion, in a context of finality: acceptance of, or yielding to grief; discouragement and depression; passive suffering; and the despair concerned with death."[19] If this section is compared to, say, the rising sequence found in act 2, scene 1 of *Tristan und Isolde* associated with Isolde's anticipation of her forthcoming meeting with Tristan, Scottie's much more ambivalent feelings are set into very sharp relief.

Judy's arrival in the corridor leading to her hotel room, seen from Scottie's point of view, is accompanied by the nadir rather than the highpoint of the cue. Flutes and clarinets intone a slow and quiet chordal passage against, first a sustained A♭ minor chord and then a very high unison B in the violins. It will come as no surprise that the first of the woodwind harmonies is a version of the "Tristan chord" (F_4–$A\flat_4$–B_4–$D\sharp_5$–$G\sharp_5$). As Judy enters the room, accompanied by a "Tristan chord" on each downbeat beneath the high, suspended octaves in the first violins, it is clear that Scottie is still not satisfied. A variant of the love theme very similar to its manifestation in "The Hair Colour" is played by divided violins as Judy agrees to put her hair in a bun. The sequential figure derived from the first four notes of "Madeline," which first appeared in "The Beach," then "Farewell" and most recently "The Hair Colour" (chapter 2, Example 2.4) slinks its way up as she slowly walks to the bathroom. Significantly, it now lacks its bass line, the cellos in the lowest voice doubling the melody two octaves lower after the first two notes; it thus sounds ungrounded and thereby neither confident nor assured.

Scottie's increasing excitement is signified musically both by the dominant pedal (G_2) in the timpani and cellos, and by the development and extension of the four-note cell from the beginning of "Madeline" interlaced with the love motif in the tremolo strings, first *sul tasto* and then *sul pont*, as the mutes are gradually removed. This passage leads to a powerful presentation of the love motif with its characteristic unprepared suspension on D resolving to C over an A♭ major chord as Judy emerges from the bathroom transformed back to Madeleine and bathed in a ghostly green light. It should be noted that we briefly see Scottie's response to Judy before we actually see her at this climactic moment. Bruce has pointed out the similarity of the proceeding waltz-like figure that rises sequentially against a chromatically descending bass line, to a section from the end of Act 2, Scene 1 of *Tristan und Isolde*.[20] In *Tristan und Isolde* this is a passage of the most extraordinary erotic charge coming close to frenzy just before the two lovers meet in the garden outside Isolde's chamber, the music propelling them towards each other. The figure is presently restated in the opera, accompanying the outpourings of the pair:

O joy of my heart, O sweetest, highest, brightest, fairest, holiest bliss! All surpassing! Overladen! Overblessed! Ever! Ne'er imagined, never known! Overflowing highest rapture! Joy o'erbrimming! Bliss entrancing! Highest heaven's world forgetting! Mine![21]

This is a world apart from the effect of the related passage in *Vertigo*. Whereas both the lovers in *Tristan und Isolde* are in a state of the highest ecstasy, Scottie and Judy seem to come together as if in a reverie. The two walk slowly towards each other, Scottie's facial expression gradually acknowledging his satisfaction and Judy smiling feebly, in a series of reverse shots. When the next major climax arrives, *molto largamente*, it is similar to that of "Farewell," with turns decorating the final notes of the two-bar phrases. A forceful rendition of the love theme follows, but it is not until the restatement of the figure that originally accompanied Judy's consent to the final adjustment of her hair that they begin to kiss.

The closing section of the cue, which is a fairly close reworking of the final section of "Farewell," begins in a similar way to the passage heard as Judy moved towards the bathroom, but now it is grounded by a bass line and thus sounds more positive and secure. A significant addition is to be found in the one-in-the-bar waltz heard as the room swirls and the scene changes to the stable at the Mission.[22] Here the strings play a series of forceful rising arpeggios that render the final climax, when it comes, even more potent. For the first time, the motif is permitted to rise assertively rather than falling passively (B_5–A_5–B_5–C_6–E_6) at the climax (chapter 2, Example 2.16), suggesting that Scottie is at last content. This impression is reinforced by the extremely positive musical closure, which, like "The Beach" cadences on a solid and unambiguous C major chord. Once again, Herrmann's music, in combination with Hitchcock's narrative technique, misleads us into thinking that we may have reached the conclusion of the film.

13C/13D/14A "THE NECKLACE"

Some time seems to have passed since the previous scene, though this is not made explicit in the screenplay. Scottie is sitting in Judy's hotel bedroom, appearing relaxed and happy, and we hear her voice coming from the bathroom, where she is putting on her make-up. Judy emerges wearing her black cocktail dress and asks for Scottie's help to put on a necklace—the necklace from Carlotta's portrait which had been given to her as a present by Gavin Elster—and finally the truth comes home to him, although he says nothing at this point to indicate that he is aware. Scottie suggests that, rather than going to Ernie's for dinner, they should go somewhere down the peninsula. The scene changes to the interior of the car as they drive south on Highway 101. Becoming increasingly concerned, Judy asks him, "Where are we going?" to which Scottie responds "One final thing I have to do and I'll be free of the past." They arrive at Mission San Juan Bautista, now shrouded in darkness.

Herrmann begins the cue just after Scottie recognises the necklace in the mirror, and we see Carlotta's picture superimposed on Judy's reflection. The second half of the film has been a distorted reflection of the first part, and so it is fitting that the mirror should be the device by which Scottie becomes aware that he has been duped. Four muted horns sustain a *sforzando* D_4, before hammering out the habanera rhythm as an ostinato, beneath which the falling segment of "Carlotta's Portrait" (C_4–B_3–$B\flat_3$–A_3) is introduced, doubled a major third lower, by clarinets and bassoons. Whereas in earlier cues, this melody had floated high up in a female register, it has now descended into the male register and is coarsened in timbre by the addition of the bassoons, in one of their few significant appearances. The adoption of the habanera rhythm in the seventh bar by two flutes low in their range, accompanying two clarinets, acts like a reverberation in Scottie's mind.

As Judy draws closer to Scottie, the time signature switches to 5/4 for only the second time in the score and a first inversion "Tristan chord" ($D^{\varnothing 7}$) is sustained by horns and strings against a rising melodic shape in the Locrian mode whose contour is adapted to the half-diminished seventh chord.[23] This is vaguely reminiscent of the melody that opened "Dawn," which was heard while Midge walked down the hospital corridor and the association between the two passages may be indicative of the imminent cure of Scottie's vertigo—in the screenplay he remarks that the reason he is driving south in the following sequence is to complete his cure.[24] The figure can also be seen to be a variant of Madeleine's motif (particularly as it appears in "Graveyard"), the rising fragment E–F♯–G–B being adjusted to D–E♭–F–G–A♭. For the last two beats of the bar the horns intone the habanera rhythm associated with Carlotta, and the figure is repeated by solo oboe and strings with the flutes playing the habanera rhythm. Judy, now clearly deeply in love with Scottie, kisses him passionately as the love motif, which has emerged from the third rendition of the rising melody, is played warmly by the strings, though he now appears to be totally indifferent to her, responding passively to her embrace.

The middle part of the sequence parallels the drive to Mission San Juan Bautista at the end of the first half of the film, but is in total contrast to their previous trip to the Mission, for now Scottie drives and Judy looks at him in apprehension, the sky is dark and ominous and even the trees seem menacing. During the lap dissolve from the hotel bedroom to the car, a new idea is heard in the horns (Example 6.8) over a "Tristan chord" (F–A♭–C♭–E♭) played tremolando by the strings. If this is compared with the motif in the violas and cellos (E_5–[F♯$_5$]–G_5–B_5–A_5–G_5) at the beginning of "Farewell," the mirroring scene, it will be noticed that this is effectively its inversion, only the passing note marked with a square bracket being omitted. Flutes and clarinets respond with a downward arpeggiation of the "Tristan chord," a passing note being placed between the final two pitches (E♭–C♭–A♭–G♭–F), which is answered by a solo horn with a sinister oscillation between C♭ and B♭, as Judy remarks, "We're going terribly far." Herrmann now introduces a significant detail in the flutes and piccolos—a rapidly descending fragment (E–C–B–A) that is sequentially repeated twice, falling a third each time. Sounding like a curiously threatening birdcall, the pattern is repeated four further times as an ostinato while the strings, *sul pont*, slither their way upward.

Example 6.8
The New Idea in the Horns, Flutes and Clarinets from "The Necklace."

Judy is clearly alarmed and remarks to Scottie "Where are you going?" Simultaneously, there is a varied and truncated repeat of the previous section of the cue beginning on the tremolo "Tristan chord" on F in the strings. Herrmann introduces one further element in the rising octave F♯'s in the cellos and basses just before the arrival at San Juan Bautista. At this stage the love motif becomes intervallically compressed, so that is simply a four-note chromatic segment (A♭–G–F♯–F) in a broad waltz rhythm marked *Molto Largamente e sost*, and the cue ends with a half-diminished seventh chord on D that is rapidly faded out.

14B "THE RETURN"

Scottie and Judy arrive at the Mission, but Judy is obviously reluctant to leave the car. Scottie points out the livery stable where they kissed and recalls Madeleine's words "If you lose me, you'll know that I loved you and wanted to go on loving you." He pushes her into the church, and up the stairs. Despite several bouts of vertigo he continues, forcing her on up the tower in front of him.

Scored for full orchestra with the exception of trombones and tuba, Herrmann gradually thickens the texture through the course of the cue from a very sparse instrumentation at the beginning to a much denser one immediately before the first appearance of the vertigo chord in bar 68, two minutes into it. For most of the movement, which is effectively a dominant preparation for the final tonality of the score (C major), a roll on G_2 is played as a pedal tone by the timpani. Against this dominant pedal, fragments of "Madeline" in a minor mode variant (F♯–G–B♭–A) are passed between violas and clarinets, and are developed as Scottie recollects the scene with Madeleine in the livery stable. A change of texture occurs in bar 11 as Scottie and Judy walk towards the church, the strings now playing nervy *sul tasto* tremolos, and the flutes soon join them with low-register flutter-tonguing. The arrival of Scottie and Judy inside the chapel is marked by a further modification to the modality and instrumentation, the melodic line now involving the motivic cell derived from "Madeline" (F♯–G–B–A) counterpointed by a rising chromatic scale in dotted minims played by clarinets and bass clarinets, and harmonically under-pinned by dyads in bassoons and lower strings.[25] Essentially, this passage is a very close reprise of the one-in-the-bar waltz used in the build up to the climax of "Farewell," but completely re-orchestrated. The highpoint of the first section arrives with the climactic figure from "Farewell" (see the four-bar passage marked *Molto Largamente* in chapter 2, Example 2.5) as Scottie, restraining Judy at the bottom of the stairs leading up to the tower, tells her "One doesn't often get a second chance. I want to stop being haunted. You're my second chance, Judy." As he forces her to climb the stairs, Herrmann splits the waltz rhythm into its two basic constituents: the dotted crotchets played *sul pont* by the violins, doubled by three flutes, articulating a rising segment of a scale of E♭ in seventh chords; and the three quavers taken by violas and cellos.[26] A third sustained element in the texture, played by clarinets on the second crotchet of each bar, works a chromatic scale downwards from $E\flat_4$ to A_3. The effect of all of this is to propel the music forward to a second and more intense statement of the climactic figure from "Farewell."

The G pedal is briefly suspended for a five-bar alternation between chords of A♭ major in second inversion with added augmented fourth (E♭–A♭–C–D) and a dominant minor ninth on D (D–F♯–A–C–E♭) marked *piu animato* and featuring pizzicato strings and hand-stopped horns. This passage has a Spanish disposition that is partly intimated by its harmony, partly by the stamped-out pizzicatos in the strings and partly by the "strummed" reiteration of the pitch D by the flutes and violas, characteristics that are redolent, in a stylised way, of flamenco.[27] The pedal G is restored as Scottie fights his way up the stairs against the vertigo that threatens to overwhelm him, though curiously the musical sequence takes a downward trajectory. When the first attack hits, trumpets superimpose a chord of A♭ major against one of D major played by clarinets, the harps playing glissandi in these two keys. The voicing of this "vertigo chord" is one of the least dissonant used by Herrmann in the score, the chord formed by clarinets and trumpets being a dominant minor ninth with sharp eleventh on D, a species that has a strong tonal function and resolves readily onto G minor—which indeed it does at the beginning of the next section. This functional voicing is perhaps suggestive that Scottie is gaining control over his fear, the chord no longer being disruptive or chaotic.

As Scottie forces himself to climb further up the stairs, a reprise of the melody that opened the cue appears in unison strings, now slowed down and with the first note of each bar articulated by trills in the flutes and clarinets. The pedal-tone G in the timpani, bass clarinets, bassoons and double basses (the latter playing a rising octave figure) accentuates the second beat of each bar, and horns fill in the rest of the harmony. Scottie's second attack of vertigo is scored in an identical way to the previous one. The final bars of the cue, marked *Largo* and scored for unison strings with hand-stopped horns doubling the first note of each bar work their way down to a final falling D–G, implying a perfect cadence. In the mixdown, the level of the final notes is attenuated to the extent that the last G is inaudible. Table 6.1 summarises the structure of the cue.

Table 6.1
Summary of the Structure of "The Return."

Bars	Instrumentation	Modality
1–10	Melody split between violas and clarinets. Pedal tone G in timpani and alternating bass clarinets and lower strinOgs	G minor
11–22	Melody sul tasto split between violas and violins. Chords on first beat in cellos, bassoons and clarinets. Flutes added flutter-tongue in bar 15. Pedal G in timpani.	G minor
24–40	Melody in violins (alternate bars dovetailing into each other). Chords on second beat in bassoons, violas and cellos. Chromatic rising scale in clarinets and bass clarinets. Pedal G in timpani. Final four bars include the climax figure from "Farewell." [28]	G Major
41–50	Chords on first beat in violins and flutes, quaver figure in violas and cellos, falling chromatic line in clarinets. Pedal G in timpani. Final four bars include second version of the climax figure from "Farewell."	B♭ Major
51–55	"Spanish" section. Melody split between crotchets played by flutes and violas and quavers in violins. Chords on the second beat in stopped horns and clarinets. Bass clarinets, bassoons and lower strings play figure that rise and fall by sevenths. Timpani silent for 5 bars.	A♭/D
56–68	Dotted crotchets trilled by unison violins and violas, quavers in flutes and clarinets. Chords in stopped horns. Pedal G in timpani, in rising octave in cellos and basses and sustained in bass clarinets, bassoons and contrabassoon. Passage ends with vertigo chord D major/A♭ major.	G
69–75	Melody in violins, violas and cellos. First note of each bar of melody doubled by flutes and clarinets. Chords in horns, sustained and not hand-stopped. Pedal G in bass clarinets, bassoons, contrabassoons and contrabassoons on the second beat of each bar. Roll in timpani. Ends with vertigo chord as before	G
76–85	Melody in all strings except basses. First note of each bar supported by horns and basses. Unison strings for last 5 bars.	G

14BI "FINALE"

The final scene begins on the steps immediately below the trap door into the bell tower. Scottie has wrung the truth out of Judy and forces her up the last few steps into the tower to see the "scene of the crime." He tells her that her mistake was her sentimentality, and that she should never have kept Elster's gift—Carlotta's necklace—the clue that finally gave her away. Tellingly, Scottie remarks "I loved you, *Maddy*" a conflation of the names of Madeleine and Judy. She responds that she had been safe when he found her and there was no evidence to connect her to the crime, but she put her life in danger and let him change her back to Madeleine because she loved him. Her final words to him are "Scottie, please! You love me now! Keep me safe!" but he replies that it is "too late … there's no bringing her back." They kiss, but Judy sees someone in the shadows from the corner of her eyes. She mumbles "No…no!" and screams as she falls from the edge of the building as the real Madeleine had done. A nun emerges from the darkness, crosses herself saying "God have mercy!" and rings the church bell. Scottie, his vertigo obviously now cured stands horror-stricken on the edge of the tower looking down on Judy's body.

In his "Additional Music Notes" for reel 14, Hitchcock advised Herrmann that "We should not have crescendo music in the Tower so that we have to take the music down in order to hear the dialogue."[29] This had not been a problem in the first scene in the tower, for there was virtually no dialogue there. Now much important narrative information is to be imparted and Herrmann adopts Hitchcock's suggestion by employing the resources of the full orchestra fairly lightly for much of the cue.

The finale is largely based on material that has been widely used in the second half of the film, though it does begin with a completely new idea. Violins and violas forcefully play trills on G_3 and Ab_3 for the first three beats of the bar and three clarinets dash up and down an eleven-note diminished-seventh arpeggio on D on the fourth beat. Meanwhile bass clarinets, bassoons, contra bassoons, cellos and basses brusquely play a pair of quavers (Eb falling to C) beginning half way through the second beat. As the texture established in the upper strings and clarinets is repeated, the bass instruments sequentially work the quaver figure down through thirds (C–Ab, Ab–F, F–D), accompanying Scottie as he forces Judy up through the trapdoor into the belfry. A falling, parallel succession of chords (Ab minor, G minor, F# minor and F minor), underpinned by a three note rising scale segment (first major, then chromatic), in the bass instruments begins as they arrive inside the tower. This sequence has been heard on two previous occasions, the most recent being at the beginning of "The Letter" where it was played as Judy slowly turned round in a state of distraction after Scottie's departure. Now, with the spine-chilling scoring for muted horns and tremolo strings, and the contrapuntal figure played on the offbeats, it takes on a much more menacing aspect.

In a lighter instrumentation of clarinets and bass clarinets, the chord sequence forms an underlay like a strange chorale for the next section of dialogue, as Scottie remarks to Judy "you were his girl." Herrmann subtly adjusts the rhythmic flow, so that the chords lie first on strong, then on weak and back to strong positions before allowing them to work their way upwards in preparation for the arrival of the love motif as Scottie says "You shouldn't have been so sentimental." The subsequent passage straightforwardly restates earlier material:

1. The love motif appears much as it did in "The Hair Colour," scored for muted strings, but the voicing is subtly different and the chords of Ab appear in the more stable first inversion. It has the same pathos-laden sequential extension that first appeared in "The Past" as Scottie noticed Madeleine's lookalike in Ernie's Restaurant and was subsequently used in both "The Hair Colour and "Scène d'amour." It now accompanies Judy's comment that she had been safe, but that her love for Scottie persuaded her to let him transform her into Madeleine.

2. The yearning, rising sequential figure based on the "Madeline" four-note cell (C♯–D–F♯–E) which has been the precursor to the climax since "The Bay" leads into the one-in-the-bar waltz in the form it took in "Scène d'amour," the opening pitches of each bar being based on a scale of E♭ ascending from the leading note up to the dominant. A falling chromatic segment appears in the bass.

3. The climax (not scored for the full orchestra) involves a continuous ascent to the climactic final couplet of the phrase (C–B) for the first time as the couple kiss, Scottie being simultaneously attracted and repelled by Judy, loving and loathing her.

Herrmann uses the "vertigo chord," the superimposition of E♭ minor and D major triads, for one final time as Judy sees the shadowy figure in the corner of the belfry. Played very quietly by the Hammond organ, it is now scarcely audible, signifying, one might propose, Scottie's final cure. The moment of silence before the coda is electrifying. We are taken right back to the music which ended "Roof-Top" with the tritone F♯–C and alternation between C and D♭ in the brass. A broad, threefold statement of the love motif with its characteristic A♭ major to Cmaj7 oscillation brings us to the score's and the film's final cadence from the flattened submediant to the tonic C major in low register in a sonorous and resonant voicing.

NOTES

1. Screenplay, p. 98.
2. Auiler, *Vertigo*, pp. 146–50.
3. There are, in fact, only eight different pitch classes in this section: C–C♯–D–E♭–F–G♭ [F♯]–A♭–A.
4. The entire figure is C–B–B♭ || A–G♯–A–C–B–B♭–A. Double bars mark the point where the material from "Carlotta's Portrait" appears in its original form.
5. Bruce, *Bernard Herrmann*, p. 175.
6. The four chords give eight notes of the chromatic scale. The addition of E♭ minor and D major glissandi in the harps adds three further pitch classes, and only C is missing from a complete chromatic scale. Bruce (p. 175) suggests that an E♭ major chord is played by upper woodwind. This is not the case, for both flutes and clarinets play E♭ minor triads.
7. It will be remembered that Scottie told Madeleine that old friends called him John and

acquaintances called him Scottie. Screenplay, p. 98.

8. In "The Beach" the melody was in Phrygian B♭ mode starting on the fifth.

9. Herrmann's orchestration of the first A♭ chord places it on the first beat for a dotted minim in brass and on the second beat, delayed by a crotchet, for a minim in woodwinds, creating a slight shuddering echo.

10. It is customary to regard moves upward through the cycle of fifths, by the addition of a sharp or the subtraction of a flat, as a tonal brightening.

11. Screenplay, p. 104.

12. Auiler, *Vertigo*, (pp. 159–61) provides details of the debate surrounding the inclusion of this scene.

13. Screenplay, p. 112.

14. The first eleven members of a harmonic series on C_2 are $[C_1]$–C_2–G_2–$[C_3]$–E_3–$[G_3]$–$B\flat_3$–$[C_4]$–D_4–$[E_4]$–$F\sharp_4$, where the brackets indicate the missing even-numbered notes from Herrmann's chord structure.

15. The bold letters represent the source pitches of the descending segment of "Good Night" in the opening phrase of "Madeline."

16. Screenplay, p. 116.

17. The B♭ is an octave lower relative to "Madeline."

18. Sterritt, *The Films of Alfred Hitchcock*, p 11.

19. Cooke, *The Language of Music*, p. 133.

20. Bruce, *Bernard Herrmann*, p. 165. The passage in question leads from the End of Act 2, Scene 1 into Act 2, Scene 2.

21. Wagner, *Tristan und Isolde*, pp. 166–69.

22. The actors were placed on a turntable which slowly rotated to shoot this scene.

23. The previous passage in 5/4 time was in "Good Night." The Locrian mode on D has the form D–E♭–F–G–A♭–B♭–C–D.

24. Screenplay, p. 133a.

25. Only F natural is missing from a complete chromatic scale on D.

26. The seventh chords are voiced (E♭$_4$–G$_4$–D$_5$; F$_4$–A♭$_4$–E♭$_5$; etc).

27. The practice (at least in imitations of flamenco style) of sliding chords up by one fret on the guitar can produce piquant chords such as the A♭ with added augmented 4th. For example, a chord of A major pushed up a fret produces, on the upper four strings, the chord F–B♭–D–E, a transposed version of Herrmann's first chord.

28. Four bars have been removed from the viola and cello parts at this point. These appeared to double the melody in the violins.

29. Auiler, *Vertigo*, p. 142.

BIBLIOGRAPHY

Auiler, Dan. *Hitchcock's Secret Notebooks* (London: Bloomsbury, 1999).

Auiler, Dan. *Vertigo: The Making of a Hitchcock Classic* (New York: St Martin's Press, 1998).

Berlioz, Hector. *A Treatise on Modern Instrumentation and Orchestration.* Translated by Mary Cowden Clarke (London: Novello, Ewer and Co., 1882).

Boileau, Pierre and Thomas Narcejac. *D'entre Les Morts*, first translated by Geoffrey Sainsbury as *The Living and the Dead* (London: Bloomsbury Publishing Plc, 1997).

Brill, Lesley. *The Hitchcock Romance: Love and Irony in Hitchcock's Films* (Princeton, NJ: Princeton University Press, 1988).

Brown, Royal S. *Overtones and Undertones: Reading Film Music* (Berkeley and Los Angeles: University of California Press, 1994).

Bruce, Graham. *Bernard Herrmann: Film Music and Narrative* (Ann Arbor, Michigan: UMI Research Press, 1985)

Chion, Michel. Edited and translated by Claudia Gorbman, *Audio-Vision: Sound on Screen* (New York: Columbia University Press, 1994).

Clynes, Manfred. *Music, Mind and Brain: The Neuropsychology of Music* (New York, London: Plenum Press, 1982).

Condon, Paul and Jim Sangster. *The Complete Hitchcock* (London: Virgin, 1999).

Cooke, Deryck. *The Language of Music* (Oxford: OUP, 1959).

Copland, Aaron and Vivian Perlis. *Copland: 1900 through 1942* (London and Boston: Faber and Faber, 1984).

Coppel, Alex and Samuel Taylor. *From Among the Dead* (screenplay).

Darby, William and Jack Dubois. *American Film Music: Major Composers, Techniques, Trends* (Jefferson, NC: McFarland, 1990).

Fletcher, Lucille. "One Iceberg Please: The Strange Case of Radio's Music Cue Man," *Detroit Free Press*, 14 May 1939.

Freedman, Jonathan and Richard Millington. *Hitchcock's America* (New York: Oxford University Press, 1999).

Gilling, Ted. "The Colour of the Music: An Interview with Bernard Herrmann," *Sight and Sound*, Winter 1971/2, p. 36.

Gorbman, Claudia. *Unheard Melodies: Narrative Film Music* (Bloomington: Indiana University press, 1987).

Hastings, Morris. "Bernard Herrmann: A CBS Institution," *485* (CBS in-house newsletter), 9 November, 1943.

Herrmann, Bernard. "Bernard Herrmann, Composer" in ed. Evan William Cameron, *Sound and the Cinema: The Coming of Sound to American Film* (New York: Redgrave Publishing Company, 1980).

Herrmann, Bernard. "Charles Ives," *Trend: A Quarterly of the Seven Arts*, vol. 1 no. 3, 1932, pp. 99–101.

Herrmann, Bernard. "Music in Films — A Rebuttal," *The New York Times*, 24 June, 1945.

Herrmann, Bernard. "Score for a Film: Composer Tells of Problems Solved in Music for 'Citizen Kane'," *The New York Times*, 25 May, 1941.

Hitchcock, Alfred. *Hitchcock on Hitchcock* (London: Faber, 1997).

Jaubert, Maurice. "Music on the Screen" from ed. Davy, Charles, *Footnotes to the Film* (London: Lovat Dickson Ltd, 1937).

Johnson, Edward. *Bernard Herrmann, Hollywood's Music Dramatist: Biographical Sketch with a Filmography, Catalogue of Works, Discography, and Bibliography* (Rickmansworth: Triad, 1977).

Kalinak, Kathryn. *Settling the Score: Music and the Classical Hollywood Film* (Madison: University of Wisconsin Press, 1992).

Kapsis, Robert E. *Hitchcock: The Making of a Reputation* (Chicago, London: University of Chicago Press, 1992).

Karlin, Fred and Rayburn Wright. *On the Track: A Guide to Contemporary Film Scoring* (New York: Schirmer, 1990).

Keller, Hans. "The State of the Symphony: Not only Maxwell Davies," *Tempo* 125 (June 1978).

Krohn, Bill. *Hitchcock At Work* (London: Phaidon, 2000).

La Valley, Albert J. *Focus on Hitchcock* (Englewood Cliffs: Prentice-Hall, 1972).

Langer, Susanne. *Philosophy in a New Key* (Cambridge, MA: Harvard University Press, 1942).

Manvell, Roger. *Film* (Aylesbury and London: Penguin, 1944, rev. 1950).

Modleski, Tania. *The Women Who Knew Too Much: Hitchcock and Feminist Theory* (New York, London: Methuen, 1988).

Murray, Lyn. *Musician: A Hollywood Journal of Wives, Women, Writers, Lawyers, Directors, Producers and Music* (Secaucus: Lyle Stuart Inc., 1987).

Nietzsche, Friedrich. *Human, All Too Human: A Book for Free Spirits*, transl. R. J. Hollingdale (Cambridge: CUP, 1986).

Ovid, *Metamorphoses*, Book 10. Translated by Sir Samuel Garth, John Dryden, et al. <http://classics.mit.edu/Ovid/metam.10.tenth.html>.

Paddison, Max. *Adorno's Aesthetics of Music* (Cambridge: CUP, 1993).

Palmer, Christopher. *The Composer in Hollywood* (London, New York: Marion Boyars, 1990).

Perlis, Vivian. *Charles Ives Remembered: An Oral History* (New Haven and London: Yale University Press, 1974.

Perry, George. *The Films of Alfred Hitchcock* (Studio Vista: Dutton, 1965).

Prendergast, Roy M. *Film Music: A Neglected Art*, second edition (New York: Norton, 1992).

Ratner, Leonard. *Classic Music: Expression, Form and Style* (New York: Schirmer Books, 1980).

Rieger, Eva. "Aus dem Reich der Toten: Geschlechterrollen in der Filmmusik." *Musik und Bildung: Praxis Musikerziehung* 28 (Jan.–Feb. 1996): 36–40.

Rohmer, Eric. *Hitchcock The First Forty-Four Films* (Oxford: Roundhouse, 1992).

Sadie, Ed. Stanley. *The New Grove Dictionary of Music and Musicians* (London: Macmillan, 1980).

Sharff, Stefan. *Alfred Hitchcock's High Vernacular Theory and Practice* (New York: Columbia University Press, 1991).

Sight and Sound, Winter 1971/2.

Skinner, Frank. *Underscore* (New York: Criterion Music Corp, 1950).

Smith, Steven C. *A Heart at Fire's Center: The Life and Music of Bernard Herrmann* (Berkeley and Los Angeles: University of California Press, 1991).

Spoto, Donald. *The Art of Alfred Hitchcock: Fifty Years of His Motion Pictures*, second edition (New York: Doubleday, 1992).

Spoto, Donald. *The Dark Side of Genius: The Life of Alfred Hitchcock* (London: Plexus,1994).

Sterritt, David. *The Films of Alfred Hitchcock* (Cambridge: Cambridge University Press, 1993).

Stam, Robert. *Film Theory: An Introduction* (Oxford: Blackwell, 2000).

Stravinsky, Igor. *An Autobiography* (London: Calder & Boyars, 1975).

Thomson, David. *Rosebud* (London: Abacus, 1997).

Taylor, John Russell. *Hitch: The Life and Times of Alfred Hitchcock* (New York: Da Capo Press, 1996).

Truffaut, François. *Hitchcock* (London: Secker & Warburg, 1968).

Wagner, Richard. *Tristan und Isolde*, translated Frederick Jameson, vocal score by Karl Klindworth (London: Schott & Co, 1906).

Waletzky, Joshua. *Music for the Movies: Bernard Herrmann* (TV programme — Sony, 1995).

Weis, Elisabeth. *The Silent Scream: Alfred Hitchcock's Sound Track* (Rutherford, Madison, Teaneck: Fairleigh Dickinson University Press, 1982).

Wood, Robin. *Hitchcock's Films* (London: A. Zwemmer, 1965, rev. 1969).

Wood, Robin. *Hitchcock's Films Revisited* (New York: Columbia University Press, 1989).

Zador, Leslie and Gregory Rose. "A Conversation with Bernard Herrmann" in ed. Clifford McClarty, *Film Music 1* (Los Angeles, California: The Film Music Society, 1998).

INDEX

About the Author

DAVID COOPER is Senior Lecturer and the Director of the Interdisciplinary Centre for Scientific Research in Music at the University of Leeds.